Patterns of Regional Economic Change

Patterns of Regional Economic Change:

A Quantitative Analysis of U.S. Regional Growth and Development

C. James Sample
System Sciences, Inc.

Ballinger Publishing Company • Cambridge, Mass.
A Subsidiary of J.B. Lippincott Company

Library of Congress Catalog Card Number: 73–21529

International Standard Book Number: 0–88410–404–4

Printed in the United States of America

Library of Congress Cataloging in Publication Data

Sample, C James.
Patterns of regional economic change.

Originally presented as the author's thesis, American University.
Includes bibliographical references.
1. United States–Economic conditions–1961–
2. Economic zoning–United States. I. Title.
HC106.6.S167 1974 330.9'73'092 73–21529

Dedication

For my beloved Mia

Contents

List of Tables xiii

List of Maps xvii

Acknowledgments xix

Chapter One
Introduction 1

Chapter Two
Spatial Units of Analysis 5

Introduction 5
Concepts of a Region 5
The OBE Economic Areas 6
Regional Groupings 8

Chapter Three
Descriptions of the Variables 11

Introduction 11
Measures of Economic Change 12
Measures of the Economic Base 14
Growth of Residentiary Employment 18
The Index of the Composition of Growth Industries 20
Coefficient of Economic Concentration 22

Measures of Industrialization 25
Change in the Labor Force Participation 26
The Net Migration Rate 28
Measures of the Loan Potential of Local Financial Institutions 30
Measures of Manufacturing Productivity 31
Measures of Manufacturing Investment 33
Measures of Agricultural Technology, Agricultural Growth Sectors, and the Character of the Agricultural Organization 34
Measures of Local Government Fiscal Effort 38
Measures of Deficit Financing by Local Governments 41
Measures of Local Government Services Provided 42
Measures of Political Participation 45
Measures of Socioeconomic Structure 48
Measures of the Level of Educational Achievement 50
Measure of Population Density 52

Chapter Four
Specifications of the Approach 55

Introduction 55
Objectives of the Study 56
Export Base Concept to be Used 56
Growth in Per Capita Income 59
Time Period 60
Approach 61

Chapter Five
Income, Employment, and Export Growth in the Continental United States: An Overview 65

Introduction 65
Growth in Total Personal Income 65
Growth in Per Capita Income 68
Employment Change and Distribution 1950–60 71
The Economic Base Model Applied to the 171 OBE Economic Areas of the Continental United States 73

Chapter Six
Economic Growth and Development of the Southeastern Regional Grouping 79

Introduction 79
Employment Growth and Distribution, 1950–60 80

Introduction to the Economic Base Model 83
Results of the Export Base Model 85
Long Term Economic Development of the Southeastern Regional Grouping 86
Long Term Economic Development: Summary 91
Growth in Total Personal Income: 1950–66 92
Short Term Economic Growth: Summary 97
Growth in Per Capita Income: 1950–66 97

Chapter Seven
Economic Growth and Development of the Northeastern Regional Grouping 101

Introduction 101
Employment Growth and Distribution, 1950–60 102
Introduction to the Economic Base Model 102
Results of the Export Base Model 103
Long Term Economic Development of the Northeastern Regional Grouping 108
Long Term Economic Development: Summary 112
Growth in Total Personal Income: 1950–66 113
Short Term Economic Growth: Summary 119
Growth in Per Capita Income: 1950–66 120

Chapter Eight
Economic Growth and Development of the Central Regional Grouping 125

Introduction 125
Employment Growth and Distribution, 1950–60 126
Introduction to the Economic Base Model 129
Results of the Export Base Model 131
Long Term Economic Development of the Central Regional Grouping 133
Long Term Economic Development: Summary 138
Growth in Total Personal Income: 1950–66 138
Short Term Economic Growth: Summary 144
Growth in Per Capita Income: 1950–66 144

Chapter Nine
Economic Growth and Development of the Far West Regional Grouping 149

Introduction 149
Employment Growth and Distribution, 1950–60 150
Introduction to the Economic Base Model 151
Results of the Export Base Model 151
Long Term Economic Development of the Far West Regional Grouping 156
Long Term Economic Development: Summary 162
Growth in Total Personal Income: 1950–66 163
Short Term Economic Growth: Summary 168
Growth in Per Capita Income: 1950–66 169

Chapter Ten
Findings: Comparative Analysis of Important Variables 173

Introduction 173
Findings: Export Base Model 174
Economic Base Model: Comparative Analysis 176
Findings: Long Term Economic Development 176
Findings: Short Term Economic Growth: 1950–66 180
Findings: Growth in Per Capita Income: 1950–66 183

Chapter Eleven
Summary of Findings and Conclusions 187

Introduction 187
Summary of Findings and Conclusions: Export Base Model 187
Summary and Conclusions: Long Term Economic Development 189
Summary of Findings and Conclusions: Short Term Economic Growth, 1950–66 192
Summary of Findings and Conclusions: Growth in Per Capita Income 194

Appendixes

A Export Industries by OBE Economic Area 197
B Variables by OBE Economic Area 201

C	List of OBE Economic Areas	235
D	Correlation Matrices	239
	Bibliography	273
	Notes	279
	Index	291
	About the Author	297

List of Tables

2–1	OBE Economic Areas Ranked by Per Capita Personal Income, 1959	9
3–1	Rate of Employment Growth by Industry Sector, 1950–60	21
3–2	Government Expenditures 1902–1967	43
3–3	Local Government Expenditure by Function	44
3–4	Variations Per Capita Expenditures in Metropolitan and non-Metropolitan Portions of Forty-five States, 1957	44
3–5	Cost Curve Studies of Scale Economies	53
4–1	Growth Industries, 1950–60	59
5–1	Geographic Distribution of Personal Income	67
5–2	Total Personal Income by Regional Grouping	68
5–3	Statistical Summary of Total Personal Income Growth, 1950–66, for the OBE Economic Areas by Nation and by Regional Grouping	68
5–4	Geographic Distribution of the Levels of Per Capita Income	69
5–5	Statistical Summary of Per Capita Income Growth, 1950–66, by Nation and Regional Groupings	70
5–6	Statistical Summary of the 1959 Levels of Per Capita Income by Nation and Regional Groupings	71
5–7	Employment Growth and Distribution by Sector; 1950–60	72
5–8	Employment Growth and Distribution by Major Sector	73
5–9	Residuals by Regional Grouping	74
6–1	Employment Growth and Distribution by Sector, 1950–60; Southeastern Regional Grouping	80
6–2	Employment Growth and Distribution by Major Sector, 1950–60: Southeastern Regional Grouping	82
6–3	OBE Economic Areas Located in the Southeastern Regional Grouping Ranked by the Percent Change in the Economic Base	84

6–4	Rotated Factor Matrix for the Level of Per Capita Personal Income in 1959: Southeastern Regional Grouping	87
6–5	Rotated Factor Matrix for the Rate of Growth of Total Personal Income, 1950–66: Southeastern Regional Grouping	94
6–6	Rotated Factor Matrix for the Rate of Growth of Per Capita Personal Income, 1950–66: Southeastern Regional Grouping	98
7–1	Employment Growth and Distribution by Sector, 1950–60: Northeastern Regional Grouping	104
7–2	Employment Growth and Distribution by Major Sector, 1950–60: Northeastern Regional Grouping	106
7–3	OBE Economic Areas Located in the Northeastern Regional Grouping Ranked by the Percent Change in the Economic Base	107
7–4	Rotated Factor Matrix for the Level of Per Capita Personal Income in 1959: Northeastern Regional Grouping	109
7–5	Rotated Factor Matrix for the Rate of Growth of Total Personal Income, 1950–66: Northeastern Regional Grouping	114
7–6	Rotated Factor Matrix for the Rate of Growth of Per Capita Personal Income, 1950–66: Northeastern Regional Grouping	122
8–1	Employment Growth and Distribution by Sector, 1950–60: Central Regional Grouping	126
8–2	Employment Growth and Distribution by Major Sector, 1950–60: Central Regional Grouping	128
8–3	OBE Economic Areas Located in the Central Regional Grouping Ranked by the Percent Change in the Economic Base	130
8–4	Rotated Factor Matrix for the Level of Per Capita Personal Income in 1959: Central Regional Grouping	134
8–5	Rotated Factor Matrix for the Rate of Growth of Total Personal Income, 1950–66: Central Regional Grouping	140
8–6	Rotated Factor Matrix for the Rate of Growth of Per Capita Income, 1950–66: Central Regional Grouping	146
9–1	Employment Growth and Distribution by Sector, 1950–60: Far West Regional Grouping	152
9–2	Employment Growth and Distribution by Major Sector, 1950–60: Far West Regional Grouping	154
9–3	OBE Economic Areas Located in the Far West Regional Grouping Ranked by the Percent Change in the Economic Base	155
9–4	Rotated Factor Matrix for the Level of Per Capita Personal Income in 1959: Far West Regional Grouping	158
9–5	Rotated Factor Matrix for the Rate of Growth of Total Personal Income, 1950–66: Far West Regional Grouping	164

9–6	Rotated Factor Matrix for the Rate of Growth of Per Capita Personal Income, 1950–66: Far West Regional Grouping	170
10–1	Variables Included in Factors that Explain 15 Percent or More of the Variance in the Levels of Per Capita Income by Regional Grouping	177
10–2	Variables Included in Factors that Explained 15 Percent or More of the Variance in the Rate of Growth of Total Personal Income by Regional Grouping	181
10–3	Variables Included in Factor that Explained 15 Percent or More of the Variance in the Rates of Growth of Per Capita Income by Regional Grouping	184
B–1	Variables by OBE Economic Area	202
B–2	Variables by OBE Economic Area	205
B–3	Variables by OBE Economic Area	208
B–4	Variables by OBE Economic Area	211
B–5	Variables by OBE Economic Area	214
B–6	Variables by OBE Economic Area	217
B–7	Variables by OBE Economic Area	220
B–8	Variables by OBE Economic Area	223
B–9	Variables by OBE Economic Area	226
B–10	Variables by OBE Economic Area	230
D–1	Correlation Coefficients: 171 OBE Economic Areas	241
D–2	Correlation Coefficients: Southeastern Regional Grouping	248
D–3	Correlation Coefficients: Northeastern Regional Grouping	254
D–4	Correlation Coefficients: Central Regional Grouping	260
D–5	Correlation Coefficients: Far West Regional Grouping	266

List of Maps

2–1	OBE Economic Areas	6a
2–2	OBE Economic Areas Ranked by the 1959 Level of Per Capita Income	8a
5–1	OBE Economic Areas Ranked by the Rate of Growth of Total Personal Income, 1950–66	66a
5–2	OBE Economic Areas Ranked by the Rate of Growth of Per Capita Income, 1950–66	70a

Acknowledgments

A book like this never represents the effort of only one person. Many have contributed to it, including those whose writings are cited throughout. First and foremost, my wife Mia has contributed immensely to this undertaking, and her support and devotion are the real forces that brought it to fruition.

An earlier draft of this book was my Ph.D. dissertation. Professor Cynthia Taft Morris was chairwoman of my committee. As a friend and advisor she contributed a tremendous amount of experience and work to every phase of the study. It would not be possible to find a more devoted and helpful advisor. Professors Vito Tanzi and James Weaver also contributed many helpful suggestions. In addition, I wish to thank Professor Warren S. Hunsberger for the help and stimulus he provided during my first years at the American University.

During the first stages of the study, discussions with Mr. Raymond Milkman, Mr. Tony Sulvetta, Mr. Jason Benderly, and Mr. Chris Bladen were most helpful. Ms. Ruth Duba typed all of the drafts during the dissertation stage. Her cheerfulness and patience in typing and correcting my errors was of tremendous assistance. Ms. Sandi Gosbee did a great job in typing the final manuscript under tight deadlines. The construction of the data files and subsequent analyses required extensive computer support. This was provided with great competence by Ms. Susan Jones and Mr. Carlis Taylor. Mr. Tom West contributed editorial comments during the final stages.

I have never been able to work without the support of family and friends. Mia and our two sons provide most of this incentive. The rest is provided by my parents Kenneth and Rosemary Sample and Dr. John and Mary Fontana and grandparents Walter and Margret Aaron. They helped me finish the study, but special thanks must go to Clifford A. Sample for getting it started.

Chapter One

Introduction

There is generally a lag in the response of science to newly recognized problems. Economics is no exception. It is useful to view the development of economics, and other social sciences as well, as theoretical and policy responses to new national issues. The very beginning of economics, as we know the field today, can be interpreted as a response by the first of the classical economists to the mercantilist policies of the early nineteenth century. Economists have been faced with a tremendous variety of issues as the economies of the world have changed since 1800. Not only have the issues been diverse, but the preconceived notions or perspectives of the economists writing about these issues have been equally diverse. One common feature, however, has been that the major advances in economic thought were made in response to issues of current interest.

Although we may now be witnessing a ceasefire in the "War on Poverty," the last two decades have brought forth a large volume of economic literature on this subject. This should not be construed as a "new issue" to economists, but at the very least, it should be recognized as a revived interest that has come to the forefront. Urban economics, for example, as a field of specialization, has become a new addition to the options of student economists. Similarly, the subject of this book, regional economic development, has recently taken a more prominent position among the interests of social scientists.

The recent development of regional economics has been typical in most respects. The initial surge of interest in regional economics—or more accurately regional science—during the 1950s was accomplished by drawing together theories developed in international economics, development economics, microeconomic theory, and macroeconomic theory.[1] These were combined with contributions from many of the other social sciences. This has been concisely expressed by Meyer as follows:

> Almost from the beginning, the convention, at least in formal discourse, has been to speak of "regional analysis" and "regional

> science" rather than "regional economics." Included and welcomed have been such diverse fields as sociology, demography, geography, and history. Indeed, at times, *the* distinguishing characteristic of regional analysis has almost seemed to be its interdisciplinary aspect.[2] (emphasis in original)

Although the theoretical sources for regional economics have been diverse, more use has been made of location theory and international trade theory than of other fields of the social sciences. This is hardly surprising, according to Meyer, since these two fields "have emphasized economic relations between geographical areas."[3]

This study attempts to maintain this tradition. It presents discussions, analyses, and interpretations of the patterns of economic change in four major geographical areas of the continental United States. It is designed on the premise that, because of very different histories, traditions, and social economic environments, major regions of the United States have undergone different patterns of economic change. The geographical boundaries of the sub-national areas selected for this study are discussed and defined in Chapter 2.

In the proposed quantitative study, three different measures of economic change will be used in the effort to present a balanced and complete analysis of economic change. These will be (1) the level of per capita income in 1959 (used as a measure of the long term structural development), (2) the average annual rate of increase in total personal income between 1950 and 1966 (used as a measure of short term growth in the total volume of economic activity), and (3) the average annual rate of increase in per capita income between 1950 and 1966 (used as a measure of the short term change in the average level of economic welfare).

Much of the literature of regional economics has emphasized the role of the continual expansion of regional exports as a primary force in regional growth. Analysis of the role of exports in determining the pattern and rate of economic growth will also be a focus of this study. Export base theory, as this theory is termed, will be analyzed separately for each sub-national area and will also become an important component in the analysis of the short term patterns in the growth of total economic activity.

The variables to be used in this study are discussed in Chapter 3. Approximately 50 variables have been included in the analyses. They represent economic, social, and political forces that have been considered to have relatively important influences on the pattern of economic growth and development by regional analysts. The set is as comprehensive as time and data availability would permit. The approach to data collection served two primary purposes. First, it enabled the selection of variables suggested by many theories of regional economic development that could not be *a priori* assigned relative importance. Second, the approach permitted the search for variables suggested as possibly important to regional economic change by the diverse fields of social science.

The statistical tools to be employed in this study will be regression analysis and factor analysis. The technique of regression analysis will be used in the analysis of a simplified export base model presented in Chapter 4. The technique of factor analysis will be used in the analyses of the patterns of long term structural development, short term growth in total economic activity, and change in the average level of economic welfare.

The variables, techniques of analysis, and spatial units to be used will enable the presentation of patterns of regional economic change from what is believed to be an original and important point of view. It will be shown that the relative importance of the export base arguments and the patterns of economic change vary according to the level of economic development obtained by the sub-national geographical areas.

In order to accomplish these objectives, primary attention will be given to the patterns of economic change experienced by each of the sub-national areas. Chapters 6 through 9 are devoted to the patterns of economic change experienced by these areas. Once this is accomplished comparisons of the patterns of economic change experienced by each regional grouping will be presented in order to specify more general properties of the patterns of economic change relevant to the United States.

This study, as stated above, is designed to be as comprehensive as possible. Yet there is little doubt that it will leave unanswered many questions concerning the patterns of economic change in regions of the United States. Adelman and Morris' *Society Politics and Economic Development* has served as a general guideline for this study. It is hoped that some of Professor Cynthia Taft Morris' contributions to this present study are recognized.

Chapter Two

Spatial Units of Analysis

INTRODUCTION

The first and possibly most important decision to be made in a study like this is to define the spatial units on which observations are to be gathered.

Economically meaningful definitions of geographical areas has been one of the most difficult problems faced by regional analysts. This difficulty arises on both theoretical and practical grounds. Theoretically, three general types of spatial units have been defined by regional analysts. However, the ever present data problem forced regional analysts to rely primarily on political boundaries when defining regions. The economic history of regions in the United States, for the most part, relied on three or four multistate regions. This has been complemented by a significant number of historical studies of states. The long term trend in regional studies has been to reduce the size of regions for analytic purposes. This was particularly evident since the 1950 Census, when reliable data were available on the basis of counties. These data permitted smaller spatial units to be defined. However, regional spatial definition remains a central problem in regional analysis.

CONCEPTS OF A REGION

The problems encountered by regional analysts in defining spatial regions are well documented.[1] The three types of spatial units most commonly used are:

1. Uniform or homogeneous regions.
2. Nodal regions.
3. Programming or planning regions.[2]

The homogeneous concept attempts to group regions having a similar characteristic. The characteristic may be economic, geographic, or sociopolitical. All that is required is that the regions are homogeneous in the specified characteristic. For example, such characteristics might include production structure, consumption patterns, climate, social attitudes, or national identity.[3] This concept is used here to group the spatial units of analysis (OBE Economic Areas) into larger regional groupings.

Nodal regions are defined with reference to a central place, usually an urban area. They are composed of heterogeneous spatial units that are functionally related.[4] This type of spatial region emphasizes the social and economic ties between the central place and the surrounding territory. The OBE Economic Areas that serve as the spatial unit of analysis in this study are an example of this type of region.

Programming, or planning, regions conform to administrative, usually political, boundaries. These regions are policy-oriented regions that have the administrative ability to carry out development plans or policies. According to Richardson, "there is a widespread view that the nodal region in general, and the metropolitan region in particular, is the optimal planning region. To the extent that this is true, then planning regions and nodal regions may coincide.[5]

In general, as Richardson also shows, there is no inherent reason why the regional definitions are mutually exclusive. However, nodal regions are most frequently combined with programming or planning regions. This stems from the importance of large metropolitan areas: spheres of regional influence. Commonly, urban areas are viewed as growth poles or growth centers and therefore set the economic growth pace for the surrounding region. This view can be traced back to the development of location and central place theory advanced by Thunen in the early 1900s.[6] "In recent years, central place theory has been extended and applied by Brian Berry and Others to a host of questions concerned with the spatial distribution of economic activities."[7] Central place theory provides the logic behind the economic areas developed by the Office of Business Economics under the direction of Brian Berry.

THE OBE ECONOMIC AREAS

The OBE Economic Areas, which were developed under the direction of Brian Berry for the Office of Business Economics of the U.S. Department of Commerce, serve as the basic observational unit for this study. These areas are presented on Map 2–1. The Alaska and Hawaii economic areas are excluded from this analysis because of their geographical isolation and because the criteria used by OBE tend to break down in these two cases.

The OBE Economic Areas are constructed on the basis of the nodal-functional concept. Each area is constructed around a central urban place, usually a Standard Metropolitan Statistical Area (SMSA). The OBE Economic Areas are based on the concept that the central place extends its sphere of economic and social influences to the surrounding area, and thus corresponds to the closed trade areas of central place theory. A sphere of influence is defined according to:

1. Journey to work patterns.
2. Comparative time and distance of travel to the center.
3. Input requirements of the area's industry, where possible.

"Each area approaches self-sufficiency in its residentiary (service) industry sector; that is, while each economic area specializes in producing goods and/or services for export to other economic areas (and abroad) most of the services (and some goods) required by the residents and businesses of the area are provided within the area."[8] The method by which the OBE areas were constructed is summarized in an unpublished memo from the Regional Economics Division of the Office of Business Economics:

> First, economic centers were identified. Standard metropolitan statistical areas were chosen where possible. Each SMSA has a large city at its center which serves both as a wholesale and retail trade center and as a labor market center. However, not all SMSA's were made centers of economic areas because some are integral parts of larger metropolitan complexes. The New York City area, for instance, encompasses not only the New York City SMSA but also Jersey City, Newark, Patterson-Clifton-Everett and the Seattle economic area includes Seattle-Everett and the Tacoma SMSA's. In rural parts of the country, where there were no SMSA's, cities of from 25,000 to 50,000 population were utilized as economic centers provided that two other criteria were met. These other criteria were: (1) that the city form a wholesale trade center for the area; and (2) that the area as a whole have a population minimum of about 200,000 people. (There are some exceptions to the size criteria in sparsely populated areas.) After identifying economic centers, intervening counties were allocated to the centers. This assignment was made on the basis of comparative time and distance of travel to the economic centers, the journey to work pattern around the economic centers, the interconnection between counties because of journey to work, the road network, the linkage of counties by such other economic ties as could be found, and certain geographic features. In places where the commuting pattern of adjacent economic centers overlap, counties were included in the economic area containing the center with which there was the greatest commuting connection. In the case of cities where the commuting pattern overlapped to a great degree, no attempt was made to separate the two cities; instead, both were included in the same economic area. In the more rural parts of the country, the journey to work information was insufficient to establish boundaries of the economic areas. In these

areas, distance of travel to the economic centers was the major determinant.[9]

The OBE Economic Areas were selected as the basic unit of analysis for this study because they represent the spatial unit most consistent with its objectives. One of the more important objectives of the study is to analyze the importance of the economic base concept in regional development. The OBE Economic Areas are spatial units that emphasize the functional interrelationships between the central place and the surrounding territory. They are, therefore, meaningful *economic* units, as opposed to the more commonly used political units. In addition, the property of closure in the residentiary sector means that the economic ties with other OBE areas are maintained primarily by exports.

REGIONAL GROUPINGS

The 171 OBE Economic Areas are grouped into four regional groupings. Two constraints were applied when forming the regional groupings. First, each regional grouping was to consist of contiguous OBE areas. Secondly, an attempt was made to maximize the degree of socioeconomic homogeneity of each regional grouping. In order to approximate homogeneous characteristics, the 1959 level of per capita income of the OBE areas was selected as the decision criterion. The procedure used was to rank the OBE areas by their 1959 per capita income (see Table 2–1). The 171 OBE areas of the continental United States are formed into regional groupings consisting, as nearly as possible, of OBE areas with similar levels of per capita income. The regional groupings formed in this way are presented in Map 2–2. The OBE areas shown on this map are coded by their quartile ranking of per capita income in 1959.

It is obvious from Map 2–2 that the boundary between the Central and Far West Regional Groupings cannot be defined by the criteria discussed above. Therefore, in order to define the western boundary of this regional grouping, the boundary of Bogue and Beale's Rocky Mountain and Intermountain Region is approximated.[10] The regional definitions developed by Bogue and Beale are drawn in order to maximize the socioeconomic characteristics. Therefore, they are applicable to this study.

It must be admitted that the regional groupings formed are somewhat arbitrary, but, in general, they approximate regions that are relatively homogeneous in terms of socioeconomic characteristics. The economic characteristics of each regional grouping are discussed in Chapters 6, 7, 8, and 9.

Table 2–1. OBE Economic Areas Ranked by Per Capita Personal Income, 1959

OBE Economic Area	*Per Capita Personal Income 1959*	*OBE Economic Area*	*Per Capita Personal Income 1959*
14.0	2872.93	61.0	2113.33
77.0	2794.18	91.0	2108.38
165.0	2783.69	154.0	2082.64
160.0	2780.62	158.0	2074.83
171.0	2773.77	156.0	2067.29
84.0	2551.95	7.0	2060.74
18.0	2540.69	75.0	2056.23
8.0	2527.59	57.0	2047.49
5.0	2517.62	95.0	2046.60
161.0	2507.09	83.0	2046.03
71.0	2470.18	64.0	2033.52
15.0	2434.32	163.0	2030.65
155.0	2433.61	58.0	2030.17
68.0	2407.33	12.0	2014.71
170.0	2402.15	16.0	2008.28
168.0	2394.31	106.0	2001.60
169.0	2387.42	54.0	1997.59
150.0	2378.03	101.0	1980.00
148.0	2375.53	153.0	1960.23
122.0	2361.00	108.0	1955.25
4.0	2358.97	159.0	1954.28
82.0	2320.82	73.0	1950.92
9.0	2312.73	90.0	1949.08
164.0	2291.56	35.0	1948.67
63.0	2278.46	105.0	1942.36
78.0	2274.63	151.0	1940.56
76.0	2271.14	2.0	1928.61
62.0	2268.82	10.0	1922.85
60.0	2260.98	59.0	1922.36
114.0	2233.47	162.0	1916.63
110.0	2225.13	119.0	1913.60
127.0	2224.76	109.0	1901.97
36.0	2224.38	152.0	1893.60
124.0	2223.01	140.0	1891.01
157.0	2218.48	146.0	1882.77
79.0	2212.50	145.0	1878.39
17.0	2205.00	44.0	1871.44
141.0	2191.51	37.0	1870.09
167.0	2187.04	69.0	1853.60
80.0	2183.32	147.0	1844.54
166.0	2180.14	102.0	1842.78
67.0	2179.92	87.0	1834.08
70.0	2174.00	85.0	1829.13
123.0	2160.80	113.0	1826.85
66.0	2157.21	72.0	1825.62
6.0	2154.79	126.0	1824.19
111.0	2140.30	149.0	1821.11
74.0	2139.54	21.0	1819.05
94.0	2138.91	11.0	1811.35
107.0	2116.18	120.0	1803.68

Table 2–1. (cont.)

OBE Economic Area	*Per Capita Personal Income 1959*	*OBE Economic Area*	*Per Capita Personal Income 1959*
125.0	1799.72	48.0	1494.10
121.0	1796.29	130.0	1483.31
34.0	1774.35	65.0	1480.34
138.0	1773.84	117.0	1477.26
25.0	1765.28	52.0	1454.33
22.0	1758.55	27.0	1438.00
3.0	1747.86	99.0	1435.79
100.0	1745.81	139.0	1421.67
39.0	1744.83	43.0	1419.44
56.0	1744.15	46.0	1399.57
13.0	1741.61	24.0	1398.54
26.0	1699.06	47.0	1397.33
88.0	1688.40	33.0	1392.29
86.0	1679.27	115.0	1388.63
128.0	1676.73	135.0	1381.56
132.0	1673.35	32.0	1352.19
89.0	1655.49	118.0	1342.86
55.0	1638.10	31.0	1327.55
103.0	1612.85	96.0	1324.91
112.0	1611.75	29.0	1321.50
1.0	1601.86	38.0	1302.19
81.0	1594.88	50.0	1301.31
116.0	1592.55	133.0	1292.27
104.0	1590.86	23.0	1288.68
142.0	1580.27	42.0	1284.51
143.0	1562.64	40.0	1281.60
19.0	1559.62	51.0	1263.95
20.0	1558.64	131.0	1240.78
28.0	1543.05	53.0	1239.91
45.0	1539.86	134.0	1206.28
92.0	1531.72	41.0	1200.85
129.0	1529.27	98.0	1199.43
137.0	1528.83	136.0	1136.78
93.0	1511.05	144.0	1096.85
97.0	1509.98	30.0	1047.98
49.0	1502.17		

Chapter Three

Descriptions of the Variables

INTRODUCTION

A basic step of any research effort is to define and justify the use of the variables to be included in the study. This chapter attempts to fulfill this requirement. In the pages that follow a discussion of the meaning, the use, and importance of each of the 49 variables that are to be used in this study will be presented.

The major objective of this study is to present a balanced analysis of economic change in regions of the United States. Therefore, the approach adopted in the selection of variables seeks to be exhaustive and eclectic, rather than restrictive. It is important to emphasize that attempts were made to include measures that are indicative of social, economic, and political forces that may be deemed as important influences on the pattern of economic change in regions of the United States. It must be admitted, however, that the final selection of variables is weighted toward the traditional economic forces. This has resulted from greater data limitations for indicators of social and political forces rather than of conscious design. Data limitations have also dictated the use of some indirect, rather than direct, measures of forces deemed important.

The variables used in this study are reported, by OBE Economic Area, in Appendix B. The basic data used to construct these variables are available at the county level in published reports. A major data constraint was the necessity of limiting variables to those for which the basic county data was available on computer tape. Keypunching, or summing by hand, data for over 3,000 counties was not feasible. Computer tapes with county data were obtained from the Office of Business Economics (OBE), the Census Department, and from files of the Economic Development Administration. In addition, a few variables were supplied by OBE at the OBE Economic Area level. The procedure used for the calculation of each variable from the basic data is reported in this chapter. In addition, a statistical summary by regional grouping of each variable is presented in order to summarize the variations in these variables.

The 49 variables used have been grouped into 19 categories representing what may be considered either major components of, or influences on, the patterns of economic change. These forces have been titled as follows:

1. Measures of Economic Change.
2. Measures of the Economic Base.
3. Growth of Residentiary Employment.
4. Index of the Composition of Growth Industries.
5. Coefficient of Economic Concentration.
6. Measures of Industrialization.
7. Estimate of the Change in the Labor Force Participation Rate.
8. The Net Migration Rate.
9. Measures of the Loan Potential of Local Financial Institutions.
10. Measures of Manufacturing Productivity.
11. Measures of Manufacturing Investment.
12. Measures of Agricultural Technology, Agricultural. Growth Sectors, and the Character of the Agricultural Organization.
13. Measures of the Local Government Fiscal Effort.
14. Measures of Deficit Financing by Local Governments.
15. Measures of Local Government Services Provided.
16. Measures of Political Participation.
17. Measures of Socioeconomic Structure.
18. Measures of the Level of Educational Achievement.
19. Measure of Population Density.

Before presenting the variables, it should be recognized that most are subject to criticism. The *a priori* meaning attached to each variable has resulted from extensive discussion and debate. There may be other interpretations than those assigned to the variables. In fact, this will generally be the case. In a few cases, the time period used to measure changes is too short. In these cases, it was believed that attempts should nevertheless be made to include them rather than exclude them completely.

MEASURES OF ECONOMIC CHANGE

This study is designed to explain variations in the patterns of economic change in regions of the United States with the use of approximately 50 variables. For this reason the estimates of economic change assume critical importance. Perloff *et al.* define six possible measures that may be used for these purposes.[1] These measures can be grouped into two types—volume and welfare measures. This study will be limited to one estimate of each type. The estimate for changes in the volume of economic activity will be the average annual rate of increase in total personal income for the period 1950–1966.[2] The estimate for the change in the average level of economic welfare for the same period will be the average annual rate of increase in per capita personal income.[3] Finally, the 1959 level of per capita income will be used to measure the variations in the structural development of each of the regional groupings.

It is necessary to include each of these estimates in the study to grasp a rounded picture of subregional growth and changes in economic welfare. All are heavily influenced by population changes, but not necessarily in the same direction. An increasing population generally has a strong positive effect on the rate of increase in total personal income. However, population increases without corresponding increases in total personal income would have a negative effect on changes in per capita income.

The use of the average annual rate of increase in total personal income as a measure of the change in the volume or growth of economic activity is not without precedent in regional analysis. According to Perloff *et al.*, "One of the most comprehensive and suggestive measures of regional economic growth is provided by total personal income."[4] The traditional or more common usage of the term economic growth may not be consistent with the way it is used in this study. However, it is suggestive, as Perloff *et al.* emphasize, of the level of total economic activity and the change in it.

Growth in per capita income has been one of the measures traditionally used to study the "economic growth" of nations.[5] The link between per capita income growth and increases in the average level of economic welfare is tenuous. However, as Perloff *et al.* argue, "The interplay between population growth and growth in total personal income within various regions is reflected in the per capita income levels and rates of increase.[6] The interplay of these forces are what will determine the average level of economic welfare. Benjamin Higgins, for example, argues that in order to have "economic development" countries must have a discernible rise in total *and* per capita income. Furthermore, he argues that the "process will be accompanied by structural change, narrowing gaps in productivity among sectors and regions, and improved education and health."[7] Therefore, the average annual rate of growth of per capita income between 1950 and 1966 will be used as a measure of the change in the average level of economic welfare.

The alternative measures discussed by Perloff *et al.* for estimates of volume changes are absolute change in income, absolute change in population, and percentage increases in population. The differences that result from use of these measures stem from the influence of the size of the base. Absolute measures overemphasize the growth of larger areas, while the percentage measures overemphasize the growth of smaller places. As this analysis is concerned with comparisons of growth between areas, the relative percentage measures are better for this purpose.

The alternative measure for welfare estimates discussed by Perloff *et al.*, is the absolute change in per capita income. Again the relative estimate is more satisfactory because of the comparative nature of this study.

There is a good case for using median family income as the measure of welfare rather than per capita income. Median family income is less influenced by the extremes of the income distribution and therefore a better indicator of the general level of economic welfare of an area. This estimate would have been used if it had been available for each OBE Economic Area. Median family income is not available on the OBE Economic Area level and cannot, of course, be determined through aggregation of data from the county level.

Statistical Summary of Variables

Rate of Increase in Total Personal Income, 1950–1966*

	Nation	*N. East*	*S. East*	*Central*	*Far West*
Mean	5.82	5.64	6.14	4.89	6.53
Standard Deviation	1.37	.66	1.10	.90	1.88
Minimum	2.71	3.54	3.84	2.71	3.50
Maximum	11.96	7.22	9.28	7.02	11.96

*Current dollars were used in the calculations.

Rate of Increase of Per Capita Personal Income, 1950–1966*

	Nation	*N. East*	*S. East*	*Central*	*Far West*
Mean	4.43	4.28	5.00	4.24	3.80
Standard Deviation	.68	.37	.64	.59	.52
Minimum	2.52	3.71	3.43	2.76	2.52
Maximum	6.73	5.35	6.73	5.28	4.75

*Current dollars were used in the calculations.

Per Capita Personal Income, 1959*

	Nation	*N. East*	*S. East*	*Central*	*Far West*
Mean	1871.00	2169.95	1484.96	1844.24	2188.07
Standard Deviation	395.32	266.98	229.38	282.38	296.63
Minimum	1048.00	1602.00	1048.00	1199.00	1821.00
Maximum	2873.00	2873.00	2192.00	2378.00	2783.00

*Current dollars were used in the calculations.

MEASURES OF THE ECONOMIC BASE

The "economic base" refers to that part, or percentage, of total income, or employment, which is accounted for by industries producing goods and/or services for export to other areas. In this study, exports refer to goods and services that are shipped or sold outside of the OBE Economic Area in which they were produced. The proposition that growth in the export base, or growth in the ratio of income earned by export industries to total income earned, is a leading force determining the rate of economic growth of the OBE Economic Areas will play an important role in this study.

The estimates of the economic base (export oriented production) to be used in this analysis were developed by the Office of Business Economics.[8] The OBE estimates are based on location quotients calculated for the two digit and some three digit Standard Industrial Classifications. Location quotients have been a common way to make base calculations, but have been widely criticized. The quotient is generally calculated as follows: first, the ratio of employment by sector to total employment for the total United States is calculated. Second, this ratio is calculated for each region. The quotient is then defined as the ratio for the region divided by the ratio for the nation.

Defined mathematically as:

$$LQ = \frac{\frac{Eij}{Ej}}{\frac{Ein}{En}}$$

Where: Eij = Employment in the ith industry in region j.
Ej = Total employment in region j.
Ein = Employment in the ith industry in the nation.
En = Total employment in the nation.

If the location quotient (LQ) for industry i is greater than 1, industry i is then interpreted to be an export oriented industry for the region because of the relatively greater concentration of that industry in the region. Conversely, if the LQ is less than 1, it is then assumed that the region must import some output of industry i from the rest of the nation. If this is the case the region is considered as less than self-sufficient in that sector and thus must be consuming all of the output from industry i produced in the region. It is therefore considered as a non-basic industry for the region.

The assumptions necessary for these interpretations are as follows:

1. Homogeneous consumption and expenditure patterns in all regions of the nation.
2. Homogeneous production functions between all regions.
3. Products consumed in all regions will be purchased from producers of those products in the same region.

In addition, the procedure underestimates the amount of exports because it addresses net exports rather than gross exports. Thus, subsectors which have been aggregated may be export oriented even though the major sector is considered as a non-basic industry. This problem is reduced as the degree of disaggregation is increased.[9]

The location quotient does not differ significantly in terms of necessary assumptions from the other methods used to estimate regional export production. In addition, according to Harry Richardson:

> The drawbacks of the method should not be overstressed. It has two important advantages. Firstly it takes care of indirect as well as direct exports. For instance, a steel plant may sell most of its output to a local car manufacturer exporting cars; this is locally sold but is tied indirectly to exports, and this fact will be revealed by the L.Q. approach. Secondly, the method is inexpensive and can be applied to historical data to reveal trends. Despite their deficiencies, L.Q. methods will yield an estimate, probably an understatement, of base activity.[10]

In addition to these advantages, the OBE estimates have attempted to minimize the drawbacks inherent in the method. First, earnings by industry source were used in preference to employment data to avoid problems with the assumption of homogeneous production functions. This assumption is necessary when using employment data, because productivity must be assumed constant between regions. When using earnings by industry sector, it is not necessary as long as we accept that productivity of wage earners is strongly related to salary, and thus earnings.

Secondly, the definition of the export sector for each OBE Economic Area is unique. This, of course, depends on the use of the location quotients. For all areas, agriculture, mining, manufacturing, and federal government activities were considered to be export activity. In addition, fourteen three digit SIC sectors, usually considered as non-basic activity, were analyzed by location quotients to determine whether or not they were to be considered non-basic activities. These sectors consist of:

1. Food Processing.
2. Printing and Publishing.
3. Railroads.
4. Trucking and Warehousing.
5. Other Transportation Services.
6. Communications.
7. Public Utilities.
8. Wholesale and Retail Trade.
9. Finance, Insurance, and Real Estate.
10. Hotels and Personal Services.
11. Business and Repair Services.

12. Amusement and Recreation Services.
13. Professional Services.
14. State and Local Government.

A list of the activities considered to be basic activities for each OBE Economic Area is included as Appendix A.

Last to be discussed here is the often debated point that not all manufacturing, mining, and agricultural activities are destined for the export market and therefore total output from those sectors should not be included in the basic sector. The rebuttal to this is that even though this is true, the output of these sectors are subject to national marketing and therefore should be distinguished from non-basic activities, which are generally marketed on a local basis. Thus, even though automobiles are purchased by residents of Detroit, the production of automobiles in Detroit is by far not as significantly influenced by local purchases as by national purchases.

This estimate does have limitations, but until export statistics are developed by region, such indirect methods must be used to estimate the actual exports by region. The base value to be used in this analysis is open to most of the criticisms, but these have been minimized by the approach taken by the Office of Business Economics, Regional Economic Division.

Statistical Summary of Variables

Economic Base 1950

	Nation	*N. East*	*S. East*	*Central*	*Far West*
Mean	44.74	42.56	46.75	46.93	41.77
Standard Deviation	6.32	5.10	5.92	6.40	5.74
Minimum	30.47	33.61	35.22	31.74	31.18
Maximum	58.04	52.41	57.49	58.04	54.15

Economic Base 1959

	Nation	*N. East*	*S. East*	*Central*	*Far West*
Mean	42.13	44.03	43.22	40.52	39.70
Standard Deviation	5.26	4.71	5.46	4.78	4.58
Minimum	28.71	36.71	31.22	28.71	32.28
Maximum	54.55	54.55	54.40	50.00	47.91

Economic Base 1967

	Nation	*N. East*	*S. East*	*Central*	*Far West*
Mean	41.96	43.30	42.92	41.43	38.82
Standard Deviation	5.04	4.84	5.53	4.34	3.97
Minimum	30.05	35.84	33.64	33.60	30.05
Maximum	55.93	54.90	55.93	51.75	46.35

Percent Change in the Economic Base, 1950–1967

	Nation	*N. East*	*S. East*	*Central*	*Far West*
Mean	−.12	−1.53	−.54	3.16	−2.64
Standard Deviation	7.49	3.71	5.48	10.85	7.85
Minimum	−16.22	−7.57	−15.99	−13.61	−16.22
Maximum	52.24	7.97	13.93	52.24	13.87

GROWTH OF RESIDENTIARY EMPLOYMENT

The residentiary sector refers to sectors that produce goods and services for local consumption. In the terminology of economic base models the residentiary sector is commonly referred to as the non-basic sector. Total employment of a given region is, therefore, the sum of the residentiary or non-basic employment and basic or export employment. In this study the following sectors are considered to be residentiary sectors since it is possible to assume that output from these sectors will be locally consumed:

1. Contract Construction.
2. Public Utilities.
3. Eating and Drinking Establishments.
4. Finance, Insurance, and Real Estate.
5. Lodging Places.
6. Other Retail Trade.
7. Business and Repair Services.
8. Amusements.
9. Private Households.
10. Educational, Medical, and Professional Services.
11. Public Administration.

In general, there has been a lack of concern about the residentiary or non-basic sector by regional analysts. Tiebout and Lane attribute this lack of concern to the emergence of two extreme points of view.[11] First, many regional analysts suggest that the basic-non-basic ratio is fixed for any given region (although few believe it is fixed and invariable as between regions).[12] As a result of this assumption, regional analysts have concentrated on the basic sector as the primary impetus in regional development. Second, other regional analysts suggest "that non-basic activity is unrelated to total activity."[13] Tiebout and Lane reject both of these interpretations. They argue that growth in the basic sector alone cannot explain regional development, especially in light of the relatively slow growth of manufacturing, which is often considered the most important of the basic sectors, over the past decade.

In addition, Tiebout and Lane stress an important behavioral characteristic of measures of the growth in the residentiary sector that will also be of major importance in this analysis. This is that the economic base multiplier is strongly influenced by the concept of income used. They have shown that this multiplier will be greater if total personal income has remained the same, as opposed to a situation where increases in total personal income have resulted from increases in per capita income. The difference, of course, results from the influence exerted on local services by movements in population. They argue that there will be greater multiplier leakages as per capita income increases. In other words, per capita increases result in more imports from other regions (i.e. automobiles), whereas total personal income increases resulting from immigration of workers result in less leakage (e.g., more expenditures on the local construction of homes). This problem will be addressed by analyzing the influence of the growth in the residentiary sector on both increases in per capita and total personal income.

In the expert base model discussed in Chapter 4, the structure of the residentiary sector is assumed to have a pronounced effect on regional growth. As mentioned above, estimates of the size of this effect will be influenced by the concept of income used as well as on the relationship between the export sector and the residentiary sector. The variable to be used in the analysis to measure the influence of growth of the residentiary sector will be the rate of employment growth in the residentiary sector between 1950 and 1960.[14]

Statistical Summary of Variables

Rate of Increase in Residentiary Employment

	Nation	*N. East*	*S. East*	*Central*	*Far West*
Mean	2.48	2.04	2.50	1.85	3.82
Standard Deviation	1.42	.53	1.15	.76	2.08
Minimum	−.14	.26	−.14	.60	.25
Maximum	9.15	3.08	6.84	3.88	9.15

THE INDEX OF THE COMPOSITION OF GROWTH INDUSTRIES

Regional analysts have focused a great deal of attention on "growth industries," considering them an important factor in regional economic development. The variable to be discussed here is designed to measure the effect of variation on the importance of national growth industries in the industrial mix of the regional economies.

Most of the literature dealing with growth industries is part of the literature on the general approach—termed shift-share analysis[15]—to regional development analysis. Regional growth, according to this approach, may be achieved by:

(1) Obtaining a greater share of the output of industries regardless of the national rate of growth of industries. Thus, these industries would grow at a greater rate within the region than they did nationally. This is commonly called the "competitive component" of regional growth. The typical example of this type of growth is southern areas that have, because of the low wage labor supply in this area, a competitive advantage in the textile industry, or

(2) By having an industrial mix that is weighted toward industries that are growing at a rate greater than the national average. Thus regions that maintain a given share of the output of these industries may also grow faster than the national average. This is commonly termed the compositional component, and the typical example could be the growth of the aerospace industry of Seattle during the 1960s.

This analysis will concentrate on the second of these types of growth, the relative compositional weight of growth industries. The two components of shift analysis are often considered to be dynamic in nature. This is not considered to be accurate, because the change in the components is analyzed rather than the time path of the change. The index to be used in this study to measure the impact of the compositional weight of national growth industries will be a static indicator for 1960. Calculated as:

$$WGS = \sum_{i=1}^{32} (Ein) \frac{(Eij)}{Ej}$$

where:

WGS = Weighted Growth Sectors

Ein = rate of growth of industry i in the nation for the period 1950–1960.[16]

Eij = employment in industry i in OBE area j in 1960.

Ej = total employment in OBE area j in 1960.

The 32 industry sectors used are listed below. The index will be relatively large when the industrial composition of the regional employment base is weighted toward growth industries. Thus if these industries have exerted a positive influence on regional growth, the index will be positively related to the measures of economic change.

Table 3–1. Rate of Employment Growth by Industry Sector, 1950–1960

Sector	*National Rate of Growth*
1. Agriculture	-4.650
2. Forestry and Fisheries	-2.589
3. Mining	-3.314
4. Contract Construction	1.222
Manufacturing:	
5. Food and Kindred Products	2.838
6. Textile Mill Products	-2.408
7. Apparel and Other Textile Products	1.152
8. Printing and Publishing	3.250
9. Chemicals	3.040
10. Lumber and Furniture	-0.930
11. Non-electric Machinery	2.216
12. Electrical Machinery	6.884
13. Transport Equipment	3.308
14. Paper and Allied Products	2.380
15. Petroleum Refining	0.075
16. Primary Metals Industry	0.723
17. Fabricated Metals and Ordinance	4.682
18. Misc.	1.614
19. Transport Services	-0.481
20. Communications	1.732
21. Utilities	1.617
22. Wholesale Trade	1.395
23. Eating and Drinking Establishments	0.889
24. Other Retail Trade	1.447
25. Finance, Insurance and Real Estate	3.758
26. Lodging Places	0.692
27. Business and Repair Services	2.353
28. Amusements and Recreation Services	0.465
29. Private Households	1.808
30. Educational, Medical and Professional Services	4.952
31. Public Administration	2.740
32. Armed Forces	5.565

Source: Calculated from basic data not reported.

Statistical Summary of Variables

The Index of the Composition of Growth Industries, 1960

	Nation	*N. East*	*S. East*	*Central*	*Far West*
Mean	1.31	1.95	1.11	.80	1.38
Standard Deviation	.69	.31	.51	.67	.71
Minimum	−.53	1.32	−.15	−.53	.43
Maximum	3.23	2.62	2.28	1.91	3.23

COEFFICIENT OF ECONOMIC CONCENTRATION

Economists have focused on the positive influence of diversification of a country's or region's economic structure as a means to avoid fluctuation in economic activity as a result of fluctuations in a single or a few commodity markets. This logic has been extended to regions that depend on a few industrial or agricultural products. Wilbur Thompson, following this reasoning, defines five stages of regional growth which essentially depend on increased diversification of production as regions grow and mature.[17]

Richard Pfister, although recognizing that diversification is desirable for a region, argues that the importance of diversification has been overemphasized.[18] On the basis of an unpublished manuscript by Stopler and Tiebout, Pfister argues that a diversified industrial structure is not sufficient to reduce cycles. Pfister's contribution makes explicit the assumption necessary for the diversification theory that commodity market fluctuations must be independent of each other. He then argues that business cycle fluctuations usually affect a wide range of commodities, and thus regions with a diversified industrial structure are not insulated from general market fluctuations.

Pfister's criticism is important, but does not destroy the diversification argument. In fact Pfister's criticism is typical of debates concerning diversification of production. It misses what may very well be the most important aspect of the diversification hypothesis. One of the most striking aspects of American economic history is the ease with which the American economy shifted from one growth sector to another. The ability to shift emphasis from one industry to another is largely a function of economic diversification. In replying to a different criticism, Douglas North alludes to this same issue by stressing that Tiebout is concentrating on the short run, which eliminates the need to consider the mobility of labor and capital.[19] It is argued here, therefore, that in the long run a region's diversified industrial or economic mix provides a better opportunity to shift resources from industry to industry within a region.

The indicators defined here are designed to measure, in aggregate terms, the extent to which regions have been able to diversify their economic structure. The index, developed by Michaely,[20] measures the degree of economic concentration on a theoretical scale of 0 to 100. The upper limit of 100 defines an economic base where all output is concentrated in one product. The lower approaches zero as the number of sectors used approaches infinity. The fewer the number of employment sectors used to calculate the coefficient, the higher will be the minimum possible value of the index. Since 32 employment categories have been used in the calculations, the lower limit is 17.66.[21]

Mathematically the index is defined as:

$$C = 100 \sqrt{\sum_{i=1}^{32} \left(\frac{x_{ij}}{x_j} \right)^2}$$

where C = degree of concentration

x_{ij} = production of commodity i in region j.

x_j = total production in region j.

Employment data for 32 industry sectors will be used as a proxy for output. Because the interest here is only in the relative degrees of concentration or, more accurately, diversification, the use of employment as a proxy for income should not significantly bias the results. The 32 employment sectors used are as follows:

1. Agriculture.
2. Forestry and Fisheries.
3. Mining.
4. Contract Construction.
5. Manufacturing: Food and Kindred Products.
6. Manufacturing: Textile Mill Products.
7. Manufacturing: Apparel and Other Textile Products.
8. Manufacturing: Printing and Publishing.
9. Manufacturing: Chemicals.
10. Manufacturing: Lumber and Furniture.
11. Manufacturing: Non-electrical Machinery.
12. Manufacturing: Electrical Machinery.
13. Manufacturing: Transport Equipment.
14. Manufacturing: Paper and Allied Products.
15. Manufacturing: Petroleum Refining.
16. Manufacturing: Primary Metals Industry.
17. Manufacturing: Fabricated Metals and Ordinance.
18. Manufacturing: Misc.
19. Transport Services.
20. Communications.
21. Utilities.
22. Wholesale Trade.

23. Eating and Drinking Establishments.
24. Other Retail Trade.
25. Finance, Insurance, and Real Estate.
26. Lodging Places.
27. Business and Repair Services.
28. Amusements and Recreation Services.
29. Private Households.
30. Educational, Medical, and Professional Services.
31. Public Administration.
32. Armed Forces.

The index will be calculated for 1950 and 1960. The percent change in this index between 1950 and 1960 will also be used. The change in the index will provide an indicator of the influence of increasing diversification on regional growth and development.

Statistical Summary of Variables

Coefficient of Concentration, 1950

	Nation	*N. East*	*S. East*	*Central*	*Far West*
Mean	31.90	26.41	33.59	36.72	30.54
Standard Deviation	6.74	3.22	5.97	7.49	4.20
Minimum	22.17	22.17	24.66	25.80	24.16
Maximum	52.75	34.37	51.85	52.75	38.42

Coefficient of Concentration, 1960

	Nation	*N. East*	*S. East*	*Central*	*Far West*
Mean	28.45	25.90	27.88	31.87	28.77
Standard Deviation	4.05	2.35	2.65	5.18	3.13
Minimum	22.59	22.59	24.15	24.75	23.80
Maximum	43.98	33.80	35.57	43.98	38.58

Percent Change in the Coefficient of Concentration, 1950–1960

	Nation	*N. East*	*S. East*	*Central*	*Far West*
Mean	−9.37	−1.80	−15.50	−12.34	−5.27
Standard Deviation	9.20	4.61	10.03	5.93	6.38
Minimum	−40.08	−13.12	−40.08	−23.94	−19.66
Maximum	6.62	4.44	1.57	3.40	6.62

MEASURES OF INDUSTRIALIZATION

Within the context of regional economic growth and development, industrialization and urbanization have generally been related. Benjamin Higgins observes that, "While it would appear that significant industrialization is not possible without some accompanying urbanization . . . . it is less clear that urbanization is impossible without industrialization."[22] The necessary link between industrialization and urbanization is, of course, the need for a stable and possibly an expanding labor force.

The process of industrialization has generally been viewed as the shifting from an agricultural economy to a manufacturing economy.[23] Higgins, for example, defines industrialization as:

> the proportion of the active male labor force engaged in manufacturing, construction, gas and electricity, or as a percentage of the total labor force working as salaried employees or wage earners in manufacturing alone.[24]

The importance of a viable manufacturing sector to the economic growth and development of a region stems from the employment and growth opportunities provided by this sector. According to Perloff *et al.*, "manufacturing is one of the largest and most dynamic sectors of total employment."[25] Industrialization may, therefore, involve both the process of urbanization and the increasing relative importance of the manufacturing sector. As we broaden the measure of industrialization from simply manufacturing to include the other industrial sectors, such as transportation, the association between industrialization and urbanization increases.[26] For this study we have selected the more restrictive measure of industrialization, since other variables to be discussed later are designed to measure urbanization. The two variables to be used in this study as measures of industrialization will be the percent of total income earned, or value added, by the manufacturing sector in 1950 and 1959. These two variables will not, of course, be used simultaneously in any analysis.

Statistical Summary of Variables

Percent Earnings from Manufacturing, 1950

	Nation	*N. East*	*S. East*	*Central*	*Far West*
Mean	15.87	25.96	16.95	7.40	10.36
Standard Deviation	11.45	9.75	9.70	6.48	9.85
Minimum	0.19	1.45	2.85	0.19	1.22
Maximum	47.06	47.06	46.80	25.96	37.28

Percent Earnings from Manufacturing, 1959

	Nation	*N. East*	*S. East*	*Central*	*Far West*
Mean	20.65	33.70	20.00	11.90	13.85
Standard Deviation	12.61	9.38	9.49	8.66	10.15
Minimum	0.89	2.24	3.87	0.89	2.68
Maximum	50.18	50.18	45.73	31.71	39.53

CHANGE IN THE LABOR FORCE PARTICIPATION

The importance of the labor force to the growth of a region cannot, of course, be understated. Richardson emphasizes three determinants of regional labor forces. They are: (1) the rate of natural increase in the population, (2) the activity rate, and (3) the rate of in- or out-migration.[27] This indicator addresses the second of these determinants, the activity rate, which we will term the labor force participation rate.

Richardson[28] and Thompson[29] argue that variation in the labor force participation rate accounts for a significant part of the per capita income differentials between states. Thompson cites empirical studies that conclude that interstate income differentials are reduced by approximately 20 to 25 percent when adjusted for non-producers.[30] Extending this reasoning Richardson argues that, "in the United States . . . a reduction in the interregional differences in labor force participation rates has been a factor promoting convergence in per capita incomes."[31]

However, it has also been shown that the labor force participation rate is strongly influenced by urbanization and other factors. Thompson argues that the reduction in interregional differences in the labor force participation rate, and thus per capita income, has largely been a result of the growth of urban areas where a more "diversified industry mix not only blends high and low wage rates, but also mixes labor demand by sex, age, color, and education to achieve similar labor force participation rates between urban areas."[32] The following factors also contribute to a higher participation rate in urban areas: (1) Under-counting of actual employment in agricultural areas where most members of farm families work on the farm but are not counted in the labor force; (2) Urban areas receiving a disproportionate share of working age persons as they migrate from the farms to find jobs in urban areas.

Since the main concern in this study is with the growth of regions, and because of the above-mentioned problems with a static estimate of the labor force participation rate, the percentage change in the rate between 1950 and 1960 will be used. The use of the percentage change avoids the criticism discussed above because it is statistically independent of the static ratio. More importantly, the percentage change measures the changes in job opportunities available in the region. Because of the close relationship between changes in the labor force participation rate and job opportunities, the Economic Development Administration at one time considered using this variable as a primary designation criterion in determining eligibility of counties for assistance. The Agency has found that changes in a county's labor force participation rate acts as one of the best indicators of the economic conditions of the county.

The labor force participation rate is defined as:

$$\frac{\text{Employed and Unemployed Persons}}{\text{Population (14 years and over)}}$$

Because of the need for consistent data for 1950 and 1960 it is necessary to use the following relationship, which is suspected to be a linear combination of the more accurate form above:

$$\frac{\text{Civilian Labor Force}}{\text{Total Population}}$$

Total labor force statistics could not be obtained in usable form for 1960. This estimate of the labor force participation rate excludes military employment and thus underestimates for areas that have gained or lost military employment over the period 1950–60. It will, however, accurately reflect changes in the participation rate for non-military activities.

In addition to the above estimator of the labor force participation rate, the change in the ratio of total employment to total population between 1950 and 1960 was also calculated. The simple correlation between this variable and the one discussed above for the 171 OBE Economic Areas is .655. The first estimator was selected because it is the change in the civilian employment that best represents the endogenous economic situation as opposed to exogenous decisions affecting the size and location of military bases. In addition, the influence of changes in military employment within an area is still reflected, although less dramatically, by the estimator used because of civilian supporting services to military installations.

Statistical Summary of Variables

Percent Change in the Civilian Labor Force Participation Rate, 1950–1960

	Nation	*N. East*	*S. East*	*Central*	*Far West*
Mean	−.03	−.03	−.02	−.03	−.01
Standard Deviation	.03	.02	.03	.02	.03
Minimum	−11.24	−9.85	−9.06	−11.24	−8.83
Maximum	8.64	8.64	4.78	3.65	7.00

Percent Change in the Ratio of Total Employment to Total Population, 1950–1960

	Nation	*N. East*	*S. East*	*Central*	*Far West*
Mean	−2.40	−3.51	−2.10	−2.68	−.37
Standard Deviation	3.33	3.17	2.82	3.34	3.76
Minimum	−.11	−.08	−.11	−.09	−.07
Maximum	.07	.02	.05	.01	.07

THE NET MIGRATION RATE

An important indicator of the economic state of a region is the migration rate. The major importance of migration stems from the type of individual that has been most prone to migrate. Since the primary incentive to leave a region has traditionally been economic opportunity in other regions, those leaving are primarily educated persons of working age.[33] "Out-migration has been highest for the 20–24 age bracket and then becomes progressively lower—owing to job protection and attachment to an area, which seems to increase with age."[34] The importance of economic considerations in migration decisions is shown in the following quotation from Sidney Sonenblum.[35]

> . . . it appears that not only total in-migration, but also in-migration of each age bracket can be reasonably well predicted by overall job opportunities in an area. This suggests either that it is the condition of the area's total labor market, rather than the opportunities in specific occupations, which is relevant to in-migration, or that an area with growing job opportunities for a variety of skills rather than concentrating opportunities in a few occupations.

Although this flow of labor force participants is often considered good for the nation as a whole, because it tends to increase the economic growth rate of the nation while equalizing labor market conditions regionally, it often is very damaging to particular regions. It is conceptually useful to break down these unfavorable effects into the following two categories.

1. Out-migration drains a region of a vital segment of the labor force, notably the more mobile young and educated person, thus greatly compounding the economic problems that may have initially induced out-migration.

2. When migration trends are disaggregated we find that, in general, the unskilled, poorly educated, often black individual tends to migrate to central cities, thus increasing the ghetto population. Conversely, the skilled and better educated person migrates to suburbia. This trend compounds the problems now faced by most of our large cities.[36]

Migration from rural areas to metropolitan areas, as a result of these two effects may lead to incorrect assumptions concerning the economic well-being of the rural areas. This stems from using the economists traditional indicator of economic growth—per capita income. Per capita incomes have been growing faster in the non-metropolitan parts of the country while personal income has grown more slowly[37] and population has decreased relatively. This, of course, is a result of rural to urban migration.

The migration rate will play a critical role as the major link between the two sets of models to be discussed in Chapter 4. Positive migration leads directly to increase in total personal income. However, depending on the socio-economic status of the in-migrants, the impact on the rate of increase of per capita personal income may be positive or negative. The out-migration of low income blacks from the South has, for that region, exerted a positive influence on the rate of growth of per capita income, but a negative influence on the rate of growth of total personal income. The influence of migration on each region will be further discussed as the growth and development of each region is analyzed.

The net migration rate will be calculated as follows:

$$\left[\frac{\sum_{i=1}^{N} (TPM)}{\sum_{i=1}^{N} (P50)}\right]_j$$

where: *TPM* = Net persons that migrated (+: meaning in-migration for each county).

P50 = Population in county in 1950.

N = Number of counties in OBE Economic Area *j*.

Inter-county migration within an OBE Economic Area will not be reflected because, when summing TPM for each county within the OBE Economic Area, this type of migration will be cancelled out.

Statistical Summary

Net Migration Rate, 1950–1960

	Nation	*N. East*	*S. East*	*Central*	*Far West*
Mean	−1.05	.78	−8.44	−7.75	15.06
Standard Deviation	18.27	5.69	15.47	8.47	20.82
Minimum	−30.38	−14.89	−30.38	−20.35	−20.42
Maximum	73.60	13.38	73.60	19.90	59.69

MEASURES OF THE LOAN POTENTIAL OF LOCAL FINANCIAL INSTITUTIONS

The three main sources of new capital financing now emphasized by investment theory are (1) internally generated funds, (2) equity financing, and (3) borrowing through financial institutions or the bond market.[38] In general, however, new or small businesses in need of risk capital must rely on local sources, usually banks, or must obtain non-local capital only on the most adverse terms.[39] The first two alternatives above are usually available mainly to the low-risk established firms.

Wilbur Thompson makes the point clearly in the following statement:

> The point is that the speed and ease with which new and small firms can gain access to the larger and lower-cost sources of short-term credit (commercial banks, for the most part) is perhaps just as important to local growth as the more dramatic supply of risk capital.[40]

Unfortunately, lack of data prevents a complete analysis of the influence of local financial institutions on local development. Available data relate to deposit accounts and savings capital accounts.[41] Therefore, what may be estimated from available data is the loan potential of banks and other financial institutions. Although loan potential statistics provide useful information concerning local financial resources, major theoretical problems arise with respect to the assumption of a causal relationship between the financial institutions' influence and development. The problem is best illustrated by the trite example of the chicken and the egg. Deposits generally must increase with development because development necessitates increases in financial resources.

In spite of these problems, an indicator will be included to measure the relative increases in local financial resources between regions. These resources must increase with development, and where they do not, their absence forms a major bottleneck in the development process.

Two variables will be used to measure loan potential and its increase. They are:

(1) demand deposits plus time deposits plus savings capital deposits per capita in 1960; and
(2) the average annual rate of increase in financial deposits, 1950–1964.

In addition, the ratio of time and demand deposits per capita in 1960 was calculated. The static variable listed above was selected over this alternative because it is more inclusive of available financial resources.

Statistical Summary of Variables

Demand, Time and Savings Capital Deposits Per Capita, 1960

	Nation	*N. East*	*S. East*	*Central*	*Far West*
Mean	1066.14	1370.70	733.02	1093.03	1153.54
Standard Deviation	393.21	437.13	214.72	174.25	335.36
Minimum	385.46	832.00	385.00	786.00	724.00
Maximum	3409.19	3409.00	1459.00	1539.00	2122.00

Rate of Increase in Time, Demand, and Savings Capital Per Capita, 1950–1964

	Nation	*N. East*	*S. East*	*Central*	*Far West*
Mean	6.61	5.78	7.23	5.58	7.91
Standard Deviation	2.11	.70	1.50	1.23	3.54
Minimum	2.97	4.56	4.26	2.97	3.96
Maximum	21.23	8.24	13.23	8.80	21.23

Demand and Time Deposits Per Capital, 1960

	Nation	*N. East*	*S. East*	*Central*	*Far West*
Mean	816.05	1064.51	538.68	855.53	901.68
Standard Deviation	332.05	412.19	167.22	120.76	255.60
Minimum	236.51	596.00	236.00	575.00	562.00
Maximum	3071.90	3072.00	1117.00	1234.00	1739.00

MEASURES OF MANUFACTURING PRODUCTIVITY

High levels of operating efficiency within the manufacturing sector may provide the source for a relatively high level of profits and growth. Ideally, productivity comparisons between similar industries would provide a means of comparing relative operating efficiency. Productivity, defined as total output per unit of total input, addresses a major proposition of microeconomic theory, that of cost minimization. In order to estimate total productivity, as stated above, all inputs must be measured. However, due to problems in accurately determining capital input, productivity is generally defined as output per unit of labor input. This convention will be followed here, which will, of course, restrict the interpretation to the efficiency of labor use.

Additional problems of measurement are imposed by the grouping of different types of manufacturers into one category. The manufacturing category used here includes all establishments primarily engaged in manufacturing, as defined in the 1957 edition of the Standard Industrial Classification Manual (as amended), except establishments owned and operated by the federal government. Thus, not only is it necessary to accept varying technologies between similar industries, but it is necessary to contend with very different technologies as a result of totally different industries.

One final limitation on the proposed variable is imposed by differences in regional wage rates. Since the estimator of manufacturing productivity will be used in cross-section analysis, it will overestimate labor productivity in regions that have relatively high wage rates. This, theoretically, results from higher capital-labor ratios in such areas influenced by a relatively high rate of substitution of capital for labor. Because of these limitations, the interpretation of the proposed variable is restricted to a relative measure of labor use efficiency.

The first variable will be the ratio of value added in manufacturing to man-hours of productive workers in manufacturing for 1958. The second variable to be used, the change in the ratio between 1958 to 1963, should be less biased. This variable can be interpreted with reasonable confidence as reflecting the changing productivity, or labor use efficiency, of the region.

The 1958 value was chosen over the same statistic for 1963 because 1958 is closer to the midpoint of the study. Data in usable form were available only for these years.

Statistical Summary of Variables

Manufacturing Productivity, 1958

	Nation	*N. East*	*S. East*	*Central*	*Far West*
Mean	5.92	6.42	5.02	6.18	6.46
Standard Deviation	1.51	1.18	1.60	1.15	1.56
Minimum	2.80	3.60	2.80	4.21	4.22
Maximum	10.71	9.17	10.71	10.16	10.53

Percent Change in Manufacturing Productivity, 1958–1963

	Nation	*N. East*	*S. East*	*Central*	*Far West*
Mean	25.53	23.24	26.10	22.27	32.53
Standard Deviation	13.50	8.18	13.33	11.53	20.26
Minimum	−5.67	−5.67	−2.14	−3.21	2.56
Maximum	79.07	43.92	79.07	45.22	78.30

MEASURES OF MANUFACTURING INVESTMENT

Economists have traditionally focused on the rate of investment in manufacturing as the most important requisite for development. This emphasis arises from two basic sources. First, economists from the time of Adam Smith have been fascinated with the attributes of capital. This traditional concern strongly influenced the evolution of development theory, as well as other fields of economics. Second, a problem most vivid in most less developed countries is the lack of domestic savings and consequently of sources for capital formation. Also contributing to these basic forces is the relatively greater importance of manufacturers *vis-à-vis* agriculture.

In recent times this emphasis on capital formation has met with growing criticism as a result of the work of Dennison and others. This criticism has been compounded by failures of economic development plans that employ the capital-output ratio, or the incremental capital output ratio, as an important tool for planning.

Nevertheless, any study of economic growth and development should consider the relative importance of capital investment. This is particularly true of the relatively capital rich U.S. economy. One variable will be used to measure the impact of manufacturing investment. It will be the average ratio of new capital expenditures in manufacturing to value added in manufacturing for 1958 and 1963. The average is used in an attempt to reduce the influence of annual fluctuations. The variable to be used is mathematically defined as:

$$\frac{\left(NKEM/_{VAM}\right)\ 1958 + \left(NKEM/_{VAM}\right)\ 1963}{2}$$

where: *NKEM* = new capital expenditures in manufacturing.
VAM = value added in manufacturing.

Therefore, the variable will be used to indicate the relative amount of manufacturing investment between regions.

Statistical Summary

Average Manufacturing Capital Investment, 1958 and 1963

	Nation	*N. East*	*S. East*	*Central*	*Far West*
Mean	7.00	5.67	7.82	6.63	8.12
Standard Deviation	2.91	1.31	3.59	2.03	3.66
Minimum	1.82	3.63	1.82	3.55	3.22
Maximum	22.13	9.20	22.13	14.14	21.84

MEASURES OF AGRICULTURAL TECHNOLOGY, AGRICULTURAL GROWTH SECTORS, AND THE CHARACTER OF THE AGRICULTURAL ORGANIZATION

Since World War II agricultural output has increased more than five percent per year.[42] Increases in domestic and foreign demand for this output have not kept pace with the increases in productivity, thus "national economic development has required that the agricultural sector decline sharply in relative share."[43] However, in some regions, particularly the Far West, the southern mountain states, and in Kansas and Nebraska, "the net gain in agricultural employment was a significant element in the upward shifts in total employment displayed by these states."[44] The variables to be discussed here are designed to measure the regional impact of the changing agricultural sector. To do this, many aspects of agricultural production must be analyzed. The following aspects will be discussed in turn: (1) the determining factors in agricultural location; (2) the growth sectors within agriculture; (3) the technological aspects of agriculture; and (4) the character of the agricultural organization.

Agriculture is, technically, a resource oriented activity, and therefore it must be located near the resource it exploits, namely fertile land. However, because of the ability of agriculture to substitute inputs (i.e. fertilizer), the market influence is exerting a significant influence on the location of agricultural activity.[45] For example, agriculture, in comparison with mining, shows a rank correlation between employment in agriculture and population of .649, whereas the same rank correlation for mining is .406.[46] This lends support to the importance of the market in determining agricultural location. But, in order to explain the changing regional share of agriculture, theories based on resources or markets are inadequate. The shift in the importance of agriculture to regions has been primarily a result of changing relative importance of particular groups of agricultural commodities.[47]

The influence of the field crop sector of agriculture has been great, as Perloff *et al.*, explain:

> The field crop sector of agriculture is, without a doubt, the most important in explaining the observed changes in agricultural activity. As measured by the value of farm products sold, it is the largest of the sectors, accounting for 40 percent of the total in 1954. It is also an important source of inputs in the livestock sectors of agriculture and therefore exerts an influence on the second largest component of agricultural production.[48]

In addition to its relatively large size, the field crop sector was the second fastest growing agricultural sector.[49] The result of the size and growth rate of the field crop sector was to stimulate agricultural development and employment in those areas specializing in these products. "Twenty-seven states showed net upward proportionality shifts in total value of farm products sold during the period 1939–54."[50] Of these, all but four specialized in field crops.[51] Conversely, 29 of the 33 states with downward shifts in the proportion of agricultural output had downward shifts in the field crops sector.

The point of this discussion is simply to emphasize the need for disaggregation of agriculture into sectors when considering the impact of agriculture on regional development of the U.S.

The rapid increase in general agricultural productivity is unquestionably a result of the increases in the capitalization of American agriculture. According to Perloff *et al.*:

> The results of our analysis imply that interstate variations in the labor incomes of agricultural workers are significantly associated with variations in marginal labor productivity reflecting variations in capital per worker used in agricultural production. They also imply that regional variations in output per worker are due to variations in capital per worker.[52]

Using the value of land and buildings as a measure of capital per worker, Perloff *et al.,* show that the relationship described holds for all two digit SIC agricultural categories.[53] The way Perloff *et al.* use the value of land and buildings as an indicator of capital per farm will be accepted in this analysis.

The final aspect of the agricultural sector to be analyzed will be the character of the agricultural organization. Here the analysis concentrates on the socioeconomic aspects of the agricultural sector. The agricultural sector in all parts of the county traces back to different periods and environments of history. This has resulted in varying structures of socioeconomic life. The plantation-tenancy situation of the South and the smaller family-owned farm in the North are prime examples in contrast. Variables have been chosen that essentially represent the result of the unique agricultural histories of each region. The variables will be measures of farm tenancy and the size distribution of farms.

The discussion has presented the basis for the use of the following variables.

1. *Value of Land and Buildings per Farm, 1959.* This variable will be used, as it was by Perloff *et al.,* as a measure of the capital investment in agriculture.

2. *Value of Total Output per Worker in Agriculture, 1959.* This variable will be used as a measure of labor productivity in agriculture.

3. *The Percent Change in Agricultural Output, 1950–64.* This variable is a measure of the relative growth of the agricultural output. It will be used to assess the relative importance of a rapidly growing agricultural sector.

4. *The Ratio of the Value of Crops to Total Agricultural Output in*

1959. Crops as discussed above, are the most rapidly growing sub-sector of agriculture. This variable is, therefore, a measure of the specialization in the growth sub-sector of agriculture. It will be used to assess the relative importance of specialization in the agricultural growth sub-sector.

5. *The ratio of Farms of 1,000 Acres or More to Farms of 10 Acres or Less.* This variable is a measure of the size distribution of farms. More particularly it will be used to assess the relative importance of large scale farming.

6. *The Percent of Farms Operated by Tenants, 1959.* This variable will be used as an indicator of the ownership characteristics of the agricultural organization.

In addition to these variables, the ratio of the value of crops plus livestock to the value of total agricultural output was also calculated. This was originally intended to be a measure of the specialization in the two agricultural growth sub-sectors. It was rejected because the values obtained were too high to be a measure of specialization. In other words, crops plus livestock component of agriculture was, in many cases, the total of all agricultural output.

There exist many possible variables that could be used to measure the technology, growth and character of the agricultural sector. The variables presented here were used because they are the best available to measure the trends discussed above.

Statistical Summary of Variables

Value of Land and Buildings Per Farm, 1959

	Nation	*N. East*	*S. East*	*Central*	*Far West*
Mean	40.67	35.95	21.30	45.24	77.23
Standard Deviation	31.40	20.83	16.74	23.27	41.05
Minimum	8.83	14.10	8.83	9.38	27.14
Maximum	186.80	96.39	96.22	106.27	186.80

Value of Total Output Per Worker in Agriculture, 1960

	Nation	*N. East*	*S. East*	*Central*	*Far West*
Mean	7.06	7.45	4.48	8.46	9.54
Standard Deviation	2.83	2.00	1.00	2.65	2.00
Minimum	2.60	4.11	2.60	3.35	6.02
Maximum	14.00	13.38	8.02	14.00	12.58

Percent Change in Agricultural Output, 1950–1964

	Nation	N. East	S. East	Central	Far West
Mean	61.51	45.58	81.02	44.83	62.22
Standard Deviation	41.90	20.76	46.45	22.77	38.33
Minimum	−12.63	.66	−12.63	−11.39	4.49
Maximum	259.50	110.30	229.79	84.86	136.74

Value of Crops per Total Output, 1959

	Nation	N. East	S. East	Central	Far West
Mean	41.77	33.80	51.75	33.90	44.55
Standard Deviation	20.04	14.56	19.52	18.16	20.40
Minimum	7.18	8.79	8.10	7.18	10.89
Maximum	89.87	68.24	89.87	85.24	76.58

Value of Crops plus Livestock per Total Agricultural Output, 1959

	Nation	N. East	S. East	Central	Far West
Mean	75.27	61.47	77.31	82.30	83.03
Standard Deviation	20.25	23.08	14.54	19.74	14.61
Minimum	19.12	19.12	30.00	29.06	40.84
Maximum	99.08	95.79	96.87	99.08	98.58

Ratio of Farms of 1000 Acres or More to Farms of 10 Acres or Less, 1959

	Nation	N. East	S. East	Central	Far West
Mean	2.79	.13	.71	8.75	2.44
Standard Deviation	8.16	.12	1.46	14.72	3.24
Minimum	.02	.02	.02	.07	.04
Maximum	69.89	.62	10.15	69.89	12.86

Percent Tenant Farms, 1959

	Nation	N. East	S. East	Central	Far West
Mean	18.28	15.40	20.86	22.77	11.53
Standard Deviation	11.50	12.55	10.75	11.07	6.50
Minimum	1.87	2.14	3.66	1.87	2.93
Maximum	48.68	42.74	48.68	48.02	33.79

MEASURES OF LOCAL GOVERNMENT FISCAL EFFORT

The variables to be discussed here are designed to measure fiscal effort and sources of funds for local governments. The ability of local governments to raise revenue is in many cases severely limited. The problems incurred by urban governments as a result of movement to suburbia and urban deterioration are well characterized by William J. Baumol.[54] He summarizes his argument as follows:

> The exodus of income to the suburbs imposes on municipal governments a double pressure—it makes it more difficult for them to obtain resources and it tends, simultaneously, to force them into heavier expenditures.[55]

It is generally recognized that local governments must rely principally on property taxes to finance local expenditures. "Prior to the 1930s, the property tax provided three-fourths or more of the general revenue of American local governments and more than four-fifths of their locally raised revenue."[56] From the early 1930s to the 1950s the share of the property tax in the general revenue of the local governments declined to approximately 50 percent because of increased intergovernment transfers. Since the early 1950s the share has stabilized near the 50 percent level.[57] Thus, the relative importance of the property tax and intergovernment transfers cannot be denied and will be used here as a measure of the fiscal effort of local governments.

However, the use of this indicator has inherent weaknesses. John Meyer, for example, argues that "The financial problems of city governments are almost certainly . . . attributable to over-reliance on property taxes."[58] Other weaknesses are well documented. The following brief list will serve as examples of other inherent weaknesses in the property tax:

1. Because it is a high regressive tax on housing consumption, it limits urban housing development and improvements.
2. The tax simulates suburban development to avoid urban property tax and thus causes loss of revenues to urban governments.
3. It poses a deterrent to industrial location because of the variations in property tax revenue.
4. The property tax is the most poorly administered of all taxes.[59]
5. Reassessment of property values are made too infrequently.

This list by no means covers all the criticisms of the property tax, but simply serves as an illustration. But it is important to recognize such weaknesses when using property taxes to indicate local government fiscal effort. In final appraisal of the property tax, it is worth quoting Netzer at length:

> The property tax does have virtues, so the public interest is in doing what can be done to minimize the defects, rather than merely describing the defects of the institution. The tax exists; it produces very large revenues; and our society and economy have adjusted to and worked through many of the baleful effects of the tax, at least of present levels of property taxation.[60]

Three variables will be used to measure and test for the relative importance of local government fiscal revenue and the sources of that revenue. These variables will be: (1) total revenue of local governments per capita in 1962; (2) property tax per capita in 1962; (3) local government transfers per capita in 1962; (These are transfers from state or federal governments to the local governments.)

In interpreting these variables it must be recognized that, in general, total revenue per capita rises with city size. Therefore, variable one above will be heavily influenced by the relative size of the system of cities within the regions.

The total revenue raised by local governments from local sources in fiscal year 1966–1967 was 44,419 million dollars. Of this, 25,180 million, or 56.5 percent consisted of revenue from property taxes.[61] This leaves 43.5 percent of local government revenue raised from local sources unexplained by analysis of the property tax. This problem was to be addressed by analyzing the extent to which local governments utilize the total available fiscal base.[62] The fiscal base of a region is a function of local income and assessed property value, since these sources provide the basis of taxation. Where local per capita income is relatively high, the revenue raised from local sales taxes or income taxes should be relatively large. Similarly, where local property value is relatively high, relatively more revenue can be raised by the property taxes.

The variable that was to be used to measure these forces was the unexplained residual from a regression equation that estimated local government revenue per capita as a function of per capita income. It was not possible to obtain estimates of property values in a form that could be used, and therefore it was assumed that the property values were closely related to the level of per capita personal income. The regression equation to be used was:

$$R/C = 3.409 + \underset{(.007)}{.096}\,(PCY59) + E \quad R^2 = .519$$

where:

R/C = local government revenue per capita.

$PCY59$ = total personal income per capita in 1959.

E = unexplained residual.

Multiple regressions were tested but the additional variance explained was not sufficient to warrant the inclusion of more independent variables.

As stated, attempts were made to use the unexplained residual (actual R/C–predicted R/C) as an indicator of the extent to which the local fiscal base is taxed by the local governments. It was to be argued, therefore, that regions that have a large, positive, unexplained residual, tax their fiscal bases to a relatively greater extent than do other regions. This reasoning was based on the hypothesis that the regression line represents the average or predicted local government redundant revenue, given the per capita income of the region.

This technique was discussed because it represents a possible means of obtaining estimates of fiscal effort. Analysis of the residuals obtained, however, negated the use of this variable here. For the most part, the residual appeared to be another estimator of urbanization. As stated above, the fiscal base of local governments increases with city size. In addition, statistical problems encountered make the use of this variable questionable for the intended purposes.

Statistical Summary of Variables

Local Government Revenue Per Capita, 1962

	Nation	*N. East*	*S. East*	*Central*	*Far West*
Mean	183.48	196.85	133.49	200.73	236.78
Standard Deviation	52.84	39.61	23.42	37.70	57.66
Minimum	88.93	121.30	88.93	124.17	158.43
Maximum	336.63	304.20	191.35	303.35	336.63

Property Tax Per Capita, Average 1957 and 1962

	Nation	*N. East*	*S. East*	*Central*	*Far West*
Mean	46.58	55.00	25.31	58.36	57.36
Standard Deviation	19.98	13.90	10.41	14.44	17.37
Minimum	8.25	23.76	8.25	25.40	18.69
Maximum	85.25	83.66	58.63	82.14	85.25

Local Government Transfers Per Capita, 1962

	Nation	*N. East*	*S. East*	*Central*	*Far West*
Mean	61.48	58.81	55.12	58.57	85.36
Standard Deviation	23.42	22.58	10.95	25.12	28.10
Minimum	19.26	22.00	33.59	19.26	34.70
Maximum	139.72	119.21	91.08	139.72	138.58

Residuals from Estimating Equation

	Nation	*N. East*	*S. East*	*Central*	*Far West*
Mean	.005	−15.32	−12.80	19.86	22.83
Standard Deviation	36.65	28.33	20.03	41.23	45.03
Minimum	−58.57	−51.58	−53.64	−58.57	−26.14
Maximum	123.45	62.98	47.71	123.46	123.45

MEASURES OF DEFICIT FINANCING BY LOCAL GOVERNMENTS

Recognizing that the taxable base of many communities and regions is inadequate to finance much of the needed social investment, the variables to be discussed here focus on the willingness of local governments to contract debt. The case for local government financing through debt is stated by John Due as follows:

> Smaller units of government are often subject to heavy, nonrecurrent expenditures for public improvements which will last over a period of years. The financing of the entire cost by taxation would result in extremely severe burdens in the short period and is considered inequitable between present and future tax payers. The use of borrowing . . . allows the spreading-out of the expenditures over a period of time and greater stability in tax rates.[63]

Because local governments must place proposals for deficit financing (the issuance of bonds) before the public for a vote, it was assumed that the level of debt of local governments represented a level acceptable both to the governments and the general voting public. In addition, it was assumed that deficit financing of local governments was used for improvements in the social overhead capital of the area.

When analyzing the relative amounts of debt incurred by local governments, an artificial barrier is imposed by varying state regulations on the debt of the local governments. Since, in effect, the use of this indicator tests for the importance of debt financing to local governments, these regulations will not be of major concern. If, in fact, growth is hindered by low debt ceilings, it should show up in the analysis.

Two variables will be used to study the interaction between local government debt on economic growth. The first will serve as a static indicator for the midpoint of the study. This variable will be the average ratio of total local government debt to total local government revenue for 1957 and 1962. The average is used to avoid the influence of fluctuations in local government revenues.

The second variable will attempt to measure the changes in local government and community attitudes toward deficit financing over the period

1957 to 1962. The variable will be the change in the ratio of total local government debt to total local government revenue between 1957 and 1962. The five year period which the variable covers is an extremely short period to measure changes in community attitudes and thus may not yield a reasonable measurement. However, since data for these two years were the only data available in usable form, the decision was made to include this variable.

Statistical Summary of Variables

Average Ratio of the Value of Local Governments Bonds Outstanding to Local Government Revenue, 1957 and 1962

	Nation	*N. East*	*S. East*	*Central*	*Far West*
Mean	123.91	116.08	144.87	108.03	116.91
Standard Deviation	48.42	33.22	53.10	45.21	53.80
Minimum	33.53	62.33	33.53	34.31	46.58
Maximum	303.00	187.28	268.03	231.31	303.00

Percent Change in the Ratio of Average Value of Local Governments Bonds Outstanding to Local Government Revenue, 1957 to 1962

	Nation	*N. East*	*S. East*	*Central*	*Far West*
Mean	−16.88	−5.85	−22.66	−17.07	−21.67
Standard Deviation	21.18	17.38	20.78	21.48	20.72
Minimum	−74.39	−36.50	−59.49	−71.93	−74.39
Maximum	45.51	41.80	45.50	24.15	27.39

MEASURES OF LOCAL GOVERNMENT SERVICES PROVIDED

The variables to be described below are designed to measure the relative level of services provided by local governments. This will require the assumption that the level of services provided are directly related to the funds dispersed for services by the local governments.

As a percent of total government expenditures at all levels, local government expenditures decreased in relative importance over most of this century and then stabilized at approximately 34 percent of Federal and state expenditures in 1950. With the exception of the World War II period, this trend is evident as is shown in Table 3–2. Many factors, economic and institutional, have produced this trend. Changes in the relative importance of local government expenditures has been determined by changes in the responsibilities assumed by the various levels of government.[64] For example, the large decreases in the relative importance of local government expenditures in the 1930s was a result of

Table 3–2. Government Expenditures 1902–1967 (Millions of Dollars)

Year	*Total Gov. Exp. (Fed., State & Local)*	*Local Gov.*	*State & Federal*	*Ratio of Local to State & Fed.*
1902	1,660	959	701	1.36
1913	3,215	1,960	1,255	1.56
1927	11.220	6,359	4,861	1.31
1932	12,437	6,375	6,062	1.05
1936	16,758	6,056	10,702	.57
1940	20,417	7,685	12,732	.60
1946	79,707	9,093	70,614	.13
1950	70,334	17,041	53,293	.32
1956	115,796	28,273	87,523	.32
1960	151,288	39,056	112,232	.35
1962–63	184,996	47,237	137,759	.35
1966–67	257,800	66,648	191,152	.35

Source: U.S. Department of Commerce, Bureau of the Census, *1967 Census of Governments,* Volume 6, No. 5, "Historical Statistics on Government Finance and Employment," pp. 33–35 and 39–41.

shifting the responsibility for public welfare from local governments to the federal government.[65] Similarly, the future trend will be determined largely by which level of government assumes primary responsibility for the growing problems resulting from increasing urbanization.

It should be noted that the trend discussed above is evident in aggregate expenditures of all governments below the state level. In 1960 there were over 100,000 such governments.[66] The estimates of the expenditures of these governments are highly reliable for recent years,[67] but become progressively weaker as we go back in time. Therefore, the trend discussed above must be used with care, but it does serve to demonstrate the impact of the changes in the assumption of responsibilities by the various levels of government.

In order to study the extent of local government expenditures they must be broken down into functional categories. This is done in Table 3–3.

The most remarkable aspect of total local government expenditures is the long term consistency in the allocation of funds between functional categories. This is particularly true for the period since 1950, but also holds fairly well for the period since 1902.[68] However, a cross-section study of local governments for 1957 shows that, in general, local governments differ in their allocation of funds. Table 3–4 presents the results of this study.[69] From this, Margolis concludes that, "urban public expenditures are more variable than one would anticipate, given the relatively high level of national integration."[70] Some of the factors giving rise to the variations in services are well known, the most important being variations in regional income. Other factors that have been found to be

Table 3–3. Local Government Expenditure by Function

	1966–67	*1963–64*	*1960*	*1952*	*1934*	*1902*
All Functions	100	100	100	100	100	100
Education	48.0	46.2	44.7	38.8	31.0	27.1
Highways	7.7	8.5	9.9	11.9	14.9	19.5
Public Welfare	6.6	6.6	6.5	7.8	10.2	3.1
Health & Hospital	5.7	5.4	5.7	6.0	4.2	3.2
National Resources	0.9	1.4	1.0	1.3	1.4	–
Financial Administration	3.6	3.8	4.3	4.7	6.3	13.4
Interest on Debt	3.4	3.5	3.3	2.3	12.0	6.6
All Other	24.1	24.6	24.6	27.2	20.1	27.2
Police	4.4	4.6	4.7	4.7	5.3	5.7
Fire	2.5	2.7	2.9	3.3	3.7	4.6
Sanitation	4.2	4.8	5.0	5.6	3.4	5.8
Recreation	2.2	2.3	2.2	1.8	2.4	3.3
Housing	2.4	2.5	2.5	4.4	–	–

Source: U.S. Department of Commerce, Bureau of the Census, *1967 Census of Governments,* Volume 6, No. 5, "Historical Statistics on Government Finances and Employment," pp. 50–1.

Table 3–4. Variations in Per Capita Expenditures in Metropolitan and Non-Metropolitan Portions of Forty-five States, 1957

	Metropolitan		*Non-Metropolitan*	
Public Services	*Mean*	*Standard Deviation*	*Mean*	*Standard Deviation*
General Expenditures	$148	$37	$134	$47
Education	63	14	69	18
Highway	15	7	20	11
Health and Hospital*	7	5	6	4
Public Welfare	7	8	8	12

*Exclusive capital outlays.
Source: Alan K. Campbell and Seymour Sacks, *Metropolitan America: Fiscal Patterns and Governmental Systems* (Syracuse University, 1966), mimeo., Table 3–10.

important are wealth, employment characteristics, age distribution, size, and density.[71]

Before the variables to be used are presented, two problems must be mentioned. Government expenditure statistics, when used to measure the services provided, are often very incomplete. This results because local governments are not the only providers of services analyzed. The federal government and private industry often provide similar services which, in some cases, outweigh the contribution of the local government.[72] Secondly, it would be better to analyze local government expenditures at the sub-county level, since aggregation often involves many quite different forms of government.

Two variables will be used, each pertaining to 1962. The first variable, total local government expenditures minus education expenditures per capita, is most often used to measure the extent of services provided by local governments. Because expenditures for education are relatively consistent between regions (Table 3–4), this will be a measure of total services, other than education, provided by local governments. The second variable is the total expenditures of local governments per capita, which will be a measure of the total operating budget of local governments. However, Seymore Sachs argues that this expenditure per capita abstracts from the important influence of urbanization.[73] He proposes that expenditure per square mile be used instead to estimate the extent of local government expenditures. This statistic has been rejected in favor of the per capita estimate, because, as Sachs states, the expenditure per square mile measure is basically a measure of urbanization. This study has sufficient measures of urbanization included in other indicators.

Statistical Summary of Variables

Non-Education Local Government

	Nation	*N. East*	*S. East*	*Central*	*Far West*
Mean	96.00	104.54	68.14	103.30	126.62
Standard Deviation	37.81	35.67	22.00	27.11	47.10
Minimum	28.38	45.06	28.38	50.85	62.19
Maximum	214.65	200.44	137.70	165.41	214.65

Total Local Government Expenditures Per Capita, 1962

	Nation	*N. East*	*S. East*	*Central*	*Far West*
Mean	190.11	205.18	141.76	202.25	245.24
Standard Deviation	54.61	42.64	29.85	38.62	60.36
Minimum	87.15	137.40	87.15	127.22	153.45
Maximum	342.53	307.79	221.46	293.19	342.53

MEASURES OF POLITICAL PARTICIPATION

The extent of political participation, as measured by voting statistics, is used here as a measure of the general level of community involvement of the population of the region. According to Lester Milbrath, " . . . evidence suggests that political participation can be thought of as a special case of general participation in social and community affairs."[74] Therefore, the variables to be discussed below are indirect measures of one effect of a host of factors that contribute to community involvement. Political scientists have constructed many models employing these factors to explain voter turnout.

The models, particulatly the one used by Milbrath,[75] Campbell *et al.*,[76] and Glaser,[77] will serve as bases for this discussion. The models emphasize that political participation is a function of the host of factors that contribute to the makeup of individual attitudes and social consciousness. Milbrath and Campbell *et al.*, emphasize that political participation, of which voting is one form, varies directly with one's social economic status. It can be generalized as does Milbrath, that:

> One of the most thoroughly substantiated propositions in all of social science is that persons near the center of society are more likely to participate in politics than persons near the periphery.[78]

Milbrath's argument focuses attention on the class of individuals that make up social economic groups that are influential members of society, or in Milbrath's terms, are near the center of society. This is related to the basic factors of education, income, job prestige, place of residence, race, etc., that make up one's personality.[79]

It has been argued that political participation is one facet of the more general community involvement and that both political participation and community involvement are functionally related to one's social economic status and spatial location in society. However, the link between voting and political involvement has yet to be established. This link is provided by Campbell *et al.* in their 1960 study. Using survey data from the Survey Research Center pertaining to the 1956 presidential election, they present the following relationship.[80]

This chart plots the percentage of persons voting against an index of political involvement. The index was constructed from a survey which addressed the following aspects of political involvement: (1) interest in the campaign, (2) concern over the election outcome, (3) sense of political efficacy, and (4) sense of citizen duty.[81] Thus, Chart 3–1 demonstrates that political participation and community involvement are directly related. This provides the basic logic for using voting statistics as a proxy for community involvement.

Two variables will be used to measure political participation and community involvement. The first will be the percent of eligible voters (persons 21 years of age and over) voting in the 1960 presidential election.

The second variable, the value of the percentage change, disregarding the sign of the change in voter turnout between the 1960 and 1964 presidential elections, will attempt to measure the average level of social negativism. As Glaser argues:

> The weaker a social group's average level of motivations, social stimuli, and role prescriptions, the more variable will be that group's turnout from one election to another.[82]

This statement is consistent with the analysis of Milbrath and Campbell *et al.* Thus, it is argued that the more a region's population is dominated

Chart 3–1. Political Attitudes and the Vote

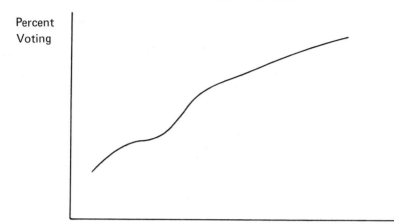

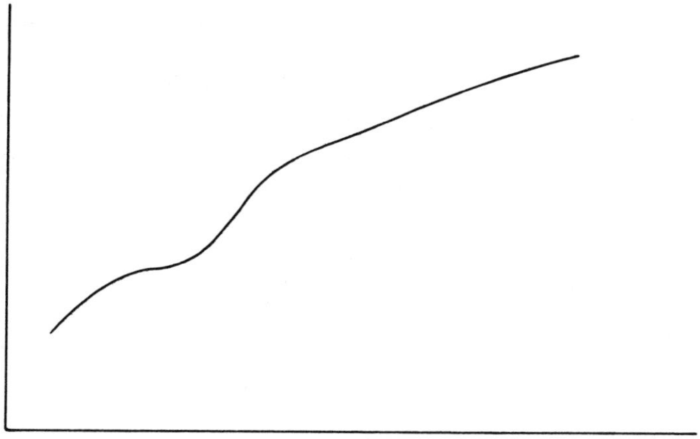

by persons in the lower range of Chart 3–1, the more variable will be election turnout. This implies, in turn, that these regions will, in general, have a population that is relatively less involved with community affairs.

Had it been possible to obtain voting statistics for more years, a better measure of the average level of social negativism would have been the variance in voter turnout. Data for the 1960 and 1964 elections was the only data available in usable form.

Statistical Summary of Variables

Percent of Persons 21 Years of Age and Over that Voted in 1960

	Nation	*N. East*	*S. East*	*Central*	*Far West*
Mean	61.29	72.13	43.65	70.46	65.48
Standard Deviation	16.92	7.85	14.25	11.61	10.21
Minimum	25.47	30.06	25.47	36.69	43.11
Maximum	82.95	82.27	80.88	82.60	82.95

Index of Voting Change, 1960–1964

	Nation	*N. East*	*S. East*	*Central*	*Far West*
Mean	5.37	3.28	8.24	4.05	4.66
Standard Deviation	4.57	3.41	5.20	2.09	4.72
Minimum	.12	.12	.34	.24	.67
Maximum	22.86	22.32	20.09	8.29	22.86

MEASURES OF SOCIOECONOMIC STRUCTURE

Social scientists have placed great emphasis on socioeconomic structure of the population base in attempting to understand and explain social interaction. The three variables to be discussed here are measures of the socioeconomic and racial structure of the population within the areas to be analyzed. These variables are presented within the same context because, although they are each separate and distinct measures of facets of socioeconomic structure, they each contribute to the form of social interaction within the areas to be analyzed. Attempts will be made, therefore, to measure the relative importance of each type in order to study the relationship to the patterns of economic change in the regional groupings.

It is possible to define socioeconomic structure with the use of many proxies. For example such proxies might make use of one or all of the following concepts:

1. blue collar (vs.) white collar workers.
2. in terms of income.
3. in terms of education.
4. in terms of race.
5. in Marxian terms of alienation.

The above classification schemes do not, of course, exhaust the possibilities.

Placing the concept in terms of alienation has merit when discussing class structure in general terms. Sociologists J. Horton and W. Thompson provide an example of how class structure may directly effect development activities.[83]

> Research on local referendums shows a consistent pattern of negative voting among the socially and economically deprived segments of the population. The research reported here tests the hypothesis that referendums may serve as institutional outlets for protest, that voting against local issues may by an expression of political protect on the part of the powerless and ordinarily apathetic members of the community. The findings from a study of defeated school-bond issues in two communities show a consistent relationship between powerlessness and negative votes in those cases where a feeling of powerlessness took the form of alienation from certain symbols of power in the community. This relationship holds independently of economic self-interest and related variables. Evidence suggests that voting down local issues does not represent an organized, class-conscious opposition, but a type of mass protest, a convergence of the individual assessments of the powerless who have projected into available symbols the fears and suspicions growing out of their alienated existence.[84]

The above quote portrays the negativism that is so often stressed when analyzing the fate of the lower classes. The point is that the alienation of a segment of society imposes costs on that society beyond the direct costs generally associated with alienation and poverty. The direct cost such as welfare payments, lost fiscal revenue, and extra police and fire protection, are probably minor when compared to the indirect human costs imposed by poverty and the loss of human dignity by this segment of society. The direct and indirect costs overlap, of course, because the indirect costs as stated here directly effect labor force participation and therefore the direct costs.

The variables used here are designed to measure major facets of socioeconomic structure. The first, a measure of income distribution, will be the ratio of families that earned $10,000 or more to families that earned $3,000 or less in 1959. The income distribution of the population base is, of course, a primary determinant of socioeconomic status, because it is a direct measure of families on the two extremes of economic well being.

The second variable describes socioeconomic structure in terms of the employment structure.[89] The variable will be the percent of employment that was white collar in 1960. The third variable, an indicator of racial mix, will be the percent of the regional population that was non-white in 1960.

Statistical Summary of Variables

Ratio of Families that Earned $10,000 or More to Families that Earned $3,000 or Less, 1959

	Nation	*N. East*	*S. East*	*Central*	*Far West*
Mean	.56	.91	.21	.41	.90
Standard Deviation	.44	.47	.11	.22	.44
Minimum	.08	.22	.08	.14	.25
Maximum	2.30	2.30	.65	1.09	1.82

Percent White Collar Employment, 1960

	Nation	*N. East*	*S. East*	*Central*	*Far West*
Mean	37.58	39.64	34.16	37.12	41.41
Standard Deviation	5.08	3.96	4.00	4.61	5.01
Minimum	26.07	33.03	26.07	29.14	32.79
Maximum	56.40	56.40	42.72	49.00	49.64

Percent Non-White Population, 1960

	Nation	*N. East*	*S. East*	*Central*	*Far West*
Mean	10.69	5.35	23.22	3.42	4.94
Standard Deviation	12.30	5.28	14.01	3.61	2.97
Minimum	.10	.18	.55	.10	.97
Maximum	52.20	24.50	52.20	15.75	11.86

MEASURES OF THE LEVEL OF EDUCATIONAL ACHIEVEMENT

The variables to be discussed here are designed to estimate the average quantity and level of quality of education provided within the areas of analysis. It is logical to hypothesize, "that no aspect of a community is more critical to its economic development status and prospects than its educational system. On the one hand, there is abundant evidence that a public school system of really high quality can act as a powerful magnet to attract and hold the kind of skilled labor force that is needed if a community is to prosper. And on the other hand, it seems very likely that a mediocre system will be an extraordinarily serious obstacle to a community's effort to attract industry and capital."[86] This reasoning is supported by Campbell and Burkhead. They argue that the business community now "perceives that an improved educational system in urban areas has a relationship to economic growth."[87]

There are, however, those that disagree with Campbell and Burkhead. A study conducted by Mattila and Thompson of 135 Standard Metropolitan Statistical Areas showed that high income manufacturing areas were characterized by low educational achievement. They conclude that this,

> suggests either that general education is not a good proxy for productivity (income) due to on-the-job training, or that relative income is more a function of market power, achieved through oligopoly and union power, than of skill.[88]

This points out one of the major failures in the present data base available on education. Data are not available on on-the-job training or on technical schools which serve a purpose similar to the formal educational institutions. Data on these two aspects of education would greatly improve knowledge about this question of the influence of education on economic growth.

It is well known that education and income are highly correlated. Mattila and Thompson extend this further by concluding the following:[89]

1. The level of family income and the degree of inequality in its distribution in an urban area are most closely associated with the educational

level and educational inequality characteristic of the adult population of the locality.

2. There is a tendency for localities with a relatively large proportion of college-educated persons to exhibit a more equal distribution of income.

Oscar Ornati provides an interpretation, although weakly supported, of the second conclusion above. He states:

> I interpret this to mean that the presence of the educated in a city leads to greater investment in human capital, but whether this is actually due to their "greater education" we do not know because of the known intercorrelation between income and education.[90]

The first two variables to be used are estimates of the quantity of education achieved by the population. They are (1) the percent of persons 21 years of age and over that completed high school, and (2) the percent of persons 21 years of age and over that completed less than five years of school.

The third variable is an estimate of the quality of educational achievement. The variable is the estimate of the percentage of persons graduating from high school that go on to college. In order to interpret this variable as a measure of educational quality, it must be assumed that it is related to the percentage of high school graduates able to meet college entrance requirements. In addition to entrance requirements, the variable also takes into account the extent to which the high school teachers have been able to motivate desire for further education. Both entrance requirements and motivation provided must be considered as complementary measures of educational quality. There is one additional limitation that should be mentioned. The data used to construct this percentage is the ratio of persons in college to persons in high school. Since both high school and college are four year institutions, this variable represents an average percent of college students for each graduating class.[91]

There are alternative measures of education available. The best of the alternatives is median school years completed. This statistic could not be calculated for the OBE Economic Areas because there is no way to arrive at a median statistic through aggregation of data from smaller units, as was necessary for all data used in this study. However, the variables used here should provide an adequate indication of the quality and quantity of the average level of educational achievement.

Statistical Summary of Variables

Percent of Persons 21 Years of Age and Over That Completed High School

	Nation	*N. East*	*S. East*	*Central*	*Far West*
Mean	39.90	41.93	31.78	43.01	47.87
Standard Deviation	7.54	4.41	4.28	5.44	4.04
Minimum	24.52	33.13	24.52	33.89	37.75
Maximum	55.55	55.55	41.01	55.07	55.52

Percent of Persons 21 Years of Age and Over That Completed Less than Five Years of School, 1960

	Nation	*N. East*	*S. East*	*Central*	*Far West*
Mean	9.30	5.31	17.10	5.35	6.34
Standard Deviation	6.62	1.70	5.76	2.33	3.67
Minimum	2.44	2.44	5.31	2.47	2.64
Maximum	40.32	10.35	40.32	11.52	14.33

Estimate of the Percent of High School Students that go on to College, 1960

	Nation	*N. East*	*S. East*	*Central*	*Far West*
Mean	28.83	36.17	24.21	28.27	27.38
Standard Deviation	17.86	23.40	16.31	14.58	10.06
Minimum	4.46	11.31	4.46	7.63	13.23
Maximum	122.36	122.36	114.06	81.56	48.13

MEASURE OF POPULATION DENSITY

The trend in per capita income to increase with city size is well documented.[92] This has been a result of industries locating in urban areas where economies of scale may be realized. The objective of the variable to be discussed here will be, therefore, to measure the relative importance of the urbanization of the pattern of economic growth.

Since it is to be assumed that urbanization is essentially a function of economies to be realized by urban industrial location, the technicalities of economies of scale will first be discussed. Private firms or the public sector will realize increased efficiency in production as a result of increasing scale as long as the economies outweigh the diseconomies. Theoretically, this results in the traditional "U" shaped average cost curve, the minimum point being established where economies and diseconomies are equal. Once this minimum point is passed, diseconomies outweigh economies, resulting in increasing cost per unit of output.

Using this reasoning, many economists have attempted to define optimum city size. Wener Hirsch, for example, argues that "in terms of economies of scale, governments serving from 50,000 to 100,000 urbanites might be most efficient."[93] In support of this, Hirsch presents his studies of urban public services and the shape of their estimated average unit cost curves.[94] (See Table 3–5.)

The variable to be used to measure the relative importance of urbanization will be the ratio of total population to total square miles. This is the specification for population density as it is generally defined.

Table 3–5. Cost Curve Studies of Scale Economies

Name and Year	*Service*	*Type*	*Result*
	Horizontally Integrated Services		
Riew (1966)	Secondary education	S	AUC is U-shaped with trough at about 1,700 pupils
Riesling (1965)	Primary and secondary education	S	AUC is about horizontal
Hirsch (1959)	Primary and secondary education	S	AUC is about horizontal
Schmandt-Stephens (1960)	Police protection	S & Q	AUC is about horizontal
Hirsch (1960)	Police protection	S & Q	AUC is about horizontal
Will (1965)	Fire protection	E	AUC is declining with major economies reached at 300,000 population
Hirsch (1959)	Fire protection	S	AUC is U-shaped with trough at about 110,000 population
Hirsch (1965)	Refuse collection	S	AUC is about horizontal
	Circularly Integrated Services		
Hirsch (1959)	School administration	S	AUC is U-shaped with trough at about 44,000 pupils
	Vertically Integrated Services		
Nerlove (1961)	Electricity	S	AUC is declining
Isard-Coughlin (1957)	Sewage plants	S	AUC is declining
Lomax (1951)	Gas	S	AUC is declining
Johnston (1960)	Electricity	S	AUC is declining

Note: The following abbreviations are used: S=statistical data; AUC=average unit cost; Q=questionnaire data; E=engineering data.

Source: Werner Z. Hirsch, "The Supply of Urban Public Services," in Perloff and Wings, eds., p. 508.

The other variable that was considered for use here was the percentage of persons living in urban area. However, data on the percentage of persons living in urban areas was available in usable form only for persons living in places of 2,500 or more population, which is the Census definition of urban places.[95] This variable was not used, because the limit of 2,500 persons is judged too low to be considered as urban for the purposes of this analysis.

Statistical Summary of Variables

Population Density, 1960

	Nation	*N. East*	*S. East*	*Central*	*Far West*
Mean	97.96	226.64	67.90	29.78	41.84
Standard Deviation	162.56	267.52	30.56	21.82	66.50
Minimum	3.76	17.82	22.18	3.76	2.16
Maximum	1641.16	1641.45	185.16	104.81	242.38

Chapter Four

Specifications of the Approach

INTRODUCTION

When an analyst sets out to specify a mathematical model, historical analysis, or simply a descriptive picture of socioeconomic events, he begins his research with a host of preconceived notions. These preconceived notions in turn determine the selection of the variables to be analyzed. On this point it is worth quoting Ronald Meek at length:

> Taking the facts which he has placed at the top of the scale as his foundation, the model builder proceeds to develop certain concepts, categories and methods of classification which he believes will help him to provide a generalized explanation of the structure and development of the economy. In this part of his work he has necessarily to rely to some extent on concept–material inherited from the past, but he also tries to work out new analytical devices of his own. The particular analytical devices which he employs—his tools and techniques, as it were—are thus by no means arbitrarily chosen. To quite a large extent they are dependent upon the nature of his vision, the nature of the primary facts which they are to be used to explain, and the nature of the general method of analysis which he decides to adopt.[1]

This somewhat lengthy quote from Meek demonstrates the methodological procedure that is implicit in most analysis. It also shows that the methodology to be used must be chosen with care. The methodology must be consistent with problem addressed and with the theoretical approach of the analysis. The theoretical approach and the general methodology from the backbone of analysis. The principle tool to be used in this study is factor analysis. The results and conclusions that follow will, of course, be influenced by the "preconceived notions" of the author. Many of the interpretations that follow will be open to debate. Only in this way can the various "preconceived notions" carried forth by regional analysts be brought to bear on the subject at hand and guide useful results.

OBJECTIVES OF THE STUDY

The primary objective of this study is to place in perspective the various forces effecting economic change and patterns of that change of regions of the United States. This will be accomplished by four separate but interrelated analyses applied to each of the four regional groupings. The first is the application of a simple export base model. This model, to be developed below, is not meant to be complete. Rather, it attempts to provide a basis for viewing the impact of changes in the relative importance of export industries on the pattern of change exhibited by each of the regional groupings.

The second approach that will be applied will be an analysis of long term structural development. In this case, 28 static variables are used in a factor analysis, with the level of per capita personnel income as the variable to be explained. This will provide clues to what factors have been related to higher levels of development in each region. It should not be surprising that no one set of factors are related to higher levels of development in all regions.

The third aspect of the study for each region will be an analysis of the factors related to the growth of the total volume of economic activity. The average annual rate of growth of total personnel income over the period 1950 to 1966 will be used as the measure of the growth in the volume of economic activity. In this case 37 variables will be used in the factor analysis. It will be in this area that the greatest variance is found in the factors related to the dependent variable.

The final aspect of the study for each region will be to analyze the factors effecting the growth in the average level of economic welfare. The dependent variable to be used in this case will be the average annual rate of growth of per capita personnel income over the period 1950 to 1966. It is in this area that the greatest similarity in predominant factors are found.

EXPORT BASE CONCEPT TO BE USED

The simplified economic base model to be used consists of the following two equations:

$$\frac{dTPY}{dt} = f(\Delta EB, CC)$$

$$\Delta EB = f(IGI, I)$$

where: $\frac{dTPY}{dt}$ = Growth in the total personal income over the period 1950–66.

ΔEB = The percent change in the economic base over the period 1950–67. (The ratio of export oriented production to total production is defined as the export base.)

CC = Coefficient of concentration in 1950.

IGI = The index of the composition of growth industries, 1960.

I = Infrastructure (Measured as non-education government expenditures per capita), 1960.

The first equation states that the growth of total economic activity is a function of the increase in the ratio of export oriented production to total production and the degree of economic diversity of the region. The basis for this argument lies in the complex of economic ties between each sector of any economy. Export base theory emphasizes the economic stimulus resulting from exports to other areas in much the same way as simple Keynesian income determination models rely on autonomous investment. Increases in the demand for an area's exports provides additional income to the area to be converted into effective demand for the services provided by the existing non-basic sector. In addition, it directly increases the demand by the exporting sectors for intermediate products. If the supplying industry sectors are also located in the area, the multiplier effects are intensified as a result of the growth in intermediate demand.

At any given point in time, the export base can act only as "a mechanical device to allocate labor"[2] or earnings between sectors. However, growth in the base initiates readjustments throughout the economy of the regions. Income is generated first through the expansion of exports, and then by iterations throughout the non-basic economy via multiplier. In terms of the forces specified in Chapter 3, there should be definite, although in most cases indirect, measurable impacts on these forces as a result of trends in the industrial structure becoming oriented toward a greater export base.

Borts and Stein have concluded that the weakness of the export base models is their inability to account for the diversity of economic activity in a region.[3] This conclusion addresses the important issue of what type of industrial structure is able to maximize the impact of multipliers initiated by growth in the export base. It is assumed here that the more diversified the economic structure of the region's economy, the greater will be the impact of the export multipliers, and therefore the greater will be the growth in total personal income. The relative degree of economic diversity will be measured by the coefficient of concentration as is discussed in Chapter 3.

By incorporating this variable into the export base model, a means has been provided to link the export base and the sector approaches. In reality these two approaches should be viewed as complementary. The sector approach, by emphasizing internal growth, focuses on the development of the total economic structure of the region. However, the essence of any growth theory, causal factors that stimulate growth, is notably lacking from the sector approaches. The causal factor is adequately supplied by the export base approach. When the sector approach is viewed as providing the foundation on which income generated from increased exports can achieve the desired multiplier effects, the two approaches become dependent.

The export base approach remains the principal causal force effecting growth. However, the export base theory has been limited by explicitly linking it with sector approach. In most applications of the export base approach, this link already exists because of the underlying assumptions with regard to the multiplier.

Most export base approaches measure exports as simply total output or total employment in the sectors of agriculture, forestry and fisheries, mining, manufacturing, and federal and state government. In addition, these studies rarely consider the growth characteristics of these industries. The OBE definitions of export sectors by Economic Area represent a significant improvement over previous measures. It will be assumed (equation 2) that the growth in the export base, as defined by the Office of Business Economics, is a function of (1) the degree to which the region's economy is weighted toward the existence of national growth industries, and (2) the development of the region's infrastructure.

The impact of national growth industries on a region's export potential becomes apparent when the growth characteristics of certain export industries are analyzed. The average annual rate of increase in employment in non-primary industries was 2.1 percent between 1950 and 1960. Thirteen of the 32 industry sectors used in this study exceeded this average. These are presented in Table 4–1. Of the thirteen growth industries, seven are always considered to be export oriented, while the remaining six will be considered as exports for some OBE areas. There should, therefore, be an association between the index of the composition of growth industries and growth in the export base.

The location of national growth industries in a region is a function of many factors. One of the more important is the quantity and quality of the public infrastructure. The infrastructure available to the region's industries influences the efficiency of the industries and may act to pull industries into the region. The public infrastructure available represents an external economy to the firm. If a region can attract and support the rapid growth industries, the impact

Table 4–1. Growth Industries, 1950–1960

Sector	*Growth Rate*	*Always Considered As Export*	*Considered As Exports For Some Regions**
Mfg. Food & Kindred Prod.	2.8		X
Mfg. Printing & Publishing	3.3		X
Mfg. Chemicals	3.0	X	
Mfg. Non-Elect. Machinery	2.2	X	
Mfg. Electrical Machinery	6.9	X	
Mfg. Transport Equipment	3.3	X	
Mfg. Paper & Allied Products	2.4	X	
Mfg. Fabricated Metals & Ord.	4.7	X	
Finance, Ins. & Real Estate	3.8		X
Business & Repair Services	2.4		X
Ed., Prof. and Med. Services	5.0		X
Public Administration	2.7		X
Armed Forces	5.5	X	

*See Appendix A.

Source: Calculated from basic data not reported.

on the export growth of the regional economy is magnified as a result of their rapid growth.

The infrastructure available to a region's industry is not, of course, limited to industry showing rapid growth. The infrastructure available provides externalities to all industries located in the region. The development of infrastructure, assuming that it is adequate in quantity and quality, reduces the costs of production of the region's industry, thereby increasing the market potential of exporting industries. As an indirect measure of the public infrastructure of the regions we are using non-education local government expenditures per capita.[4]

GROWTH IN PER CAPITA INCOME

In the discussion of the export base model developed above, no mention was made concerning growth in the per capita income. The assumption made in this study is that growth in the total economic activity of an area, measured by growth in total personal income, is the primary determinant of the economic condition of the region. However, since this study is an attempt to analyze the determinants of the economic growth and the change in the average level of welfare of the regional groupings, independent analysis of each income growth concept is necessary. The procedure that will be used is discussed below.

The assumption that growth in the total level of economic activity is the primary determinant of the economic condition of the region is not unreasonable. Exceptions to this are most relevant in cases where out-migration of labor force participants reduces the supply of labor and, therefore, tends to increase the wages and general level of welfare of those that remain. This, strictly stated, is the neo-classical view of labor markets. It has also been used to help explain the convergence of regional per capita income levels. More recent research on the effect of out-migration from depressed areas suggests that this view is inaccurate. Muth, for example, in an analysis of 50 depressed counties, argues that "In-migration tends to increase median family income and out-migration to reduce it. In particular, statistically significant relationships were uncovered showing that a ten percent reduction in population, attributable to out-migration, tended to reduce median family income by about $200."[5] Three explanations are possible: The first deals with the socioeconomic characteristics of the out-migrants. The second alleges a simple Keynesian income determination model that, as a result of a decrease in demand for goods and services, results in decreased earnings for those that remain. Finally, the areas may be in such a state of deterioration that the effect of out-migration, even if it exerts a positive influence on those that remain, is insufficient to counteract the trend toward further deterioration.

More complete analysis done by Borts and Stein also supports that done by Muth.[6] They have argued that for large cities differential rates of employment are induced by differential rates of in-migration. In other words, persons migrating to cities increase the demand for goods and services, thus inducing employment opportunities that may, or may not, have been available before their arrival.

To summarize, growth in the volume of economic activity of a given area affects the economic condition of the area by providing employment opportunities before or after the fact of migration, and affects the average welfare levels of all areas as a result of the trends in migration. There are, of course, many other determinants of the interrelationship between volume and welfare changes, and many of these will be discussed in later chapters. In fact, the determinants of migration, and the results thereof are still largely unknown at this time. However, as the above points demonstrate, explanations of migration to an area must deal explicitly with the job opportunities provided by that area. It will not be a major concern, in this study, whether persons migrate because of an actual job opportunity, or because they believe better opportunities exist in their new location. Rather, the focus of this study will be on the impact of such factors as migration on the two income concepts.

TIME PERIOD

The time period to be used will be 1950–66. The selection of this time period was based on data availability and consideration of the economic trends over the past three decades. Most of the data used to construct the variables discussed in Chapter 3 are available in the 1940 Census publications. This provided the option of extending the data base back to that year, but the option was rejected. This was not done because this would have involved accounting for the impact of armament and readjustment caused by World War II.

In addition, time period of the dependent variables, growth in total personal income, and growth in per capita personal income have been extended to 1968. This was rejected because the year 1966 preceded the major upturn in the inflationary period of the late 1960s.

This choice of the period to be analyzed is consistent with that chosen by the Advisory Commission on Intergovernmental Relations:

> In selecting a time period for study, two major considerations prompted the choice of the period 1950–1966. For the purpose of this analysis, recent experience is most relevant and, equally important, a period long enough to reveal the trend rather than cyclical change is necessary. If the time period were extended to include earlier years, World War II and the dislocations it produced would have to be reckoned with, while going even further back into the 1930s would involve the Great Depression. Since historical comparability is not essential to this analysis, it is proper to begin with 1950.
>
> Other years, of course, could have been chosen as the base point. Despite the beginning of the Korean War and is essentially "random" disturbance, 1950 was selected because of the greater availability of data. Moreover, the relatively high 1950 unemployment rate of 5.3 percent indicates the economic impact of the Korean War was not immediately felt. Indeed, since the unemployment rate for 1966 was down to 3.9 percent, some of the economic growth that transpired represents more favorable cyclical developments. Nonetheless, the unemployment rates for the two years are sufficiently comparable to draw meaningful conclusions for the period as a whole. Modifications of this time span would yield, of course, different results in terms of the numerical growth recorded. It is reasonably safe to assume, however, that no strikingly different results than reached here would emerge in the recorded growth profile among various governmental levels and this comparative aspect is the essential concern.[7]

APPROACH

The approach to be specified in this section will be applied to each of the four regional groupings of OBE Economic Areas. The sequence, as presented above, will be to analyze the impact of changes in the economic base on the growth of total economic activity. This will be followed by analyses of regional factors affecting long term structural development, growth in total economic activity, and growth in the average level of economic welfare.

The use of factor analysis in studies like this has not been without controversy. Therefore, it might be wise to begin with a brief explanation of the technique and its advantages and shortcomings. Factor analysis is essentially an analysis of interdependence. The technique breaks down the variance of all variables into variance components which provide the basis for grouping associated variables into factors. The factors formed by the variance analysis become the final explanatory vectors of the dependent variable. The choice of the number of factors to include in the final analysis has important effects on the result, as does the number of independent variables in a multi-regression equation. Therefore, strict requirements must be placed on the amount of overall variance explained by each factor before it is included in the analysis. The choice of how many variables to include thus involves the same decision-making process that is used in deciding how many independent variables to be used in regression analysis.

The danger of misusing this technique is well known; however, it is worth quoting at length Adelman and Morris concerning its applicability:

> It should be emphasized that, like all multi-variant analyses, factor analysis is a study of mutual association rather than a study of causality. The decomposition of the original set of variables into smaller subsets of factors partitions the totality of variables into essentially independent subgroups. In this sense the analysis can be used to infew the extent of independence of a given variable from a given set of forces within a single factor. However, the association found may arise in more than one way. Causality may run from any subset of variables within the factor to any other non-overlapping subset in the same factor; or the association may arise from some common cause (or causes) omitted from explicit consideration in the factor analysis. Thus, like correlation analyses, factor analyses can provide only information concerning the extent of mutual interdependence. Additional information not contained in the statistical analysis must be used to infer the existence and direction of causality.[8]

Therefore, factor analysis can be used only as a basic tool to group a relatively large number of variables into a smaller number of factors. The interpretation of the factors must be based on the *a priori* logic specified, and on historical and theoretical knowledge of the economic events being analyzed. Factor analysis, like all statistical techniques, is simply a tool that the analyst may use to specify properties of his observations, which will aid him in his approach to the problem he is dealing with.

In order to establish the components of the pattern of economic growth and the pattern of change in the average level of welfare, and to define the relationship between these components, or forces, three factor analysis runs for each of the regional groupings will be made. The first will have as the variable to be explained the per capita personal income of OBE Economic Areas in 1959. This year was selected because it is the midpoint of the period, and because the available static variables cluster at that year. Although this is a static measure of the level of development, it represents the cumulation of long term trends more so than do the variables that measure the changes in income over the period 1950–1966.

The logic for the use of cross-section analysis to obtain insights into the forces that have contributed to the long run development of the regional groupings is supplied by Adelman and Morris:

> One may view cross-country results as representations of patterns of change typical of individual countries at a given point in time when access to technology and opportunities for trade are, at least in principle, common to all. Historically, however, the process of development occurs in an environment of concurrent change in all aspects relevant to national development. In order to interpret cross-sectional analyses as indications of historical transformations one must therefore conceive of successive points along the statistical fit as successive levels of socioeconomic-political development achieved by a typical underdeveloped country in the process of structural change. More specifically, corresponding to each country is a point in *n*-dimensional space which is determined by a set of *n* attributes related to the country's stage of social, political, and economic development. The factor analysis fitted to these points in the *m*-dimensional space of common factors yields a representation of the average relationship among the several factors for the countries in the sample. Since we interpret consecutive points along the factor analysis fit to represent consecutive stages of development, we treat the fit as a representation of the historical path that would be traversed by an average country undergoing socioeconomic and political transformation.[9]

The use and interpretation of the factor analysis runs on the static level of per capita personal income in 1959 for the OBE Economic Areas will be approached in the way explained by Adelman and Morris.

The second factor analysis run will use the rate of growth of total personal income as the dependent variable. This will provide the statistical grouping of variables that will be used as the basis for analyzing the patterns of economic growth. The final factor analysis to be completed for each regional grouping will have the rate of growth of per capita income as the dependent variable. This, also as discussed above, will provide the statistical basis for analyzing the change in the average level of welfare in each of the regional groupings.

Chapter Five

Income, Employment, and Export Growth in the Continental United States: An Overview

INTRODUCTION

In order to place regional economic growth and development in proper perspective, it is necessary to discuss the income and employment trends of the continental United States. As presented in Chapter 2, there are 171 OBE Economic Areas located in the continental United States. The following brief analysis of the income and employment trends for these areas provides a foundation on which the trends of the four regional groupings may be compared and contrasted. It is presented only for use in the following chapters and is not meant to be an analysis of growth and development in the continental United States.

The remainder of this chapter demonstrates the importance of the regional viewpoint. An analysis of the economic base model is presented and shows that, although the statistical results are acceptable, economically meaningful results are not obtained when applied to all 171 OBE Economic Areas.

GROWTH IN TOTAL PERSONAL INCOME

During the 16 years covered by this study, total personal income in the continental United States grew from $227 billion to $578 billion, or at an average annual rate of 6.05 percent. However, this growth was not uniform throughout the nation. The mean rate of growth for the 171 OBE Economic Areas was 5.8 percent per annum and ranged from a high of 11.96 percent to a low of 2.5 percent. Map 5–1 provides a quartile ranking of the OBE Economic Areas according to their rates of growth of total economic activity over the period.

With some exceptions, the most rapid growth areas were in the Southeast and in the Far West. Growth in total personal income paralleled population movements. The continued westward movement was the dominant characteristic of U.S. population redistribution and growth. This, to some degree, concealed the continued and substantial growth in population of the eastern and midwestern sections of the country.[1] The percentage of population and total personal income growth over the period 1950–66 for the regional groupings were:

Region	*Percent Population Growth*	*Percent Total Personal Income Growth*
Far West	61.6	206.5
Northeast	25.7	141.6
Southeast	21.4	164.2
Central	17.3	132.8

The Far West Region dominated these measures. The Southeast, however, ranked second in terms of total personal income growth but third with respect to population increases. In addition, 44 of the 55 OBE Economic Areas located in the Southeastern Region experienced out-migration during the 1950s. The compensating factors leading to the growth in total personal income in this region appears to be intraregional migration and relatively high rates of natural increases in population.

In terms of the nine Census Geographical Regions of the United States, four (the Pacific, South Atlantic, West South Central, and the Mountain Regions) have shown significant increases in the share of total personal income earned. The Pacific Region accounted for 4.6 percent of total personal income earned in 1880 and 14.4 percent in 1965. The South Atlantic Region increased its share from 7.9 percent in 1880 to 12.8 percent in 1965. The West South Central Region came close to doubling its 1880 share by increasing it from 4.0 percent to 7.8 percent in 1965. The share of the Mountain Region increased 2.2 percent to 3.6 percent. The share of total personal income earned by all other regions decreased (see Table 5–1).

The regional groupings show similar but less decisive trends for the period 1950–1966. Table 5–2 presents total personal income by regional groupings for the initial, midpoint, and final years covered by this study.

The Far West Regional Grouping increased its share of total personal income while the Northeastern decreased. However, in 1966, over 50 percent of total personal income earned was earned in the Northeastern Regional Grouping. This shows the dominance of this region in terms of the total economic activity of the continental United States.

Within each of the regional groupings, the variation in the rates of total personal income growth is low. Table 5–3 presents a statistical summary of the growth in total personal income for the OBE Economic Areas by the 171 OBE Economic Areas (Nation) and by regional grouping.

The average rate of total personal income growth for the OBE Economic Areas was highest in the Far West and Southeastern Regional Group-

Table 5–1. Geographic Distribution of Personal Income

Year of Cycle	United States (millions of current dollars)	Geographic Distribution of Personal Income (percent								
		New England	Middle Atlantic	East North Central	West North Central	South Atlantic	East South Central	West South Central	Mountain	Pacific
1880	$ 8,740	11.3	30.4	22.8	11.1	7.9	5.7	4.0	2.2	4.6
1900	15,390	9.9	29.0	22.4	13.3	7.1	4.9	5.2	3.1	5.2
1919-21[1]	69,277	8.7	28.5	22.2	10.3	8.4	4.4	7.0	3.2	7.3
1929	85,661	8.3	29.6	23.6	8.9	8.5	4.0	6.1	2.5	8.5
1929-37	62,650	8.8	30.0	22.1	8.5	9.3	3.9	6.0	2.5	8.8
1937-44	100,492	7.8	25.4	22.4	8.4	11.0	4.4	6.9	2.9	10.8
1944-48	178,465	6.9	23.7	22.1	8.7	11.4	4.8	7.5	3.0	11.9
1948-53	240,435	6.6	23.1	22.7	8.7	11.4	4.7	7.9	3.2	11.8
1953-57	310,828	6.5	22.7	22.9	8.1	11.6	4.6	7.8	3.3	12.6
1957-60	371,010	6.4	22.3	22.0	8.1	11.9	4.5	7.9	3.6	13.3
1960-65[1]	454,542	6.4	21.7	21.2	7.9	12.4	4.6	7.8	3.7	14.4
1965	527,890	6.3	21.2	21.4	7.8	12.8	4.6	7.8	3.6	14.4

[1] Period does not cover a complete business cycle.

Source: U.S. Department of Commerce, Bureau of the Census, *Long Term Economic Growth,* (Washington: Government Printing Office, 1966), p. 70.

Table 5–2. Total Personal Income by Regional Grouping (000,000)

Year	Total	Northeast	Southeast	Central	Far West
1950	226,580	127,961	37,240	28,508	31,274
1959	381,858	209,141	61,899	44,358	61,680
1966	577,990	309,209	98,406	66,369	95,843

Percent

Year	Total*	Northeast	Southeast	Central	Far West
1950	99.28	56.47	16.43	12.58	13.80
1959	98.72	54.76	16.20	11.61	16.15
1966	98.57	53.49	17.02	11.48	16.58

*Sums to less than 100% because of the deletion of OBE Economic Areas 35 and 36 from the Southeastern Regional Grouping.

Source: Calculated from basic data not reported.

Table 5–3. Statistical Summary of Total Personal Income Growth, 1950–66, for the OBE Economic Areas by Nation and by Regional Grouping

	Nation	N. East	S. East	Central	Far West
Mean	5.82	5.64	6.14	4.89	6.53
Standard Deviation	1.37	.66	1.10	.90	1.88
Coefficient of Variation	.235	.117	.179	.184	.287
Minimum	2.71	3.54	3.84	2.71	3.50
Maximum	11.96	7.22	9.28	7.02	11.96

Source: Calculated from Appendix A, Table A–1.

ings, thus reflecting the trends discussed above. Although the range of growth rates is high within most groupings, the coefficient of variation is low. This reflects, as does Map 5–1, that the OBE Economic Areas within each grouping are, with a few exceptions, following similar trends in terms of growth in total personal income.

GROWTH IN PER CAPITA INCOME

Per capita income in the United States grew from $1,498 in 1950 to $2,965 in 1966, or at an annual rate of 4.35 percent. The regional growth trend was one of convergence of the level of per capita income for all regions. Table 5–4 summarizes this trend from 1880 to the initial period of this study for the nine Census Geographical Regions. This table expresses the per capita income level of the Census Regions in terms of the percentage of per capita income of the United

Table 5–4. Geographic Distribution of the Levels of Per Capita Income

Year of Cycle	United States (current dollars)	Percent Geographic Division is of United States								
		New England	*Middle Atlantic*	*East North Central*	*West North Central*	*South Atlantic*	*East South Central*	*West South Central*	*Mountain*	*Pacific*
1880	$ 174	141	146	102	90	52	52	60	168	205
1900	202	135	143	107	98	51	50	61	140	163
1919-21[1]	650	125	136	109	87	64	53	72	101	136
1929	703	125	139	114	81	66	50	62	83	130
1929-37	500	133	140	108	79	72	48	60	84	129
1937-44	756	121	125	112	85	78	55	70	91	134
1944-48	1,278	109	120	110	93	80	62	77	94	125
1948-53	1,576	107	116	112	95	81	63	81	96	120
1953-57	1,890	108	115	112	91	82	66	82	92	118
1957-60	2,120	109	116	108	93	82	67	83	95	118
1960-65[1]	2,425	110	115	107	94	85	69	82	94	117
1965	2,724	109	113	109	95	86	70	81	91	114

[1] Period does not cover a complete business cycle.

Source: U.S. Department of Commerce, Bureau of the Census, *Long Term Economic Growth,* (Washington: Government Printing Office, 1966), p. 69.

States. The strong tendency toward convergence did not begin until the early part of the 20th century.[2] The delay in continued convergence that occurred between 1860 and 1880 is attributed to the devastation of the South resulting from the Civil War.[3] In concluding a major study of per capita income trends, Richard Easterlin concludes that:

> Product and resource mobility appears to have played a part in the convergence since 1880, as has the differing income elasticity of demand for agricultural and non-agricultural products. The role of dynamic factors such as technological change, resource discovery and exhaustion, and transportation developments is difficult to unravel, although in the small number of cases considered here, there was little indication that these factors tended systematically to favor the low-income regions.[4]

This leaves product and resource mobility as the primary cause for the convergence of per capita income.

The trend toward convergence of per capita income continued during the period of this study. Map 5–2 presents quartile groupings of per capita income growth of the OBE Economic Areas for the period 1950–66. Comparing this map with Map 2–2, which presents quartile groupings of the level of per capita income in 1959 of the OBE Economic Areas, a mirror image becomes evident. The simple correlation between the level of per capita income in 1959 and the growth of per capita income between 1950 and 1966 is −.63 for the 171 OBE Economic Areas. This high inverse relationship holds for each of the regional groupings of this study except for the Far West, where the simple correlation was a low −.11. This exception is explained by the relatively higher income and education of migrants to the Far West Region. These trends may also be interpreted to support Easterlin's conclusion that the convergence is primarily due to product and resource mobility.

Table 5–5 presents statistical summaries of the rates of per capita income growth for the OBE Economic Areas in the nation and within the four regional groupings. This table presents, in a different way, the trends under discussion. The OBE areas grouped into the Southeastern regional grouping had the

Table 5–5. Statistical Summary of Per Capita Income Growth, 1950–66, by Nation and Regional Groupings

	Nation	*N. East*	*S. East*	*Central*	*Far West*
Mean	4.43	4.28	5.00	4.24	3.80
Standard Deviation	.68	.37	.64	.59	.52
Coefficient of Variation	.153	.087	.128	.139	.137
Minimum	2.52	3.71	3.43	2.76	2.52
Maximum	6.73	5.35	6.73	5.28	4.75

Source: Calculated from Appendix A, Table A–1.

Table 5–6. Statistical Summary of the 1959 Levels of Per Capita Income by Nation and Regional Groupings

	Nation	*N. East*	*S. East*	*Central*	*Far West*
Mean	1871	2170	1485	1844	2188
Standard Deviation	395	267	229	282	297
Coefficient of Variation	.211	.167	.154	.153	.136
Minimum	1047	1602	1048	1199	1821
Maximum	2873	2783	2192	2375	2783

Source: Calculated from Appendix A, Table A–1.

highest average growth rate in per capita income. The OBE Economic Areas grouped into the Far West had the lowest average growth rate of per capita income. When these trends are compared with Table 5–5, which presents a statistical summary of the levels of per capita income of the OBE Economic Areas by nation and regional grouping, the trend toward convergence is evident. The relatively low coefficients of variation for per capita income growth rates, and the inverse relationship between the average rate of growth and the average level of per capita income, show the trend toward convergence.

EMPLOYMENT CHANGE AND DISTRIBUTION 1950–1960

During the 1950s total employment grew by 14.6 percent. However, major changes occurred in the distribution of employment between the 32 employment sectors used in this study. Tables 5–7 and 5–8 present the employment growth and distribution by industry sector and major sector for the period 1950–60. Most dramatic was the redistribution of employment from the primary sectors to other sectors. A notable trend was the increasing share of employment taken by the service sector.[5] In terms of percentage growth in employment during the 1950s the service sector's growth was matched only by the major sector of public administration and the armed forces (Table 5–8).

Many studies define services to include public administration and government. When this is done the growth of services is highlighted even more. The growth of the service sector has often been attributed to a relatively higher income elasticity of demand for services than for other products, particularly agricultural and other necessity products.[6] Victor Fuchs argues from an extensive empirical study of the growth of the service sector that this is a misinterpretation. According to Fuchs:

> Examination of cross-sectional buying patterns, and of trends in output over time, suggests that the growth of income and a consequent shift in demand has not been a major source of the relative growth of service employment. Measured in dollars of constant

Table 5–7. Employment Growth and Distribution by Sector; 1950–60

Sector	*Employment 1950 (000)*	*Percent of Total*	*Employment 1960 (000)*	*Percent of Total*	*Percent Change 50–60*
Agric.	7,013	12.25	4,356	6.62	–37.88
Forest & Fish.	122	0.21	94	0.14	–22.95
Mining	944	1.64	673	1.02	–28.70
Construction	3,491	6.10	3,942	5.99	12.91
Manufacturing					
Food & Kindred	1,419	2.40	1,877	2.85	32.27
Textile Mill	1,257	2.19	949	1.44	–24.66
Apparel	1,079	1.88	1,210	1.84	12.14
Printing	865	1.51	1,191	1.81	37.68
Chemicals	668	1.16	902	1.37	35.02
Lumber & Furn.	1,208	2.11	1,100	1.67	–8.94
Elect. Machinery	800	1.40	1,556	2.36	94.50
Mach. Non-Elect.	1,312	2.29	1,634	2.48	24.54
Transport Eq.	1,365	2.38	1,890	2.87	38.46
Paper Prod.	475	0.83	601	0.91	26.52
Petro. Refin.	292	0.51	294	0.44	0.60
Primary Metals	1,184	2.07	1,272	1.93	7.43
Fab. Metals	852	1.49	1,347	2.04	58.09
Misc. Mfg.	1,999	3.49	2,347	3.57	17.40
Transport Serv.	2,983	5.22	2,843	4.32	–4.69
Communications	718	1.25	852	1.29	18.66
Utilities	793	1.38	931	1.41	17.40
Wholesale Trade	2,004	3.50	2,031	3.09	1.34
Eating Places	1,710	2.99	1,869	2.84	9.29
Other Retail	6,987	12.23	8,067	12.27	15.45
Fin. Ins. & Real Est.	1,943	3.40	2,810	4.27	44.62
Lodging Places	1,881	3.29	2,015	3.06	7.12
Business Repair	1,328	2.32	1,676	2.55	26.20
Amusements & Rec.	499	0.87	523	0.79	4.80
Priv. Households	1,659	2.90	1,985	3.02	19.65
Ed., Med. & Prof.	4,847	8.48	7,860	11.96	62.16
Public Admin.	2,525	4.42	3,308	5.03	31.00
Armed Forces	994	1.74	1,708	2.59	71.83
Totals	*57,216*	*100.00*	*65,713*	*100.00*	*14.85*

Source: Calculated from basic data not reported.

purchasing power, the Service sector's share of output was the same in 1965 as in 1929. Measured in current dollars, it grew only from 47 to 50 percent. As a share of non-agricultural output in constant dollars, the Service sector actually declined over the same period, while in current dollars its share rose by less than 1 percentage point. If gross product is classified by type of final output rather than by industrial origin, the share accounted for by "services" increased only slightly between 1929 and 1965, whether measured in current dollars or after adjustments for changes in price.[7]

Table 5–8. Employment Growth and Distribution by Major Sector, 1950–60

Major Sector	*1950 Employment*	*%*	*1960 Employment*	*%*	*% Change*
Primary	8,079	14.12	5,123	7.79	–36.58
Construction	3,491	6.10	3,942	5.99	12.91
Manufacturing	14,775	25.82	18,170	27.65	22.97
Transportation, Communications, & Utilities	4,494	7.85	4,626	7.03	2.93
Wholesale & Retail Trade	10,701	18.70	11,967	18.21	11.83
Services	12,157	21.24	16,869	25.67	38.75
Government & Armed Forces	3,519	6.15	5,016	7.63	42.54
Totals	*57,216*	*100.00*	*65,713*	*100.00*	*14.85*

Source: Calculated from Table 5–7.

Fuchs attributes the rise in the service sector's share of total employment to slower growth of labor productivity in services rather than in agriculture and industry.[8] Therefore, relative growth in service employment was necessary to maintain a constant relative demand for services. Although the latest employment data used in this study is for 1960, all indications, including those of Fuchs, are that this trend continued over the period of this study.

Employment in the manufacturing sector increased by 23 percent, while the relative share of employment in the manufacturing sector increased slightly during the 1950 decade from 25.8 percent in 1950 to 27.7 percent in 1960. However, the relative shares of the 14 employment sectors within manufacturing remained relatively constant over the decade.

The only major sector that declined was the primary sector. The components of the primary sector, agriculture, forestry and fisheries, and mining declined by 38, 23, and 29 percent, respectively. This is a continuation of the long term decline of the primary sector in terms of employment. The reason for the decline is the well established income inelasticity of agricultural products combined with rapid growth in agricultural productivity. Fuchs estimates that the average annual rate of increases in labor productivity in agriculture was 3.4 percent since 1929. This compares to average annual increases of 2.2 percent for industry and 1.1 percent for services.[9]

THE ECONOMIC BASE MODEL APPLIED TO THE 171 OBE ECONOMIC AREAS OF THE CONTINENTAL UNITED STATES

The influence that the economic base concept has had on regional economic theory was expressed in previous chapters. However, most empirical studies concerned with the relationship between export growth and regional growth have concluded that the growth in exports is not a critical force in regional growth. Most of these studies were done on a national rather than a regional basis. In addition, they were concerned with the static export base ratio, rather than the change in the ratio used in this study. It is agreed that studies designed to use the static ratio of observations from areas or cities scattered throughout the United States show negative results. These studies, if the static ratio is used, abstract from the iterative adjustments so important to the economic base arguments. If the studies do not focus on sub-national areas, they miss relationships that are unique to each of the major geographical areas of the United States, and therefore often overlook associations altogether.

Using the 171 OBE Economic Areas as observations, the following regression was used to estimate the growth of total personal income as a function of the change in the economic base.

$$\frac{dTPY}{dt} = 6.17 + \underset{(.009)}{.065}\,(Pct.\ Ch.\ EB) \qquad R^2 = .244$$

where $\frac{dTPY}{dt}$ = growth rate of total personal income, 1950–66.

Pct. Ch. EB = percent change in the economic base, 1950–67.

The relatively low coefficient of determination, common in cross-section analysis,[10] is not of major concern. The regression does not accurately portray the true economic relationship between growth in total personal income and change in the economic base, although the beta coefficient and the coefficient of determination are statistically significant. If the unexplained residuals are disaggregated by regions, definite patterns emerge. Table 5–9 presents the

Table 5–9. Residuals by Regional Grouping

Regional Grouping	*Number of OBE Econ. Areas With Positive Residuals*	*Percent*	*Number of OBE Econ. Areas With Negative Residuals*	*Percent*
Northeast	9	19.6	37	80.4
Southeast	41	74.5	14	25.5
Central	9	21,9	33	78.1
Far West	17	65.4	9	34.6

Given these results, the same regression was run for each of the regional groupings in order that the problem signalled by the grouping of the residuals might more specifically be defined. The results are depicted in Chart 5–1 below.

Chart 5–1.

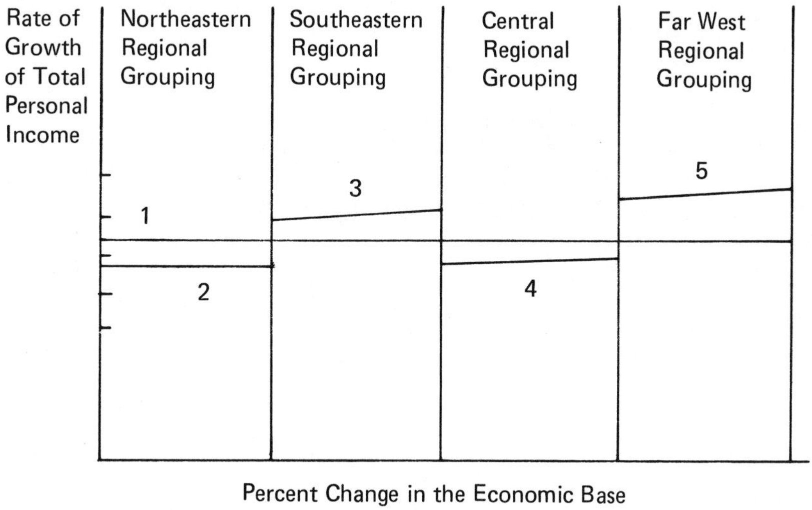

number of positive and negative residuals from this regression by regional grouping.

The grouping of the residuals by regional grouping shows that the regression has been fit through four separate relationships. This problem, technically defined as autocorrelation, is most commonly observed and applied to time series analysis. However, it is also relevant to cross-section analysis if meaningful groupings of the residual terms are obtained. The groupings of residuals found here meet that requirement.

Statistical Summaries

Equation (1) Regression fit against the 171 OBE Economic Areas and reported above.

(2) *Northeastern Regional Grouping*

$$\frac{dTPY}{dt} = 5.61 + .015\,(\Delta EB)$$

Standard error of beta = .010
Coefficient of determination = .051
F Ratio = 2.368

(3) *Southeastern Regional Grouping*

$$\frac{dTPY}{dt} = 6.97 + .104\,(\Delta EB)$$

Standard error of beta = .017
Coefficient of determination = .40
F Ratio = 35.659

(4) *Central Regional Grouping*

$$\frac{dTPY}{dt} = 5.597 + .065\,(\Delta EB)$$

Standard error of beta = .010
Coefficient of determination = .50
F Ratio = 39.50

(5) *Far West Regional Grouping*

$$\frac{dTPY}{dt} = 7.393 + .129\,(\Delta EB)$$

Standard error of beta = .028
Coefficient of determination = .47
F Ratio = 20.86

Where: $dTPY$ = The rate of growth of total personal income for the OBE Economic Areas for the period 1950–66.

ΔEB = The percentage of change in the Economic Base for the OBE Economic Areas during the period 1950–67.

The regressions are drawn to reflect their relative slopes and intercepts accurately. It should be obvious that five separate relationships are depicted in Chart 5–1. It will be shown in the following chapters that the relationships between the change in the economic base and growth in total personal income have different characteristics for each regional grouping. This is true for the underlying relationships as well as the statistical estimating equations.

Since the argument stated above is that the importance of the economic base of regions cannot be assessed when seen from a national point of view, discussion will not continue. However, this is not an attempt to disprove the concept. In fact, it may be argued that regression (1) of Chart 5–1 supports the economic base theory.[11] It is not being so argued because it is believed that the relationship between the growth in total personal income and change in the economic base expressed by this regression is a composite of more meaningful regional relationships.

Chapter Six

Economic Growth and Development of the Southeastern Regional Grouping

INTRODUCTION

During the period of this study (1950–66), the Southeastern Regional Grouping made major readjustments in its industrial structure. Total personal income increased by 6.2 percent per year. Per capita personal income increased from \$1,016 in 1950 to \$2,213 in 1966, an average annual rate of 5.0 percent. The growth rate of per capita income in this region is the highest exhibited by any of the regional groupings, while the growth rate of total personal income is second only to the Far West Regional grouping. Underlying these growth rates was a readjustment of industrial structure from primary output to manufactured and service goods.

The Southeastern Regional Grouping defined in Chapter 2 contains 55 Office of Business Economics (OBE) Areas which, in 1959, were among the lowest in terms of per capita income. The mean per capita income of the OBE Economic Areas in this regional grouping was \$1,485. This is significantly lower than the other three regional groupings defined for this study.

The two southernmost OBE Economic Areas in Florida, the Orlando and Miami Areas, were deleted from this regional grouping. As explained in Chapter 2, an attempt was made to define the boundaries of the regional groupings so as to maximize the homogeneity of the socioeconomic characteristics. These areas have significantly higher per capita incomes than the regional average and their industrial structure differs greatly from the OBE Economic Areas included in the Southeastern Regional Grouping. Because it was required that the regional groupings consist of contiguous OBE Economic Areas, these two Areas were deleted rather than adding them to another regional grouping which had socioeconomic characteristics more similar to their own.

Table 6–1. Employment Growth and Distribution by Sector, 1950–1960:

	(1) *Employment 1950 (000)*	*(2)* *Percent of Total 1950*
Agriculture	2,847	22.63
Forestry and Fisheries	54	0.42
Mining	389	3.09
Contract Construction	796	6.32
Manufacturing		
Food and Kindred Products	226	1.79
Textile Mill Products	605	4.80
Apparel and Other Textile Products	138	1.09
Printing and Publishing	90	0.71
Chemicals	159	1.26
Lumber and Furniture	529	4.20
Non-electrical Machinery	25	0.19
Electrical Machinery	71	0.56
Transport Equipment	52	0.41
Paper and Allied Products	86	0.68
Petroleum Refining	76	0.60
Primary Metals Industry	103	0.81
Fabricated Metals and Ordinance	54	0.42
Misc.	225	1.78
Transport Services	559	4.44
Communications	107	0.85
Utilities	147	1.16
Wholesale Trade	350	2.78
Eating and Drinking Establishments	297	2.36
Other Retail Trade	1,413	11.23
Finance, Insurance and Real Estate	265	2.10
Lodging Places	395	3.14
Business and Repair Services	234	1.86
Amusements and Recreation Services	83	0.65
Private Households	594	4.72
Educational, Medical and Professional Services	908	7.21
Public Administration	441	3.50
Armed Forces	260	2.06
Totals	*12,578*	*100.00*

Source: Calculated from basic data not reported.

EMPLOYMENT GROWTH AND DISTRIBUTION, 1950–60

Total employment grew by only 9.14 percent between 1950 and 1960 as compared with an increase of 14.9 percent for the continental U.S. over the same period. The relatively small increase must be attributed to the large decline in employment in the primary sectors, which accounted for 26 percent of total employment in 1950 (see Tables 6–1 and 6–2).

Southeastern Regional Grouping

(3) Share of Industry Less Share of Industry in U.S. 1950	(4) Employment 1960 (000)	(5) Percent of Total 1960	(6) Share of Industry Less Share of Industry in U.S. 1960	(7) Percent Change in Employment 1960–60
10.38	1,466	10.67	4.05	−48.50
.21	40	0.29	.15	−25.92
1.45	263	1.91	.89	−32.39
.22	939	6.84	.85	17.96
−.25	344	2.50	−.35	52.21
2.61	599	4.36	2.92	−0.99
−.79	281	2.04	.20	103.62
−.80	133	0.96	−.48	47.77
.10	232	1.68	31.00	45.91
2.09	444	3.23	1.56	16.06
−1.21	115	0.83	−1.53	360.00
−1.73	112	0.81	−1.67	57.74
−1.97	127	0.92	−1.95	144.23
−.15	131	0.95	.04	52.32
.11	81	0.59	.15	6.57
−1.26	132	0.96	−.97	28.15
−1.07	124	0.90	−1.14	129.62
−1.71	307	2.23	−1.34	36.44
−.78	537	3.91	−.41	−3.95
−.40	137	0.99	.30	28.03
−.22	196	1.42	.01	33.33
−.72	433	3.15	.06	23.71
−.63	327	2.38	−.46	10.10
−1.00	1,726	12.57	.30	22.15
−1.30	440	3.20	−1.07	66.03
−.15	438	3.19	.13	10.88
−.46	281	2.04	.51	20.08
−.22	82	0.59	−.20	−1.20
1.82	729	5.31	2.29	22.72
−1.27	1.458	10.62	−1.34	60.57
−.92	602	4.38	−.65	36.50
.32	472	3.43	84.00	81.53
–	*13,728*	*100.00*	–	*9.14*

In 1950, the primary sector was the largest major sector, accounting for 26 percent of total employment (Table 6–2). By 1960 the primary sector was fourth (13 percent) in terms of total employment, following services (25 percent), manufacturing (23 percent), and wholesale and retail trade (18 percent). This represents a major readjustment of the productive structure away from the primary sector. Comparison of columns (3) and (6) of Tables 6–1 and 6–2 highlights this readjustment process. These columns compare the employment distribution in the regional grouping with the employment distribution in the U.S. for

Table 6–2. Employment Growth and Distribution by Major Sector 1950–60: Southeastern Regional Grouping

Major Sector	*(1) Employment 1950 (000)*	*(2) Percent of Total 1950*	*(3) Share of Major Sector Less Share of Major Sector in U.S. 1950*	*(4) Employment 1960 (000)*	*(5) Percent of Total 1960*	*(6) Share of Major Sector Less Share of Major Sector in U.S. 1960*	*(7) Percent Change in Employment 1950–60*
Primary	3,290	26.15	12.03	1,769	12.88	5.09	−46.23
Construction	796	6.32	.22	939	6.84	.85	17.96
Manufacturing	2,439	19.39	−6.43	3,162	23.03	−4.62	29.64
Transportation Communications and Utilities	813	6.46	−1.39	870	6.33	−.70	7.01
Wholesale and Retail Trade	2,060	16.37	−2.33	2,486	18.10	−.11	20.67
Services	2,479	19.70	−1.54	3,428	24.97	−.70	38.28
Government and Armed Forces	701	5.57	−.58	1,074	7.82	.19	53.20
Totals	*12,578*	*100.00*	–	*13,728*	*100.00*	–	*9.14*

Source: Calculated from Tables 6–1 and Table 5–7.

1950 and 1960. In 1950 the Southeastern Regional Grouping had nine employment sectors which were relatively larger than other similar sectors in the continental United States. Five of these agriculture, forestry and fisheries, mining, textile mill products, and lumber and furniture products declined nationally in terms of total employment between 1950 and 1960. By 1960, each of these sectors decreased in relative size (columns 2 and 5 of Table 6–1) in the Southeastern Regional Grouping. Conversely, the manufacturing sectors as a group increased in terms of employment from 19 percent in 1950 to 23 percent in 1960 and services from 20 percent in 1950 to 25 percent in 1960.

This shows that the relative importance of the various employment sectors within this regional grouping is moving from the declining sectors and toward a distribution similar to that exhibited by the U.S. economy.

INTRODUCTION TO THE ECONOMIC BASE MODEL

Before presenting the actual results of the export base model discussed in Chapter 4, the general underlying relationships must first be explored. Table 6–3 presents the rates of growth of total personal income of the OBE Economic Areas ranked by the percentage change in the economic base. This shows that 49 of the 55 OBE Economic Areas in this regional grouping experienced a decline in the ratio of export oriented production to total production over the period 1950–67. However, it is also apparent that areas experiencing an increase, or a smaller decrease, in the economic base generally realized more rapid growth in total personal income. This is shown by disaggregating the OBE Economic Areas listed in Table 6–3 by quartiles based on the percentage change in the economic base. The average rate of total personal income growth for the OBE Areas in the highest quartile was 7.9 percent annually. For the remaining quartiles the average percentages of total personal income growth were 6.38, 5.94, and 5.1, respectively. The simple correlation between the change in economic base and growth in total personal income for this regional grouping was .634, which also confirms the expected positive relationship between these two variables.

This general pattern of decline in the ratio of export oriented production is most likely a result of the trends in primary output. The primary sector, considered an export sector, declined in terms of employment by 46.2 percent from 1950 to 1960. It was anticipated that this trend continued throughout the period of the study and, therefore, had a strong negative influence on the growth of the export base. The interpretation is supported by simple correlations between the size of the export base and the percentage of earnings from the manufacturing sector in 1950 and 1960. In 1960 the size of the manufacturing sector exhibited a greater association with the relative size of the economic base than it did in 1950. For 1950 the simple correlation between these two variables

Table 6–3. OBE Economic Areas Located in the Southeastern Regional Grouping Ranked by the Percent Change in the Economic Base

OBE Economic Area	*Percent Change Economic Base 1950–67*	*Rate of Increase TPY 50–66*
32.0	8.22	7.275
141.0	5.93	6.828
139.0	5.01	7.290
140.0	4.12	6.047
47.0	1.06	8.868
138.0	1.02	6.680
39.0	−.57	8.695
42.0	−1.09	6.571
29.0	−1.14	7.413
24.0	−1.58	6.926
34.0	−1.60	7.523
44.0	−2.02	7.493
48.0	−2.22	6.475
55.0	−2.36	5.129
31.0	−2.51	7.315
37.0	−4.13	9.285
134.0	−5.15	4.789
131.0	−5.43	5.560
46.0	−6.18	5.833
38.0	−6.39	7.092
22.0	−7.06	6.261
143.0	−7.31	5.733
21.0	−7.35	6.228
25.0	−7.78	6.563
43.0	−7.93	5.720
49.0	−8.04	6.726
20.0	−8.22	5.805
117.0	−8.55	6.475
33.0	−8.63	5.706
142.0	−8.80	6.039
40.0	−8.97	5.695
129.0	−9.21	6.083
27.0	−9.30	5.529
130.0	−9.57	5.626
133.0	−10.27	5.812
137.0	−10.51	7.299
28.0	−10.67	6.216
41.0	−10.93	6.252
56.0	−11.05	4.655
26.0	−11.63	6.467
135.0	−11.72	6.187
45.0	−11.93	5.645
136.0	−12.40	5.378
30.0	−13.57	6.052
65.0	−13.94	4.071
51.0	−13.97	4.838
118.0	−14.35	5.174
50.0	−14.89	4.965

Table 6–3. (cont.)

OBE Economic Area	*Percent Change Economic Base 1950–67*	*Rate of Increase TPY 50–66*
115.0	–16.27	4.754
144.0	–16.98	4.942
132.0	–17.35	4.701
23.0	–17.86	5.916
19.0	–19.33	5.679
53.0	–20.25	6.109
52.0	–21.75	3.836

is .335, but increased to .489 for 1960. This increase in the association of manufacturing and the relative size of the export base may be interpreted as reflecting and decreasing importance of primary production on exports of the regions. If this is the case, relative growth in non-primary exports must be able to absorb the losses in primary exports before any net increases in the basic sector may be achieved. This did not occur in most of the OBE Economic Areas in the Southeastern Regional grouping during the period 1950–1967.

RESULTS OF THE EXPORT BASE MODEL

In order to test the export base model as defined in Chapter 4, regressions were fitted to both of the specified equations. The statistically significant results were as follows:

$$\frac{dTPY}{dt} = 6.97 + \underset{(.017)}{.104}(\Delta EB) \qquad R^2 = .40 \qquad (5.1)$$

$$\Delta EB = -17.96 + \underset{(1.77)}{3.6}(IGI) + \underset{(.04)}{.09}(I) \qquad R^2 = .225 \qquad (6.2)$$

where: $\frac{dTPY}{dt}$ = Average Annual Rate of Growth in Total Personal Income, 1950–66.

ΔEB = Percent Change in the Economic Base over the period 1950–67.

IGI = Index of the Composition of Growth Industries, 1960.

I = Infrastructure (Measured as Non-education Government Expenditures per capita in 1960).

CC = Coefficient of Concentration.

Forty percent of the variance in the rates of growth of total personal income of the OBE Economic Areas in this regional grouping is explained by the variance in the percentage change in the economic base (Equation 6.1). This equation, as specified in Chapter 4, originally included the coefficient of concentration as an independent variable. This was excluded because of the statistical insignificance of the beta coefficient for this variable. This leaves the more simple form of this relationship as expressed by equation 6.1. From this equation it appears that a 1.0 percent average annual increase in the economic base was associated with a .3 percent annual average rate of increase in total personal income between 1950 and 1966.

Equation 6.2, as specified in Chapter 4, is statistically significant. The reasoning that the growth in the economic base is a function of the existence of growth industries in the region and the development of the region's infrastructure cannot be rejected. However, variation in these two independent variables used in combination explains only 22 percent of the variance of the change in the economic base. The addition of more independent variables does not significantly increase the explained variance.

The results of these tests are not inconsistent with the major aspects of the economic base hypotheses stated in Chapter 4. The coefficient of concentration did not meet the statistical tests as required in equation 6.1, leaving the percentage change in the economic base as the only variable used to explain the difference in the rates of growth of total personal income. Although the resulting equation is consistent with the hypothesis that growth in the export base is a primary force determining the rate of growth of total personal income, the amount of explained variance is relatively low.

It was also found that growth in the export base was significantly associated with the index of the composition of growth industries and the measure of the development of the area's infrastructure. The degree of association was again very low. However, the relatively low coefficients of determination demonstrate the need for the more complete analysis of the economic growth of this regional grouping that follows.

LONG TERM ECONOMIC DEVELOPMENT OF THE SOUTHEASTERN REGIONAL GROUPING

The results of the factor analysis, using the 1959 level of per capita income as the variable to be explained, are presented in Table 6–4. Four factors are used which explain 89.5 percent of the variance in the levels of per capita income of the

Table 6–4. Rotated Factor Matrix for the Level of Per Capita Personal Income in 1959: Southeastern Regional Grouping

	Factor 1	*Factor 2*	*Factor 3*	*Factor 4*	h^2
Per Capita Personal Income, 1959	*.713*	*.499*	*–.342*	*.142*	*.895*
Demand, Time and Savings Capital Deposits per Capita, 1960	.616	.519	–.039	.211	.695
Manufacturing Productivity, 1958	.572	.172	.239	.292	.499
Value of Land and Buildings per Farm, 1959	.679	–.080	.551	.168	.800
Output per Worker in Agriculture, 1960	.574	.164	.152	.258	.446
Local Government Revenue per Capita, 1962	.894	.097	.057	.077	.818
Property Tax per Capita, Average 1957 and 1962	.809	.167	.116	.352	.820
Non-Education Government Expenditures per Capita, 1962	.862	.135	–.091	–.194	.808
Total Government Expenditures per Capita, 1962	.919	.121	–.048	–.024	.802
Average Bonds per Total Revenue, 1957 and 1962	.631	.045	.205	–.079	.449
Ratio of Families with Income of $10,000 to $3,000, 1960	.746	.438	–.284	.029	.829
Percent High School Graduates, 1960	.648	.546	–.125	–.205	.776
Index of the Composition of Growth Industries, 1960	.357	.673	–.020	–.296	.668
Coefficient of Concentration, 1960	.198	–.681	.023	–.047	.506
Value of Crops per Total Agriculture Output, 1959	.275	–.657	.085	–.382	.660
Percent White Collar Employment, 1960	.552	.723	225	–.081	.885
Percent of Persons 21 and Older that Completed Less Than 5 Years of School, 1960	.108	.650	.479	–.261	.731
Percent Tenant Farms, 1959	.060	.562	.100	–.554	.637
Economic Base, 1959	–.274	–.524	–.442	.085	.552
Population Density, 1960	.375	.054	–.685	.001	.613
Percent Earnings From Manufacturing, 1959	.167	–.077	–.723	.352	.680
Ratio of Farms of 1000 Acres to 10 Acres, 1959	.284	–.011	.697	.126	.583
Percent Voting, 1960	.067	.122	–.134	.822	.712
Index of Voting Change, 1960–64	.116	.226	.089	–.734	.611
Percent Non-White Population, 1960	–.106	–.191	–.094	–.866	.806
Average Manufacturing Capital Investment, 1958 and 1963	.397	.154	.049	.008	.184
Government Transfers per Capita, 1962	.015	–.276	.113	–.207	.131
Estimate of the Percent College Students	.011	.380	.235	.013	.200

OBE Economic Areas in this regional grouping. Each of the first three factors explain a significant part of the explained variance.

Table 6–4 is a rotated factor matrix.[1] Each entry of the matrix, *aij*, shows the net correlation between variable *i* and factor *j*. These coefficients are termed "factor loadings" and provide the basis for the grouping of the variables into the factors. Each variable is included in the factor on which it has the highest partial correlation. In other words, it is grouped into the factor that has the highest correlation with the variable. In cases where this cannot be done, because variables assume equal association with two factors, the variable is included in the factor in which it is theoretically best suited.

Each factor loading *(aij)* represents the partial correlation of variable *i* on vector *j*, given the preceding vectors. Thus the square of the factor loading *(aij)* represents that part of the variance of variable *i* explained by vector *j*, given the preceding vectors. The communality (h^2), or total variance explained, for each variable is provided by the right hand column of Table 6–4. Therefore, it appears that 89 percent of the variance in the levels of per capita personal income in the Southeastern Regional grouping is explained by the four vectors of Table 6–4. This is calculated as follows:

$$(.713)^2 + (.499)^2 + (-.342)^2 + (-.142)^2 = .895$$

The First Factor

The first factor explains 51 percent of the total explained variance. The factor consists of the following eleven variables, all of which are positively related to each other and to the level of per capita income.

1. The percentage of persons 21 years of age and over that completed high school.
2. Ratio of families that earned $10,000 or more to families that earned $3,000 or less.
3. Financial deposits per capita.
4. Local government revenue per capita.
5. Average property tax per capita.
6. Non-education local government expenditures per capita.
7. Total local government expenditures per capita.
8. Ratio of local government bonds outstanding to local government revenue.
9. Manufacturing productivity.
10. Output per worker in agriculture.
11. Value of land and buildings per farm.

The first variable, percentage of high school graduates, represents the stock of secondary level education available in the higher per capita income areas. The next two (2. and 3.) represent the potential source and stock of savings and financial capital. It is to be expected that as the level of educational achievement increases, the ratio of families that earned $10,000 or more to families that earned $3,000 or less would also increase. This ratio, based on income flows, provides the source for the relatively higher level of financial deposits. Variables listed 4. through 8. are closely related measures of the level of local government services and the public infrastructure provided. They represent the long term accumulation of a stock of infrastructure available in the higher per capita income areas. Also included are the local government revenue variables that provide the source of this stock of government services.

Variables 9. through 10. are measures of manufacturing and agricultural productivity and the level of capital stock in the agricultural sector. It is reiterated that this factor includes variables representing the stocks of secondary education and financial capital. Both of these stocks may contribute to higher levels of manufacturing productivity as measured by the ratio of value added to man hours of productive workers. The higher levels of financial capital available may provide the source for higher levels of capital invested in the manufacturing sector. Similarly, higher levels of educational achievement should provide for a more productive labor force. The last variable included, the value of land and buildings per farm (11), a measure of capital investment in the agricultural sector, is positively related to the level of agricultural productivity.

This factor may be interpreted as representing variations in the abundance of capital supply, human resources, and local government services available in the OBE Economic Areas in the Southeastern Regional Grouping. Related to the variables measuring the accumulated stocks of capital and human resources are variables representing the levels of productivity in manufacturing and agriculture. In general, this factor may be interpreted as a dimension that highlights the interrelationship between the higher levels of human and other capital stocks available and the higher levels of productivity achieved. It is this dimension that explains the greatest part of the variance in the levels of the 1959 per capita income of the OBE Economic Areas in this regional grouping.

The Second Factor

The second factor consists of seven variables and explains 28 percent of the total explained variance in the levels of per capita income. The variables included are:

1. Coefficient of concentration (−).
2. Index of the composition of growth industries (+).
3. Economic base (−).
4. Percentage of white collar employment (+).
5. Value of crops per total agricultural output (−).
6. Percentage of tenant farms (+).
7. Percentage of persons 21 years of age and over that completed less than five years of school (+).

Variable one, the coefficient of concentration, has a negative factor loading indicating that the trend toward greater diversification is positively related to the factor. Variable two, an index of the composition of growth industries, has a positive factor loading. Taken together, these two variables describe the extent to which regions have developed an industrial structure that is economically diversified as well as reflective of a greater proportion of national growth industries. It was to be expected that such characteristics would be negatively associated with the relative size of the economic base. Increased diversification has typically involved an increase in the relative importance of non-basic sectors. It is also to be expected that the increased relative importance of non-basic, or residentiary, sectors would be associated with an increasing percentage of white collar workers, represented by variable 3. The relationship between the percentage of white collar occupations and the percentage of residentiary income results from the fact that most residentiary occupations are also white collar in nature.

The remaining three variables do not seem to fit with the four variables described above or into a group by themselves. The negative factor loading on the value of crops per total agricultural output is indicative that crops, used here as an indicator of an agricultural growth sector, are not associated with the industrial growth sectors. The positive factor loading on the percentage of persons 21 years of age and over that completed less than 5 years of school may be an indication that the type of industrial structure described is related to the more urban areas. The congregation of lower income and more poorly educated persons in the more urban areas could have caused the association discussed. There does not seem to be a sound theoretical basis for the inclusion of the percentage of tenant farms with a positive factor loading.

This factor, therefore, may be interpreted as representing the shift in industrial structure characterized by greater economic diversification, greater relative importance of national growth industries, and greater relative importance of residentiary, or non-basic, output.

The Third Factor

The third factor accounts for 13 percent of the total explained variance in the levels of per capita income. The three variables included in the factor are the population density, percentage of total income earned by the manufacturing sector, and the ratio of farms of 1,000 acres or more to farms of 10 acres or less. The first two variables are positively related to each other and to the level of per capita income. The third variable included in the factor, the ratio of 1,000 acres or more to farms of 10 acres or less is negatively related to the other variables and to the level of per capita income. The associations of these variables represent the trend toward greater urbanization and industrialization of the higher income OBE Areas of this regional grouping. The indication that these areas may also be characterized by relatively smaller scale farming is to be expected. The Southeastern Regional Grouping, in general, is not characterized by large scale farming techniques. The OBE Economic Areas that are experiencing the trend toward industrialization and urbanization should, as this factor indicates, be those that were least characterized by large scale farming.

The Fourth Factor

The fourth factor explains only 2.3 percent of the total explained variance in the level of per capita income. It consists of three variables interpreted to represent social influences. The first, the percentage of persons 21 and over that voted in 1960, is positively associated with the level of per capita income. This is consistent with the expected behavior of this variable, as expressed in Chapter 3, that community involvement increases with the level of per capita income. The remaining two variables, the index of voting change and the index of the relative importance of non-white population, are negatively associated with the level of per capita income and the level of community involvement. The index of voting change is used in this analysis as a measure of social negativism. It is expected that variations in this measure would be positively associated with the proportion of non-white members of the population. This factor may, therefore, be interpreted as representing the positive association between the variations in the measure of social negativism and the relative share of the non-white population. These measures are negatively associated with the measure of the level of community involvement.

LONG TERM ECONOMIC DEVELOPMENT: SUMMARY

The long term structural development of the Southeastern Regional Grouping is presented in terms of four factors. The most important factor represents the inter-OBE Area variability in the accumulated stock of private, public, and human capital investment. Positively related to this higher level of stock accumulation are higher levels of agricultural and manufacturing productivity. The third factor represents the trend toward greater levels of urbanization and industrialization and the reduced relative importance of agriculture. Finally, the second factor of Table 6–4 represents the positive association between the variations in the level of per capita income and the variations in the measures of greater economic diversification, relative importance of national growth industries in the industrial mix of the economy, and the greater relative importance of non-basic industries. The last factor, which is not related to the level of per capita income, expresses the interrelationships between community involvement and the racial mix and irregular voting behavior of the population.

The three factors that explain the variation in the 1959 levels of per capita income may be expressed as representing the growth of the stocks of human, public, and private capital. Related to the growth of these stocks is the modernization of the economic structure. This may be summarized as: greater industrialization, urbanization, and the related trend toward greater relative importance of non-basic industry sectors; greater economic diversification; and the greater relative importance of national growth industries.

GROWTH IN TOTAL PERSONAL INCOME, 1950–66

The rotated factor matrix, with the rate of growth of total personal income as the variable to be explained, is presented in Table 6–5. The rate of growth in total personal income is used as the measure of short term economic growth. Three factors are included in the factor analysis presented in Table 6–5. Increasing the number of factors does not significantly affect the factor components of this table. Seventy-five percent of the variance in the rates of growth of total personal income of the OBE Economic Areas in the Southeastern Regional Grouping is explained by the three factors. Virtually all of this is explained by the third factor.

The First Factor

The first factor contains 16 variables not related to the growth rates of total personal income. The factor contains the same 11 variables found in the first factor of Table 6–4. In addition it also contains the following five variables:

1. Economic base, 1950 (+).
2. Coefficient of concentration, 1950 (+).
3. Percent change in the coefficient of concentration. 1950–60 (–).
4. Percent white collar employment, 1960 (–).
5. Ratio of farms of 1,000 acres or more to farms of 10 acres (–).

The discussion of the relationships of the 11 variables included in the first factor of Table 6–4 will not be repeated. In that discussion it was concluded that these variables represented variations in human, public, and private capital investment. Two of the additional variables, the economic base and the coefficient of concentration, are inversely associated with the other variables included in the factor. Positively associated with the other variables, except those two mentioned above, are the percent white collar employment, the percent change in the coefficient of concentration, and measure of large scale agriculture. The negative relationship of the economic base with the other variables implies that the relative importance of the residentiary sector is positively related to the other variables. The variation of each of these with the measures of the stock of human, public, and private capital investment implies that the levels of these stocks increase with the increase in the relative importance of non-basic industries. The positive relationship between the measure of large scale farming with the other variables should be expected because of the importance assigned to agricultural capital investment and productivity in the discussion of the second factor of Table 6–4. Finally, the positive association between the percent change in the coefficient of concentration and the other forces discussed above shows the relationship between these variables and increasing degrees of economic concentration.

Therefore, it may be interpreted that this factor represents the positive relationship between the variations in the levels of private, public, and human capital investment and the relative importance of the non-basic sectors. The factor also includes variables representing the positive relationship between these forces and the relative importance of a large scale, capital intensive agricultural sector. The agricultural variables may explain the association of the trend toward greater economic concentration. The factor must therefore be considered as representing variations in a conglomerate of forces that are most closely associated with differences in levels of per capita income, rather than with the rate of growth of total economic activity.

The Second Factor

The second factor contains eight variables. The factor explains 5.4 percent of the total explained variance. The variables are:

1. Value of crops per total agricultural output.
2. Percent tenant farms.
3. Percent of persons 21 years of age and over that voted in 1960.
4. Index of voting change.
5. Percent non-white population.
6. Percent of persons 21 years of age and over that completed less than five years of school.
7. Percent of total earnings accounted for by the manufacturing sector.
8. Percent change in the labor force participation rate.

This factor contains all the variables contained in factors 3 and 4 of Table 6–4, with the exception of population density. It appears that this factor is somewhat a conglomerate representation of the impact of the levels of industrialization and community involvement discussed earlier. The single additional variable, the percentage of change in the labor force participation rate has a high loading on this factor and may represent the greater trend toward community involvement of the growing labor force in the industrial areas of the Southeastern Regional Grouping during the 1950s.

This factor, therefore, contains elements that represent the basic social attitudes and related racial mix indicators, as well as indicators of the economic structure. Directly related to the degree of manufacturing is the measure of community involvement and the measure of the changes in job

Table 6–5. Rotated Factor Matrix for the Rate of Growth of Total Personal Income, 1950–66: Southeastern Regional Grouping

	Factor 1	*Factor 2*	*Factor 3*	h^2
Rate of Increase of Total Personal Income, 1950–66	–.131	–.202	.832	.751
Economic Base, 1950	.536	–.078	–.216	.340
Coefficient of Concentration, 1950	.552	–.544	–.295	.688
Percent Change in the Coefficient of Concentration, 1950–60	–.572	.445	.300	.616
Demand, Time and Savings Capital Deposits per Capita, 1960	–.663	.410	.228	.661
Manufacturing Productivity, 1958	–.710	.097	–.195	.552
Value of Land and Buildings per Farm, 1959	–.793	–.210	–.094	.684
Output per Worker in Agriculture, 1960	–.591	.170	.019	.379
Ratio of Farms of 1000 Acres or More to Farms of 10 Acres or Less, 1959	–.527	–.249	–.349	.462
Local Government Revenue per Capita, 1962	–.833	.064	.144	.719
Property Tax per Capita, Average 1957 and 1962	–.841	.249	–.063	.772
Non-Education Government Expenditures per Capita, 1962	–.741	–.050	.350	.674
Total Government Expenditures per Capita, 1962	–.820	.055	.224	.726
Average Bonds Outstanding per Total Government Revenue, 1957 and 1962	–.633	–.115	.049	.416
Families with Income of $10,000 or More to Families with $3,000 or Less, 1960	–.689	.341	.391	.744
Percent White Collar Employment, 1960	–.732	.231	.324	.694
Percent of Persons 21 and Over that Completed High School or More	–.644	.199	.521	.725
Percent Change in the LFPR, 1950–60	.268	.560	–.106	.397
Value of Crops per Total Agricultural Output, 1959	–.084	–.703	.067	.506
Percent Tenant Farms, 1959	.193	–.770	–.096	.640
Percent Voting, 1960	–.128	.679	–.336	.590
Index of Voting Change, 1960–64	.106	–.426	.450	.396
Percent Non-White Population, 1960	.256	–.662	.368	.639
Percent of Persons 21 and Over that Completed Less Than 5 Years of School, 1960	.087	–.724	–.346	.651
Percent Earnings from Manufacturing, 1960	.388	.528	.095	.439
Percent Change in the Economic Base, 1950–67	–.298	–.200	.560	.443
Rate of Increase in Residentiary Employment, 1950–60	–.270	–.305	.719	.683
Index of the Composition of Growth Industries, 1960	–.456	.156	.553	.539

Rate of Growth of Time, Demand & Savings Capital Deposits per Capita, 1950–64	−.043	−.027	.738	.547
Percent Change Agricultural Output, 1950–64	.113	.002	.607	.381
Net Migration Rate, 1950–60	−.534	.148	.707	.807
Percent Change in Manufacturing Productivity, 1958–63	.065	.223	.295	.146
Percent Change in Bond Investment, 1957–62	−.230	.013	−.147	.074
Government Transfers per Capita, 1962	.121	−.189	.001	.050
Percent College Students, 1960	−.169	.179	−.096	.078
Average Manufacturing Capital Investment, 1958 and 1963	−.327	−.126	.090	.131
Population Density, 1960	−.112	.249	.325	.180

opportunities. Conversely, related to the measures of the relative importance of agriculture are the social variables of race, social negativism, and lower levels of educational achievement. The factor is not, however, related to the rates of growth of total personal income.

The Third Factor

The third factor explains 93 percent of the total explained variance in the rates of growth of total personal income. The factor contains the following six variables, all of which are positively related to each other and to the rate of growth of total personal income:

1. Percent change in the economic base.
2. Rate of increase in the residentiary employment.
3. Index of the composition of growth industries.
4. Rate of growth of financial deposits.
5. Percent change in agricultural output.
6. Net migration rate.

These variables provide the basis for the description of the short term pattern of economic growth in the Southeastern Regional Grouping. This pattern is consistent with the cluster of variables included in the economic base model. The first three variables provide the basic structure of the economic base model. As expressed in Chapter 4, the association between the percentage of change in the economic base and the index of the composition of growth industries may be presented in terms of the type of industry most likely to lead to growth in the export base. The inclusion of the rate of growth of residentiary employment in this factor is consistent with this interpretation. At the center of the export base arguments is the need for income generated by exports to be transmitted by iterations throughout the economy, and especially throughout the residentiary sectors, via the multiplier.

The inclusion of the remaining three variables in this factor highlights other forces associated with the growth in the export base. Since agriculture is always considered as an export sector, the rate of growth in total agricultural output should be positively associated with the growth in the export base. However, the general decline of the relative importance of agriculture has, for most OBE Areas in this regional grouping, resulted in an actual decline in the economic base. Where growth in total agricultural output was greater, the economic base declined less.

The inclusion in this factor of the net in-migration rate between 1950 and 1960, and rate of increase of demand, time, and savings capital deposits per capita between 1950 and 1964, represent increases in the labor and financial capital supplies available in the more rapidly growing OBE Economic Areas. Increases in job opportunities associated with growth in the level of economic activity may have acted as an attraction to migrants, or as a force restricting out-migration. Exceptions to this interpretation, which are consistent with the general interpretation of this factor, are those expressed by Muth and Borts and Stein. They have argued, as stated in Chapter 4, that persons migrating to areas increase the need for services and therefore jobs as a result of the migration.

Growth in financial deposits per capita, also included in the factor, provide additional capital that may continually feed the growth of economic activity. These deposits represent an increasingly prosperous population base. Thus, this factor represents the interaction between the growth of the economic base and growth of the residentiary sector, together with the supporting growth of factor supplies.

SHORT TERM ECONOMIC GROWTH: SUMMARY

The three factors of Table 6–5 explain 75 percent of the variance of the rates of growth of total personal income in this regional grouping. Virtually all of the explained variance is accounted for by the third factor. This factor is interpreted as being consistent with the export base model. In addition, this factor highlights variables not originally included in the export base model and suggests possible improvements in the original model.

The first factor explains an additional 1.7 percent of the total explained variance. Another 4 percent is added by the second factor. Therefore, it may be concluded that the influences accounting for growth in total personal income represent the interaction between growth in the economic base and growth of the residentiary sector together with the supporting growth of factor supplies.

GROWTH IN PER CAPITA INCOME: 1950–1966

The rotated factor matrix using the rate of growth of per capita income as the variable to be explained is presented in Table 6–6. The rate of growth of per capita income is used as the measure of short term changes in the average level of economic welfare. The three factors explain only 48 percent of the variance in the rates of growth of per capita income. Increasing the number of factors does not appreciably effect the factor components of those included in Table 6–6. The factors are identical to those of Table 6–5, but assume very different relationships to the variable being explained.

Virtually all of the explained variance in the rates of growth of per capita income is explained by the first factor of Table 6–6. However, 14 of the 16 variables included in the factor are inversely related to the rate of growth of per capita income. In the analysis presented above, this factor was interpreted to represent the interrelationships between the stocks of human, private, and public capital and the extent of the shift in industrial structure toward residentiary and

Table 6–6. Rotated Factor Matrix for the Rate of Growth of Per Capita Personal Income, 1950–66: Southeastern Regional Grouping

	Factor 1	*Factor 2*	*Factor 3*	h^2
Rate of Increase of Per Capita Personal Income, 1950–66	*.686*	*–.109*	*.028*	*.483*
Economic Base, 1950	.483	–.054	–.286	.318
Coefficient of Concentration, 1950	.528	–.481	–.433	.697
Percent Change in the Coefficient of Concentration, 1950–60	–.578	.383	.395	.637
Demand, Time, and Savings Capital Deposits per Capita, 1960	–.622	.371	.363	.656
Manufacturing Productivity, 1958	–.712	.143	–.122	.542
Value of Land and Buildings per Farm, 1959	–.820	–.163	–.114	.712
Output per Worker in Agriculture, 1960	–.550	.174	.124	.348
Ratio of Farms of 1000 Acres of More to Farms of 10 Acres of Less, 1959	–.557	–.158	–.376	.476
Local Government Revenue per Capita, 1962	–.802	.044	.235	.701
Property Tax per Capita, Average 1957 and 1962	–.823	.263	.066	.751
Non-Education Government Expenditures per Capita, 1962	–.703	–.110	.414	.678
Total Government Expenditures per Capita, 1962	–.788	.017	.314	.720
Average Bonds Outstanding per Total Government Revenue, 1957 and 1962	–.641	–.106	.050	.425
Families with Income of $10,000 or More to Families with $3,000 or Less, 1960	–.663	.269	.491	.754
Percent White Collar Employment, 1960	–.698	.181	.414	.691
Percent of Persons 21 and Over that Completed High School or More	–.608	.103	.599	.740
Percent Change in the LFPR, 1950–60	.296	.584	–.036	.429
Value of Crops per Total Agricultural Output, 1959	–.113	–.702	–.073	.510
Percent Tenant Farms, 1959	.170	–.749	–.229	.642
Percent Voting, 1960	–.121	.737	–.203	.600
Index of Voting Change, 1960–64	.147	–.513	.401	.446
Percent Non-White Population, 1960	.270	–.742	.271	.697
Percent of Persons 21 and Over that Completed Less than 5 Years of School, 1960	.016	–.643	–.513	.677
Percent Earnings from Manufacturing, 1960	.396	.491	.156	.422
Percent Change in the Economic Base, 1950–67	–.245	–.285	.531	.610
Rate of Increase in Residentiary Employment, 1950–60	–.256	–.411	.612	.543
Index of the Composition of Growth Industries, 1960	–.420	.056	.603	.697

Rate of Growth of Time, Demand & Savings Capital Deposits per Capita, 1950–64	.003	–.141	.684	.488
Percent Change Agricultural Output, 1950–64	.184	–.118	.635	.452
Net Migration Rate, 1950–60	–.501	.035	.719	.769
Percent Change in Manufacturing Productivity, 1958–63	.084	.167	.334	.147
Percent Change in Bond Investment, 1957–62	–.210	.027	–.067	.049
Government Transfers per Capita, 1962	.118	–.194	–.029	.053
Percent College Students, 1960	–.164	.203	–.057	.071
Average Manufacturing Capital Investment, 1958 and 1963	–.316	–.145	.090	.126
Population Density, 1960	–.126	.176	.347	.167

national growth industries. The accumulation of these stocks and the direction of these trends are inversely related to the rate of growth of per capita income.

The reason for this result is that the rate of growth of per capita income of the OBE Economic Areas in the Southeastern Regional Grouping during the period of 1950 to 1966 was primarily influenced by the level of per capita income in 1950 and the trends in migration during the same period. Each of the ten OBE Areas that achieved the most rapid growth rates of per capita income experienced out-migration between 1950 and 1960. The median net migration rate for the ten most rapid per capita income growth rate areas was −15 percent. However, of the ten OBE Economic Areas that experienced the slowest growth rates of per capita income, four experienced net in-migration between 1950 and 1960. The median net migration rate of these areas was only −4.6 percent.

It should be noted that 11 of the 16 variables included were also included in the factor of Table 6–4 to explain the greatest part of the variance in the levels of per capita income. These variables, negatively related to the rate of growth of per capita income, are shown to be positively related to level of per capita income in the first factor of Table 6–4. The variables included in the first factor of Table 6–6 assume the negative relationship with the rate of growth of per capita income because the behavior of these variables reflects the level, rather than the rate of growth, of per capita income. The correlation between the level of per capita income and the rate of growth of per capita income of the OBE Areas in the Southeastern Regional Grouping is −.500. This is another way of presenting this basic relationship.

The higher income areas, generally urban, have attracted poorer migrants leaving the farm and other areas. The initial, and potentially lasting, effect of this trend is to reduce the rate of growth of per capita income in the area of in-migration. Conversely, this trend increases the rate of growth of per capita income in the areas left by the migrants because there are now fewer people to share the total income.

Chapter Seven

Economic Growth and Development of the Northeastern Regional Grouping

INTRODUCTION

The OBE Economic Areas in the Northeastern Regional Grouping account for over 50 percent of total personal income earned in the U.S. in 1967. This regional grouping embraces an area of the United States that was first to experience industrialization. For these reasons it may be expected that the economic trends, both long term and short term, will differ significantly from the other regional groupings.

During the period 1950–66 total personal income increased by approximately 5.6 percent per year. Only the Central Regional Grouping experienced a lower average annual rate of growth. Consequently, the share of total personal income earned in the continental U.S. decreased from 56.5 percent in 1950 to 53.5 percent in 1960. Per capita personal income in this region was $2,170 in 1966. The average annual rate of growth of per capita personal income during the period 1950–66 was approximately 4.3 percent. Although the level of per capita income was above the national per capita income level in 1966, the rate of increase between 1950 and 1966 was less than that for the nation. The two statistics are related. The higher per capita income areas experienced relatively high net migration, which, as proposed, exerts a downward pressure on the rate of increase in per capita income.

This region includes the "manufacturing belt"—the outgrowth of the long history of industrialization. Between 1950 and 1960 there were no major shifts in the relative importance of industrial sectors. Although employment in the primary sectors decreased by 37 percent between 1950 and 1960, the relative share of this major sector declined from only 6.4 percent to 3.6 percent.

The boundaries of the Northeastern Regional Grouping are defined in Chapter 2. The Regional Grouping contains 46 OBE Economic Areas. Only eight of the 46 OBE Areas were below the national median in terms of the 1959 per capita personal income. Conversely, 23 of the 46, or exactly 50 percent of the Areas, ranked in the highest quartile in terms of the 1959 per capita personal income of the OBE Economic Areas.

EMPLOYMENT GROWTH AND DISTRIBUTION, 1950–60

During the 1950s total employment grew by 12.7 percent. This was slightly below the employment growth for the continental United States, which was 14.85 percent over the same period. However, the dominance of this region on statistics for the continental United States biases the comparisons to be made between these two geographical elements.

Tables 7–1 and 7–2 present the trends in employment growth and distribution in the Northeastern Regional Grouping by 32 definitive sectors and seven major sectors. The largest major sector in 1950 and 1960 was manufacturing (Table 7–2), which grew by 13.5 percent over the decade, but maintained the same relative share (34 percent) of total employment in the regional grouping. There was, however, significant variation in the percentage growth of employment in the 14 manufacturing sectors (column 7 of Table 7–1). The manufacturing sectors that experienced the largest increases were electrical machinery, with a 64 percent increase in employment, printing and publishing (32 percent), chemicals (30 percent), and fabricated metals and ordinance (28 percent). Only four of the manufacturing sectors showed a decline in employment during the decade. They were: textile mill products (42 percent), petroleum refining (13 percent), lumber and furniture (7.0 percent), and apparel and other textile products (6.0 percent).

The 37 percent decline in employment in the primary sector between 1950 and 1960 did not exert the negative influence on the total employment trend that it did in other regional groupings. This was because of the relatively minor share of the primary sector in the economy of the Northeastern Regional Grouping. In 1950, the primary sector accounted for only 6.4 percent of total employment and decreased to 3.6 percent in 1960.

Services increased in employment by 32 percent, slightly below the national increase of 39 percent over the decade. The remaining major sectors (construction, wholesale and retail trade, and government and armed forces) all increased, but at percentage rates less than those for the same major sectors in the continental United States.

INTRODUCTION TO THE ECONOMIC BASE MODEL

Before presenting the actual tests of the export base model, the basic underlying relationships should be explored. Table 7–3 presents the OBE Economic Areas in the Northeastern Regional Grouping ranked by the percentage of change in the economic base between 1950 and 1967. Unlike the Southeastern Regional Grouping, one half of the OBE Economic Areas experienced an increase in the economic base over the period 1950–67. However, the simple correlation between the percentage of change in the economic base and the growth in total personal income was a low .226. For 46 degrees of freedom, this correlation is not significant. Disaggregating Table 7–3 into quartiles, based on the percentage of change in the economic base and calculating the mean rate of increase of total personal income, confirms that the change in the base is unrelated to total personal income growth. The mean rate of increase in total personal income for the first quartile was 5.70 percent, for the remaining three quartiles the mean rates were 5.78 percent, 5.71 percent, and 5.36, respectively.

RESULTS OF THE EXPORT BASE MODEL

In order to test the economic base model as discussed in Chapter 4, regressions are fitted to each of the specified relationships with the following results:

$$\frac{dTPY}{dt} = 3.86 + \underset{(.010)}{.021}\,(\Delta EB) + \underset{(.030)}{.066}\,(CC) \qquad R^2 = .148 \qquad (7.1)$$

$$\Delta EB = -13.65 + \underset{(4.550)}{8.162}\,(IGI) \qquad R^2 = .068 \qquad (7.2)$$

where: $\frac{dTPY}{dt}$ = Growth in Total Personal Income, 1950–66.

ΔEB = Percent Change in the Economic Base, 1950–67.

IGI = Index of the Composition of Growth Industries, 1960.

CC = Coefficient of Concentration.

Although the coefficient of determination of the first equation (7.1) is only .148, the beta coefficients are statistically significant. However, the beta coefficient on the coefficient of concentration has a positive sign, whereas a negative sign was expected. In addition, based on simple correlation analyses, there is some doubt concerning the validity of the specified relationship between the growth in total personal income and the change in the economic base.

The equation to test association between change in the economic base and the two independent variables (the index of the composition of growth industries and the measure of public infrastructure) was rejected. The equation accepted explains only 6.8 percent of the variance in the percent change in the economic base. Therefore, the economic base model as presented in Chapter 4

Table 7–1. Employment Growth and Distribution by Sector, 1950–60:

Sector	*(1)* *Employment 1950 (000)*	*(2)* *Percent of Total 1950*
Agriculture	1,571	5.30
Forestry and Fisheries	34	0.11
Mining	304	1.02
Contract Construction	1,615	5.45
Manufacturing		
Food and Kindred Products	769	2.59
Textile Mill Products	620	2.09
Apparel and Other Textile Products	830	2.80
Printing and Publishing	580	1.95
Chemicals	424	1.43
Lumber and Furniture	357	1.20
Non-electrical Machinery	1,075	3.63
Electrical Machinery	721	2.43
Transport Equipment	1,074	3.62
Paper and Allied Products	306	1.03
Petroleum Refining	135	0.45
Primary Metals Industry	966	3.26
Fabricated Metals and Ordinance	687	2.31
Misc.	1,533	5.17
Transport Services	1,598	5.39
Communications	403	1.36
Utilities	423	1.42
Wholesale Trade	1,051	3.54
Eating and Drinking Establishments	889	3.00
Other Retail Trade	3,626	12.24
Finance, Insurance and Real Estate	1,159	3.91
Lodging Places	947	3.19
Business and Repair	689	2.32
Amusements and Recreation Services	247	.83
Private Households	700	2.36
Educational, Medical and Professional Services	2,569	8.67
Public Administration	1,369	4.62
Armed Forces	342	1.15
Totals	*29,613*	*99.84*

Source: Calculated from basic data not reported.

Northeastern Regional Grouping

(3) Share of Industry Less Share of Industry in U.S. 1950	(4) Employment 1960 (000)	(5) Percent of Total 1960	(6) Share of Industry Less Share of Industry in U.S. 1960	(7) Percent Change in Employment 1950–60
−6.95	1,035	3.10	−3.52	−34.11
−.10	23	0.06	−.15	−32.35
−.62	145	0.43	−.59	−52.30
−.65	1,753	5.25	−.74	8.54
.19	950	2.84	−.01	23.53
−.10	358	1.07	−.37	−42.25
.92	779	2.33	.49	−6.14
.44	764	2.28	.47	31.72
.27	552	1.65	.28	30.18
−.91	332	.99	−.68	−7.00
1.34	1,243	3.72	1.24	15.62
1.03	1,181	3.53	1.17	63.80
1.24	1,263	3.78	.91	17.59
.20	350	1.04	.13	14.37
−.06	118	0.35	−.09	−12.59
1.19	1,004	3.00	1.03	3.93
.82	879	2.63	.59	27.94
1.68	1,660	4.97	1.40	8.28
.17	1,464	4.38	.06	−8.38
.11	450	1.34	.05	11.66
.04	456	1.36	−.05	7.80
.04	1,147	3.43	.34	9.13
.01	938	2.81	−.03	5.51
.01	3,936	11.79	−.48	8.54
.51	1,538	4.60	.33	32.70
−.10	937	2.80	−.26	−1.05
–	858	2.57	.02	24.52
−.04	247	.74	−.05	0.00
−.54	742	2.22	−1.00	6.00
.19	4,037	12.09	.13	57.14
.20	1,692	5.07	.05	23.59
−.59	537	1.60	−.99	57.01
–	*33,368*	*99.82*	–	*12.68*

Table 7–2. Employment Growth and Distribution by Major Sector, 1950–60: Northeastern Regional Grouping

Major Sector	*(1) Employment 1950 (000)*	*(2) Percent of Total 1950*	*(3) Share of Major Sector Less Share of Major Sector in U.S. 1950*	*(4) Employment 1960 (000)*	*(5) Percent of Total 1960*	*(6) Share of Major Sector Less Share of Major Sector in U.S. 1960*	*(7) Percent Change in Employment 1950–60*
Primary	1,909	6.44	–7.68	1,203	3.60	–4.19	–36.98
Construction	1,615	5.45	–.65	1,753	5.25	–.74	8.54
Manufacturing	10,077	34.02	8.20	11,433	34.26	6.61	13.45
Transportation Communications and Utilities	2,424	8.18	.33	2,370	7.10	.07	–2.22
Wholesale and Retail Trade	5,566	18.79	.09	6.021	18.04	–.17	8.17
Services	6,311	21.31	.07	8.359	25.05	–.62	32.45
Government and Armed Forces	1,711	5.77	–.38	2,229	6.68	–.95	30.27
Totals	*29,613*	*100.00*	–	*33,368*	*100.00*	–	*12.68*

Source: Calculated from Tables, 7–1 and 6–7.

Table 7–3. OBE Economic Areas Located in the Northeastern Regional Grouping Ranked by the Percent Change in the Economic Base

OBE Economic Area	*Percent Change Economic Base 1950–67*	*Rate of Increase TPY 50–66*
63.0	29.14	6.323
78.0	24.96	5.111
61.0	20.02	5.813
84.0	18.67	5.729
69.0	16.11	5.669
60.0	15.30	6.471
10.0	14.49	4.707
8.0	12.38	6.261
79.0	10.54	5.198
77.0	8.29	5.729
68.0	8.16	5.707
75.0	7.83	6.366
12.0	7.13	5.313
82.0	6.02	6.146
62.0	4.74	5.706
17.0	3.75	6.095
4.0	3.25	5.402
72.0	2.88	6.610
64.0	2.63	6.231
9.0	1.62	4.889
5.0	.92	6.025
67.0	.83	5.231
7.0	.76	5.390
15.0	.63	5.635
6.0	−.12	5.047
14.0	−.74	5.608
114.0	−1.64	5.489
83.0	−1.75	6.287
54.0	−2.14	6.311
70.0	−2.46	5.172
74.0	−3.17	6.358
73.0	−3.22	5.833
57.0	−3.54	5.254
59.0	−3.82	6.166
76.0	−4.02	5.372
58.0	−4.88	5.984
3.0	−5.32	5.645
1.0	−5.37	5.628
11.0	−5.60	4.483
71.0	−7.06	6.170
66.0	−7.13	4.483
16.0	−7.42	5.049
18.0	−7.79	7.221
80.0	−8.93	5.748
2.0	−12.17	5.043
13.0	−16.54	3.545

must be rejected. This demonstrates the need for more indepth analysis of the patterns of economic change in the Northeastern Regional Grouping presented below.

LONG TERM ECONOMIC DEVELOPMENT OF THE NORTHEASTERN REGIONAL GROUPING

The results of the factor analysis using the 1959 level of per capita income as the variable to be explained are presented in Table 7–4. Four factors are used which explain 89.7 percent of the variance in the levels of per capita income of the OBE Economic Areas in this regional grouping. Increasing the number of factors to five raises the explained variances by two percent. Reducing the factors to three lowers the variance by five percent. Four factors are selected over these alternatives because they are better defined and because the variables were more easily assigned to one factor.

The First Factor

The first factor contains ten variables and explains 87 percent of the total explained variance in the levels of per capita income. The variables are positively related to each other and to the level of per capita income. They include:

1. Index of the composition of growth industries.
2. Ratio of families that earned $10,000 or more in 1960 to families that earned $3,000 or less.
3. Financial deposits per capita.
4. Percentage of white collar employment.
5. Local government revenue per capita.
6. Local government property tax revenue per capita.
7. Non-education local government expenditures per capita.
8. Total local government expenditures per capita.
9. Local government transfers per capita.
10. Population density.

The first variable listed above, the index of the composition of growth industries, shows that variations in the degree to which areas are able to attract and maintain rapid growth industries are positively related to the level of per capita income. The second and third variables are measures of the private capacity to save and the actual savings per capita. Higher rates of savings increase the availability of financial capital available for investment. The higher growth rate industries, as noted by the first variable, represent a potential demand source for these deposits. The higher savings rate, coupled with a potentially high rate of investment, provides the basis for the relatively higher levels of per capita income.

Table 7–4. Rotated Factor Matrix for the Level of Per Capita Personal Income in 1959: Northeastern Regional Grouping

	Factor 1	*Factor 2*	*Factor 3*	*Factor 4*	h^2
Per Capita Personal Income, 1959	*.875*	*.221*	*.076*	*–.076*	*.897*
Index of the Composition of Growth Industries, 1960	.663	.270	.223	.090	.570
Demand, Time and Savings Capital Deposits per Capita, 1960	.760	.291	.071	–.131	.684
Local Government Revenue per Capita, 1962	.932	–.192	–.042	.043	.908
Property Tax per Capita, Average 1957 and 1962	.618	–.347	–.307	–.287	.679
Government Transfers per Capita, 1962	.512	–.179	–.079	.542	.594
Non-education Government Expenditures per Capita, 1962	.929	–.092	.122	.095	.895
Total Local Government Expenditures per Capita, 1962	.919	–.200	.008	.137	.903
Families that Earned $10,000 or more to Families that Earned $3,000 or less, 1960	.855	.096	.253	–.103	.815
Percent White Collar Employment, 1960	.712	–.139	.602	–.119	.903
Population Density	.677	.402	.195	–.099	.668
Coefficient of Concentration, 1960	.035	–.696	.317	.020	.586
Average Local Government Bonds per Total Revenue, 1957 and 1962	.366	.665	.331	–.187	.721
Estimate of the Percent College Students, 1960	.003	–.600	–.087	–.220	.416
Percent High School Graduates, 1960	.230	–.828	.164	–.098	.775
Percent Persons 21 Years of Age and over that Completed Less than 5 Years of School, 1960	.134	.744	.361	.115	.715
Percent Voting, 1960	–.163	–.009	–.852	–.142	.773
Index of Voting Change, 1960–64	–.096	–.205	.688	.313	.622
Percent Non-white Population	.421	.346	.673	–.143	.771
Percent Earnings from Manufacturing, 1960	.047	.368	–.702	.260	.668
Manufacturing Productivity, 1958	.345	–.029	.027	–.492	.362
Value of Land and Buildings per Farm, 1959	.169	–.242	.006	–.899	.895
Output per Worker in Agriculture, 1960	–.238	–.394	–.320	–.707	.814
Value of Crops per Total Agriculture Output, 1959	.169	–.242	.006	–.899	.895
Percent Tenant Farms, 1959	.017	–.263	–.087	–.851	.801
Economic Base, 1959	–.133	–.161	–.391	.277	.273
Farms of 1000 Acres to Farms of 10 Acres, 1959	–.375	–.391	.248	–.095	.364

The fourth variable listed, the percent of white collar employment, contributes to this interpretation because this type of employment is likely to be a source for higher income and a higher rate of savings.

Variables five through nine are measures of the stock of local government services and infrastructure available in these areas. The revenue obtained for these services and infrastructure is related to the higher income potential resulting from the characteristics represented by the first four variables. In addition, the 10th variable indicates that these variables are associated with the more urbanized areas of the Northeastern Regional Grouping. It is the urban areas that require greater services from local governments and, at the same time, provide greater revenue sources through the generally higher property values.

This factor, therefore, combines the influences of rapid growth industries, greater stocks and sources of financial capital, and greater services and infrastructure provided by local governments. These forces are the basis for a greater income flow by providing greater savings and utilizing the savings by investment.

The Second Factor

The second factor contains five variables and explains 5.4 percent of the total explained variance in the levels of per capita income:

1. Coefficient of concentration (−).
2. Average bonds per total local government revenue (+).
3. Estimate of the percent of high school graduates going on to college (−).
4. Percentage of persons 21 years of age and over that completed high school (−).
5. Percentage of persons 21 years of age and over that completed less than five years of school (+).

These variables characterize the higher per capita income OBE Economic Areas as being more economically diversified and having a relatively higher stock of accumulated public investment, and a lower level of educational achievement.

As noted in the first factor, the greatest part of the inter-OBE Area variation in income levels is explained by variations in capacities to save and invest, both publicly and privately. The first two forces, greater economic diversity and greater accumulation of public investment, are also representative of the more urbanized areas of this regional grouping. This relative importance of the urban areas may also be used to interpret the relationship of these forces and the educational variables.

The three variables in the second factor that are used to measure the quantity and quality of the educational system vary between themselves as expected, but not as expected with the level of per capita income. The estimate of the percentage of college students and the percentage of persons 21 years of age and over that completed high school are negatively related to the 1959 level of per capita income. The percentage of persons 21 years of age and over that completed less than 5 years of school is positively associated with the level of per capita income. A possible explanation for this unexpected result is that these variables reflect the migration of low income, poorly educated persons from the other areas of the United States. When migration trends are disaggregated it is found that, in general, the unskilled, poorly educated individual migrates to the central cities. This migration trend toward the higher per capita income cities in the Northeastern Regional Grouping could very well influence the percentage measures of educational quantity and quality used in this analysis. Disregarding the effects of migration, the variables reflect the generally acknowledged poorer condition of most of school systems of our central cities.

Therefore, some of the variation in the levels of per capita income not explained by the first factor is explained by the counteracting tendency for per capita incomes in urban areas depressed by the low income status of in-migrants.

The Third Factor

The third factor contains four variables not related to the dependent variable:

1. The percentage of persons 21 years of age and over that voted in 1960 (−).
2. Index of voting change, 1960–64 (+).
3. The percentage of non-white population in 1960 (+).
4. The percentage of total income earned accounted for by the manufacturing sector (−).

The index of voting change and the percentage of non-white population are positively related (both have negative factor loadings). They are inversely related to the percent voting as expected. The index of voting change, as expressed in Chapter 3, is a measure of erratic and negative voting behavior. This behavior is characteristic of the more impoverished minority classes, and the variables vary inversely with the measure of the average level of social awareness and community involvement, and with the percentage of voting participation.

The percentage of total earnings accounted for by the manufacturing sector is directly related tᵒ the percentage of voting participation. This may reflect the tendency for higher income, blue collar workers to be more involved in community affairs, yet also demonstrates more erratic voting behavior.

This factor explains less than one percent of the total explained variance in the levels of per capita income in the OBE Economic Areas of the Northeastern Regional Grouping.

The Fourth Factor

The fourth factor has five variables that are not associated with the level of per capita income. Each of its variables has a negative factor loading, and they are therefore directly related:

1. Value of land and buildings per farm.
2. Output per worker in agriculture.
3. Value of crops per total agricultural output.
4. The percent of farms operated by tenants.
5. Manufacturing productivity.

These are primarily measures of the capital investment and productivity and the type of output produced in the agricultural sector. The first variable is used as an indicator of the relative amount of capital investment in the agricultural sector. The output per worker in agriculture is a measure of agricultural productivity. The value of crops per total agricultural output is an indicator of the growth sub-sector in agriculture. Also included is a measurement of the ownership characteristic of the agricultural sector.[1] The last variable, manufacturing productivity, is positively associated with all of the other variables.

This factor represents the association of the greater level of capital investment in the agricultural sector and higher agricultural productivity with the most rapidly growing agricultural sector. In addition, the variable measuring manufacturing productivity, with a very low factor loading, is included. However, these influences do not vary consistently with the variations in per capita income not already explained by the dimensions of the first two factors.

LONG TERM ECONOMIC DEVELOPMENT: SUMMARY

Variations in the 1959 levels of per capita income of the OBE Economic Areas in the Northeastern Regional Grouping were discussed earlier in terms of the influence of rapid growth industries, greater stocks of financial capital, and higher levels of services and infrastructure provided by local governments. The impact of these forces provided a greater supply of and demand for investible funds, thus generating an income flow resulting in a higher average level of per capita income. These forces were active primarily within the more urbanized areas of the Northeastern Regional Grouping and provided the inducement for poorer educated, lower income migrants from other areas to locate in these areas. This migration produced a countervailing influence on level of per capita income of these OBE Areas.

GROWTH IN TOTAL PERSONAL INCOME: 1950–66

The results of the factor analysis run which describe the short term pattern of economic growth, and which use the rate of growth of total personal income as the variable to be explained, are presented in Table 7–5. The five factors used represent the most clearly defined of any possible number of factors. Increasing the number of factors does not increase the explained variance. The five factors of Table 7–5 explain 72 percent of the variance in the rates of growth of total personal income of the OBE Economic Areas located in the Northeastern Regional Grouping.

The First Factor

The first factor contains 10 variables, but explains only 2 percent of the explained variance in the rates of growth of total personal income:

1. Economic base.
2. Percent white collar employment.
3. Population density.
4. Financial deposits per capita.
5. Ratio of families that earned $10,000 or more to families that earned $3,000 or less.
6. Local government property tax per capita.
7. Local government revenue per capita.
8. Non-education local government expenditures per capita.
9. Total local government expenditures per capita.
10. Percent change in agricultural output.

This factor is similar in composition to the first factor of Table 7–4,[2] which is most important in explaining the variance in the levels of per capita income.

The first factor is interpreted as representing the stock of private and public capital and the influences exerted by residentiary industry sectors in the industrial mix of the area. Although the accumulation of these stocks and the related influences were the primary forces that were the distinguishing aspects of the long run pattern of structural development, they are not distinguishing aspects of the variations in the short term rates of growth of total personal income. The long term accumulation of stocks should play a major role in the long term development of a region. However, over the shorter period the growth *rate* of a region's economy is subject to much shorter range influences. It is these influences that are the subject of the factor analysis presented in Table 7–5.

Table 7–5. Rotated Factor Matrix for the Rate of Growth of Total Personal Income, 1950–66: Northeastern Regional Grouping

	Factor 1	*Factor 2*	*Factor 3*	*Factor 4*	*Factor 5*	h^2
Rate of Increase in Total Personal Income, 1950–66	*.124*	*.279*	*.055*	*.051*	*.787*	*.719*
Economic Base, 1950	–.537	.295	.218	–.215	–.063	.473
Demand, Time, and Savings Capital Deposits per Capita, 1960	.886	–.229	–.024	.071	–.109	.856
Percent Change in Agricultural Output, 1950–64	–.691	.067	–.120	.154	.128	.537
Local Government Revenue per Capita, 1962	.829	.169	–.192	–.252	.292	.902
Property Tax per Capita, Average, 1957 and 1962	.579	.343	–.462	.077	.119	.686
Non-education Government Expenditures per Capita, 1962	.842	.091	–.019	–.270	.328	.898
Total Government Expenditures per Capita, 1962	.784	.175	–.121	–.348	.341	.898
Families that Earned $10,000 or More to Families that Earned $3,000 or Less, 1960	.743	–.132	.087	–.029	.481	.809
Percent White Collar Employment, 1960	.762	.139	.397	.085	.366	.899
Population Density, 1960	.729	–.301	.150	.057	.032	.650
Coefficient of Concentration, 1950	–.130	.711	.265	–.016	.144	.613
Percent Change in the Coefficient of Concentration, 1950–60	.388	–.457	–.077	–.022	–.016	.366
Average Bonds per Total Local Government Revenue, 1957 and 1962	.412	–.616	.220	.234	.029	.725
Estimate of the Percent College Students, 1960	.107	.676	.062	.181	–.079	.510
Percent High School Graduates	.202	.798	.064	.032	.239	.739
Percent of Persons Completing Less than 5 Years of School, 1960	.260	–.649	.430	–.008	–.176	.705
Percent Change in the Economic Base, 1950–67	.122	–.203	–.619	.063	.362	.574
Percent Voting in 1960	–.161	.076	–.751	.033	.438	.788
Index of Voting Change, 1960–64	–.064	.129	.730	–.124	.120	.584
Percent Earnings from Manufacturing, 1960	–.226	–.464	–.568	–.390	.057	.745
Value of Land and Buildings per Farm, 1959	.236	.305	–.251	.789	.200	.874
Output per Worker in Agriculture, 1959	–.269	.409	–.479	.611	–.004	.818
Value of Crops per Total Agricultural Output, 1959	.101	–.088	.016	.521	.376	.431
Percent Tenant Farms, 1960	.019	.303	–.312	.738	.205	.789
Percent Change in Bond Investment, 1957–62	–.166	.218	–.067	–.570	.206	.477

Government Transfers per Capita, 1962	.343	.100	−.061	−.661	.188	.604
Rate of Growth of Residentiary Employment, 1950–60	−.162	.307	−.062	−.113	.771	.732
Index of the Composition of Growth Industries, 1960	.505	−.363	.098	−.156	.522	.693
Percent Change in the Labor Force Participation Rate, 1950–60	.229	.401	−.067	.085	−.564	.543
Rate of Growth of Demand, Time and Savings Capital Deposits per Capita, 1950–64	.040	.171	.169	−.117	.780	.682
Manufacturing Productivity, 1958	.168	−.009	−.207	.308	.586	.510
Percent Non-White Population, 1960	.366	−.368	.493	.187	.571	.874
Net Migration Rate, 1950–60	.440	−.107	−.074	−.006	.806	.860
Percent Change in Manufacturing Productivity, 1958–63	.223	−.084	−.134	−.386	.067	.233
Ratio of Farms of 1000 Acres to 10 Acres, 1959	−.192	.389	.217	.242	−.205	.336
Average Manufacturing Capital Investment, 1958 and 1963	−.258	.121	.278	.351	−.055	.285

The Second Factor

The second factor accounts for approximately 11 percent of the total explained variance in the rates of growth of total personal income, using six variables:

1. Coefficient of concentration, 1950 (+).
2. Percentage of change in the coefficient of concentration, 1950–60 (–).
3. Estimate of the percentage of high school graduates going on to college, 1960 (+).
4. Percentage of persons 21 years of age and over that completed high school, 1960 (+).
5. Percentage of persons 21 years of age and over that completed less than five years of school, 1960 (–).
6. Average bonds outstanding per total local government revenue, 1957 and 1962 (–).

The level of economic *concentration* in 1950 is positively related to the rate of growth of total personal income. However, there is an inverse relationship between the coefficient of concentration in 1950 and the percentage of change in this coefficient between 1950 and 1960. Based on this it appears that the higher growth rate OBE Economic Areas in this regional grouping had a relatively concentrated economic structure in 1950 and experienced a trend toward greater diversity of economic structure between 1950 and 1960. This trend parallels the national trend toward greater economic diversity. Only 29 of the 171 OBE Economic Areas in the continental United States experienced a trend toward greater economic concentration during the period.

The next three variables, representing a higher level of educational achievement, are directly related to the dependent variable. The association between each educational variable is as expected. The estimate of the percentage of high school students going on to college is directly associated with the percentage of persons 21 years of age and over that completed high school, and with the rate of growth of total personal income. Each of these variables is indirectly associated with the percentage of persons 21 years of age and over that completed less than 5 years of school.

This factor is interpreted as representing an adjustment process in the economic structure of the more rapidly growing OBE Economic Areas in this regional grouping over the period 1950 to 1966. The expansion of economic activity into a more diversified set of pursuits carried with it a potential for more rapid growth of total economic activity. This should be expected since it was the economically concentrated areas in 1950 that had the greater potential to expand their economic activity into other industrial pursuits.

The set of educational variables included in this factor is interpreted as representing the accumulation of a stock of higher quality human capital. It is expected that this stock of human capital would be an important input into the expansion of the labor force related to the more rapid growth of total economic activity.

The Third Factor

The third factor, containing four variables, is not closely associated with the rate of growth of total personal income in the Northeastern Regional Grouping:

1. The percentage of change in the economic base, 1950–67 (–).
2. The percentage of total earnings accounted for by the manufacturing sector, 1960 (–).
3. The percentage voting, 1960 (–).
4. The index of voting change, 1960–64 (+).

This factor is interpreted as representing the higher degree of community involvement in the more industrialized areas of the Northeastern Regional Grouping. The positive association of the percentage of change in the economic base with the percentage of total earnings accounted for by the manufacturing sector is to be expected because it is this sector that accounts for the greater share of total exports. The inverse relationship of the index of voting change with the other variables indicates that it is the industrial areas that also experienced the greater variability in voter turnout. However, the variation in these forces is not related to the variation in the rates of growth of total personal income in this regional grouping.

The Fourth Factor

The fourth factor contains six variables and is also not related to the rate of growth of total personal income:

1. The value of land and buildings per farm.
2. The output per worker in agriculture.
3. The value of crops per total agricultural output.
4. The percentage of tenant farms.
5. The percentage of change in local government bond investment.
6. Local government transfers per capita.

The first four variables, indicators of the characteristics of the agricultural sector, are all positively related to each other. These variables are measures of capital stock of agriculture, agricultural productivity, the most rapid growth sector of agricultural output, and the ownership characteristic of the agricultural sector. The positive association between capital investment, productivity, and the more rapidly growing crop sector is to be expected.[3] However, the variations of these is not consistent with the variations in the rates of growth of total personal income.

The last two variables are negatively related to the agricultural variables included in the factor. This association appears to reflect the smaller amount of deficit financing and government transfers in the rural agricultural areas in comparison with the urban areas of the Northeastern Regional Grouping.

This factor, therefore, represents the characteristics of the agricultural sector in this regional grouping. In addition, it contains variables that indicate lesser local government deficit financing and intergovernmental transfers in the more rural areas of this regional grouping.

The Fifth Factor

The fifth factor contains seven variables and is most important in explaining the variance in the rates of growth of total personal income of the OBE Economic Areas in the Northeastern Regional Grouping. It explains 86 percent of the total explained variance:

1. The rate of growth of residentiary employment.
2. The index of the composition of growth industries.
3. Manufacturing productivity.
4. The rate of growth of demand, time, and savings capital deposits per capita.
5. Percentage of non-white population.
6. The net migration rate.
7. The percentage of change in the labor force participation rate.

Each of these variables, except the percentage of change in the labor force participation rate, is directly related to the rate of growth of total personal income.

The first two variables summarize the most important components of the growth of total personal income, while the remainder summarize the productivity element and the critical changes in the supplies of savings and labor, without which the rate of growth obtained could not have taken place. This factor is interpreted as representing the importance of growth in residentiary employment and production in national growth industries in the pattern of economic growth of the Northeastern Regional Grouping over the period 1950 to 1966. Supporting this growth is an efficient manufacturing sector (undoubtedly related to the existence of the high national growth rate industries), growth in the level of financial capital, and growth in the labor force through migration. The high positive factor loading on the net in-migration rate is an indicator of a major component of the population and labor force growth. Related to this is the percentage of non-white population. A significant part of the migration may, therefore, be accounted for by black migrants.

The only variable that is negatively related to the other variables and the rate of growth of total personal income is the percentage of change in the labor force participation rate. This reflects, as it does across the nation, the trend toward delaying entrance into the labor force by extending the educational period. This variable changes inversely with the other variables because it reduces the growth of income by reducing the growth rate of the active labor supply.

This factor, therefore, represents the growth of residentiary employment and the related forces that are responsible for the higher rates of growth of the OBE Economic Areas in the Northeastern Regional Grouping. The factor provides indications of the sources of financial capital and labor that accelerate the growth process. This finding is particularly important to the objectives of this study because it is inconsistent with the hypothesis that a primary force affecting the rate of growth of total personal income was increases in the economic base. As this factor indicates, in the Northeastern Regional Grouping it was the growth of residentiary, or non-basic, employment and the related growth in financial and factor supplies that were the primary elements in the growth pattern from 1950 to 1966.

SHORT TERM ECONOMIC GROWTH: SUMMARY

The five factors of Table 7–5 explain 72 percent of the variance in the rates of growth of total personal income of the OBE Economic Areas located in the Northeastern Regional Grouping. The greatest part of this variance, 86 percent, is explained by the fifth factor. The second factor accounts for most of the remaining explained variance. The fifth factor is interpreted as representing the major components of the growth—the growth of residentiary employment in particular and growth of national growth industries in general. This factor also highlights the supporting aspects of this growth process—more productive manufacturing, growth in financial capital, and growth in the labor supply through migration.

In addition, the second factor demonstrates that the more rapidly growing OBE Areas in this regional grouping had a relatively concentrated economic structure in 1950, but were able to increase the degree of economic diversity during the period 1950 to 1960. A logical explanation for this seemingly contradictory relationship is that those areas that were relatively concentrated in economic structure in 1950 had the greatest potential to improve their industrial mix and thus positively affect their rates of growth. Compared to the OBE Economic Areas in the other three regional groupings, those in the Northeastern Regional Grouping were the most diversified in economic structure in 1950. This association between the rates of growth and increased diversification is consistent with the two hypothesized functional relationships. First, as discussed in Chapters 3 and 4, increased diversification of the economic structure permits greater inter-industry substitution of the factors of production in response to changes in the relative levels of demand. Second, as discussed in Chapter 4, the greater the degree of economic diversity, the greater is the internalization of income multipliers. However, it must be stressed that the income multipliers may not be considered as originating in the export sector. These multipliers most likely have their origin in the growth of the residentiary sectors and other rapidly growing industry sectors.

GROWTH IN PER CAPITA INCOME: 1950–1966

The factor analysis used to explain the variance in the rates of growth of per capita income is presented in Table 7–6. using five factors. As expressed in Chapter 4, the growth in per capita income is used as a general indicator of the change in the average level of economic welfare during the period 1950–66. The use of this variable permits description of the pattern of economic growth from a different point of view. Analysis may be made of the interrelationship between the growth in the total volume of economic activity, as measured by the growth in total personal income, and the growth in the average level of economic welfare, as measured by the growth in per capita income.

Forty-six percent of the variance in the rates of growth of per capita income are explained by the five factors included in Table 7–6. The factor components are identical to those of Table 7–5. A review is made only of those factors that explain a significant proportion of the variance in the rates of growth of per capita income.

The first factor, which explained only a small part of the variance in the rates of growth of total personal income, explains 8.2 percent of the variance in the rates of growth of per capita personal income. This factor is interpreted as representing the stock of private and public capital and their association with non-basic industry sectors. In addition, these forces are found within the more urbanized areas of the Northeastern Regional Grouping. However, they are negatively related to the rate of growth in per capita income. It is this same set of variables, with minor exceptions, that explain 87 percent of the total explained variance in the levels of per capita income in Table 7–4. Therefore, it appears that these variables are primarily related to the level, rather than the rate of increase, of per capita income. It was found throughout this study that the high per capita income areas are the areas that are growing more slowly in terms of per capita income. The variables included in this factor are negatively related to the dependent variable of Table 7–6.

The second factor explains 18.2 percent of the variance in the rates of growth of per capita income. The variables included in the factor vary in the same direction in both Table 7–5 and Table 7–6, and the same reasoning is applied. In the above case, it is argued that the variables included in the second factor represent the contributions made by the accumulation of a higher quality stock of human capital. In addition, the influences exerted by the expansion of economic activity into a more diversified set of economic pursuits are noted.

Inter-OBE Area variations in the rates of growth of per capita income are also positively related to variations in these forces.

The fifth factor of Table 7–6 explains an additional 17.1 percent of the variance of the rates of growth of per capita income. This factor is interpreted as representing the growth of the residentiary sectors and, more generally, the influences exerted by an industrial mix consisting of relatively more national growth industries. Closely related to these forces, and providing the critical inputs into the growth process, is the growth of financial capital and the growth of the labor force. These variables are, however, negatively related to the rates of growth of per capita income. The logical interpretation of these results is that the growth of total economic activity increases the employment opportunities and in turn increases the rate of in-migration. (Note the very high .805 factor loading on the net migration rate and its negative association with growth in per capita income.) For the most part, the in-migrants command a relatively lower income than the average of the areas, thus bringing down the rate of increase of the per capita income.

This analysis shows that three factors explain approximately 50 percent of the variance in the rate of growth of per capita income. Positively associated with the rate of increase in per capita income are the variables included in the second factor—those representing higher levels of educational achievement and an increase in the degree of economic diversity. The variables that are closely related to the level of per capita income (the accumulated level of stocks of private and public capital and the orientation of the economy toward residentiary industry sectors) and those that are related to the growth in residentiary employment (primarily net in-migration) are negatively related to the rates of growth of per capita income.

Table 7–6. Rotated Factor Matrix for the Rate of Growth of Per Capita Personal Income, 1950–66: Northeastern Regional Grouping

	Factor 1	*Factor 2*	*Factor 3*	*Factor 4*	*Factor 5*	h^2
Rate of Increase in Total Personal Income, 1950–66	–.287	.427	.018	.160	–.414	.462
Economic Base, 1950	–.522	.334	.197	–.231	–.043	.478
Demand, Time, and Savings Capital Deposits per Capita, 1960	.856	–.330	–.007	.069	–.080	.853
Percent Change in Agricultural Output, 1950–64	–.672	.160	–.116	.164	.092	.526
Local Government Revenue per Capita, 1962	.858	.152	–.160	–.179	.296	.904
Property Tax per Capita, Average, 1957 and 1962	.628	.318	–.410	.156	.069	.693
Non-education Government Expenditures per Capita, 1962	.861	.071	.008	–.212	.326	.898
Total Government Expenditures per Capita, 1962	.814	.170	–.096	–.277	.351	.901
Families that Earned $10,000 or More to Families that Earned $3,000 or Less, 1960	.718	–.153	.116	.013	.521	.824
Percent White Collar Employment, 1960	.757	.075	.445	.111	.337	.902
Population Density, 1960	.686	–.376	.160	.047	.064	.644
Coefficient of Concentration, 1950	–.079	.713	.302	.016	.082	.613
Percent Change in the Coefficient of Concentration, 1950–60	.345	–.487	–.093	–.038	.055	.370
Average Bonds per Total Local Government Revenue, 1957 and 1962	.412	–.689	.213	.189	.094	.734
Estimate of the Percent College Students, 1960	.163	.623	.112	.211	–.180	.504
Percent High School Graduates	.270	.778	.124	.098	.156	.728
Percent of Persons Completing Less than 5 Years of School, 1960	.179	–.700	.394	–.087	–.113	.698
Percent Change in the Economic Base, 1950–67	.127	–.134	–.604	.132	.373	.555
Percent Voting in 1960	–.128	.086	–.764	–.010	–.427	.790
Index of Voting Change, 1960–64	–.087	.108	.724	–.164	.159	.596
Percent Earnings from Manufacturing, 1960	–.247	–.371	–.626	–.374	.186	.765
Value of Land and Buildings per Farm, 1959	.238	.250	–.166	.841	.140	.873
Output per Worker in Agriculture, 1959	–.185	.400	–.419	.660	–.065	.810
Value of Crops per Total Agricultural Output, 1959	–.114	–.047	.065	.547	.299	.408
Percent Tenant Farms, 1960	.024	.272	–.259	.790	.160	.790
Percent Change in Bond Investment, 1957–62	–.136	.300	–.093	–.534	.268	.473

Government Transfers per Capita, 1962	.376	.146	−.080	−.619	.230	.605
Rate of Growth of Residentiary Employment, 1950–60	−.109	.422	−.029	−.027	.686	.662
Index of the Composition of Growth Industries, 1960	.471	−.339	.100	−.128	.568	.685
Percent Change in the Labor Force Participation Rate, 1950–60	−.193	.341	−.068	.059	−.612	.536
Rate of Growth of Demand, Time and Savings Capital Deposits per Capita, 1950–64	.062	.258	.200	−.050	.741	.662
Manufacturing Productivity, 1958	.152	.029	−.162	.373	.606	.556
Percent Non-White Population, 1960	.308	−.371	.514	.182	.579	.865
Net Migration Rate, 1950–60	.434	−.062	−.042	.068	.805	.847
Percent Change in Manufacturing Productivity, 1958–63	.257	−.059	−.153	−.365	.052	.229
Ratio of Farms of 1000 Acres to 10 Acres, 1959	−.144	.373	.252	.232	−.348	.399
Average Manufacturing Capital Investment, 1958 and 1963	−.258	.113	.304	.328	−.124	.294

Chapter Eight

Economic Growth and Development of the Central Regional Grouping

INTRODUCTION

During the period of this study, 1950–66, the OBE Economic Areas brought into the Central Regional Grouping did not make major adjustments in their productive structures. However, total personal income increased by 4.89 percent annually. This was the lowest average annual rate of growth of total personal income experienced by any of the regional groupings over the period. Population growth also lagged behind other regional groupings, increasing by only 17.3 percent between 1950 and 1966. In 1966 this regional grouping accounted for 17 percent of the total income earned in the continental United States.

Growth in per capita personal income did not lag behind other regional groupings largely because of out-migration. The per capita income of the regional grouping was $1,844 in 1959 and increased over the period 1950–66 by 4.25 percent per year. This rate of increase was higher than the Far West Regional Grouping, about equal to the Northeastern Regional Grouping, but below the Southeastern Regional Grouping.

The boundaries of the Central Regional Grouping were defined in Chapter 2. The Regional Grouping contains 42 OBE Economic Areas and covers an area extending north to Canada and south to Texas. It is bordered on the west by the Rocky Mountains and extends eastward to the Ozarks and the western tip of the manufacturing belt. It is considered the most heterogeneous of the regional groupings. In terms of the 1959 per capita personal income, this regional grouping contains OBE Economic Areas that fell into all four quartile rankings. As explained in Chapter 2, the western boundary could not be defined on the basis of homogeneous levels of per capita income. Therefore, Bogue and Beale's definition of the Rocky Mountain and Intermountain Region is used. However, the boundary defined in this way is only an approximation of Bogue and Beale's Regional Boundary.

Table 8–1. Employment Growth and Distribution by Sector, 1950–60:

	(1) Employment 1950 (000)	*(2)* Percent of Total 1950
Agriculture	1,891	24.38
Forestry and Fisheries	6	0.07
Mining	141	1.81
Construction	512	6.60
Manufacturing		
Food & Kindred Products	242	3.12
Textile Mill	17	0.21
Apparel	52	0.67
Printing	96	1.23
Chemicals	38	0.48
Lumber & Furniture	80	1.03
Electrical Machinery	25	0.32
Mach. Non-Electric	100	1.28
Transport Equipment	74	0.95
Paper Products	48	0.61
Petroleum Refining	38	0.48
Primary Metals Industry	46	0.59
Fabricated Metals	45	0.58
Misc. Manufacturing	131	1.68
Transport Services	439	5.66
Communications	98	1.26
Utilities	106	1.36
Wholesale Trade	296	3.81
Eating Places	248	3.19
Other Retail	988	12.73
Finance, Insurance & Real Estate	232	2.99
Lodging Places	246	3.17
Business & Repair	202	2.60
Amusements & Recreation	63	0.81
Private Households	170	2.19
Educational, Medical & Professional Services	682	8.79
Public Administration	301	3.88
Armed Forces	103	1.32
Total	*7,756*	*99.85*

Source: Calculated from basic data not reported.

EMPLOYMENT GROWTH AND DISTRIBUTION, 1950–60

Total employment grew by only 9.3 percent over the period 1950–60. This compares with an increase of 14.9 percent for the continental United States over the same decade. The employment growth and distribution for this regional

Central Regional Grouping

(3) Share of Industry Less Share of Industry in U.S. 1950	*(4) Employment 1960 (000)*	*(5) Percent of Total 1960*	*(6) Share of Industry Less Share of Industry in U.S. 1960*	*(7) Percent Change in Employment 1950–60*
12.13	1,264	14.90	8.28	–33.15
–.14	5	0.05	–.09	–16.66
.17	144	1.69	.67	2.12
.50	536	6.32	.33	4.68
.72	306	3.60	.75	26.44
–1.98	12	0.14	–1.30	–29.41
–1.21	67	0.79	–1.05	28.84
.28	137	1.61	.20	42.70
–.68	44	0.51	–.86	15.78
–1.08	73	0.86	–.81	8.75
–1.08	78	0.92	–1.44	212.00
–1.01	142	1.67	.81	42.00
–1.43	133	1.56	–1.31	79.72
–.22	64	0.75	–.16	33.33
–.03	44	0.51	.07	15.78
–1.48	43	0.50	–1.43	6.52
–.91	106	1.25	–.79	135.55
–1.81	180	2.12	–1.45	37.40
.44	401	4.72	.40	–8.65
.01	109	1.28	–.01	11.22
–.02	127	1.49	.08	19.81
.31	325	3.83	.74	9.79
.20	263	3.10	.34	6.04
.50	1,119	13.19	.92	13.25
–.41	336	3.96	–.29	44.82
–.12	264	3.11	.05	7.31
.28	197	2.32	–.23	–2.47
–.06	60	0.70	–.09	–4.76
–.71	224	2.64	–.78	31.76
.31	1,065	12.56	.60	56.15
–.54	393	4.63	–.40	30.56
–.42	217	2.55	–.04	110.67
–	*8,478*	*99.83*	–	*9.30*

grouping by 32 sectors and by 7 major sectors are presented in Tables 8–1 and 8–2.

The agricultural sector was the largest in terms of employment in 1950, accounting for 24.4 percent of total employment. By 1960 the employment share of agriculture decreased to 14.9 percent of the total, but still remained the largest sector. Although employment in the agricultural sector

Table 8–2. Employment Growth and Distribution by Major Sector, 1950–60: Central Regional Grouping

(1) Major Sector	*(2)* 1950 Employment (000)	*(3)* Percent of Total 1950	*(4)* Share of Industry in Reg. Less Share in U.S. 1950	*(5)* 1960 Employment (000)	*(6)* Percent of Total 1960	*(7)* Share of Industry in Reg. Less Share in U.S. 1960	*(8)* Percent Change 1950–60
Primary	2,038	26.27	12.15	1,413	16.66	8.87	–30.66
Construction	512	6.60	.50	536	6.32	.33	4.68
Manufacturing	1,032	13.30	–12.52	1,429	16.85	–10.80	38.46
Transportation, Communications and Utilities	643	8.29	.44	637	7.51	.48	–0.93
Wholesale & Retail Trade	1,532	19.75	1.05	1,707	20.13	1.92	11.42
Services	1,595	20.56	–.68	2,146	25.31	–.46	34.54
Government & Armed Forces	404	5.20	–.95	610	7.19	–.44	50.99
Totals	*7,756*	*100.00*	–	*8,478*	*100.00*	–	*9.30*

Source: Calculated from Table 8–1 and Table 5–7.

decreased by 33 percent over the decade, no major readjustments were made in the employment structure of this regional grouping. Columns 4 and 7 of Tables 8–1 and 8–2 show the differences between percentages of employment by sector and major sector in the Regional Grouping, and the employment share by sector and major sector in the Continental United States. The positive values for the agricultural sector and the consistently negative values for the manufacturing sectors show that the employment structure of this Regional Grouping has a greater share of agricultural employment and a lesser share of manufacturing employment than was true for the continental United States. However, most important is the consistency and the signs of these values for 1950 and 1960. In short, the industrial structure of this regional grouping did not significantly change over the decade. With reference to the economy of the continental United States, each employment sector and major employment sector maintained nearly the same relative importance.

Analysis shows that the 30.1 percent decline in agricultural employment, which reflects the change in the relative importance of this sector, had a major influence on the change in the economic base.

INTRODUCTION TO THE ECONOMIC BASE MODEL

Before actual tests of the export base model can be presented, the general underlying relationships must be explored. Table 8–3 presents the rates of growth of total personal income for the OBE Economic Areas in the Central Regional Grouping, ranked by the percent change in the economic base. This table shows that 37 of the 42 OBE Economic Areas in this regional grouping experienced a decline in the ratio of export oriented production to total production over the period 1950–67. However, it can be derived from the table that, in general, the greater the decline in the export base, the less the rate of growth of total personal income. Disaggregating the OBE Economic Areas listed in Table 8–3 into quartiles based on the percentage of change in the economic base confirms this statement. The mean rate of growth of total personal income for the OBE Economic Areas ranked in the first quartile was 5.790 percent per year. The mean rate of growth for the remaining quartiles was 5.092, 4.598, and 4.110 respectively. Additional support for the direct association between growth (in this case the smaller the decline) in the economic base and the rate of growth of total personal income is provided by the simple correlation between these two variables of .705.

The dominance of the agricultural sector on the economic base in 1950 can be shown from different viewpoints. The correlation between the economic base in 1950 and the percentage of earnings from manufacturing in 1950 is −.344. This negative relationship may be interpreted as reflecting the dominance of agriculture *vis-à-vis* manufacturing, since both are considered as

Table 8–3. OBE Economic Areas Located in the Central Regional Grouping Ranked by the Percent Change in the Economic Base

OBE Economic Area	*Percent Change Economic Base 1950–67*	*Rate of Increase TPY 50–66*
120.0	12.12	5.712
128.0	11.27	5.369
147.0	9.04	6.487
127.0	7.90	6.795
121.0	.01	5.033
148.0	–1.92	7.024
85.0	–1.94	5.648
87.0	–1.99	4.440
91.0	–3.30	6.064
110.0	–3.93	5.340
90.0	–5.43	5.311
111.0	–5.72	5.632
100.0	–5.81	4.865
113.0	–7.60	4.818
150.0	–8.82	4.013
107.0	–9.27	5.409
89.0	–9.45	5.044
119.0	–9.69	5.639
88.0	–10.11	4.973
86.0	–10.31	5.850
105.0	–10.60	4.461
106.0	–11.12	5.039
123.0	–13.11	6.185
116.0	–13.92	4.468
92.0	–14.15	4.672
125.0	–14.20	4.152
109.0	–15.87	4.408
108.0	–16.07	5.208
98.0	–16.29	3.832
97.0	–16.70	3.877
104.0	–17.36	4.696
102.0	–18.68	4.044
99.0	–19.03	4.323
122.0	–19.36	5.041
93.0	–19.81	4.303
103.0	–20.25	3.439
95.0	–20.88	3.703
94.0	–20.95	4.242
112.0	–24.08	4.682
96.0	–24.54	4.289
81.0	–25.28	4.373
101.0	–26.82	2.706

export sectors. The correlation between the economic base in 1960 and the percentage of earnings from manufacturing in 1960 was .163. Although this correlation is not significant at the 95 percent confidence level, it does reflect the increasing relative importance of the manufacturing sector on the economic base.

If, as was the case for the Southeastern Regional Grouping, the argument is to favor the importance of growth in the economic base as a primary force effecting the growth of total personal income, it must be shown that the dominance of negative values in the change in the export base results from the decline of agriculture. In addition, it must be demonstrated that growth of more viable exports absorbed most of the loss in agricultural exports in the more rapidly growing OBE Economic Areas. This, as will be demonstrated, is the export pattern followed by the more rapidly growing OBE Economic Areas in this regional grouping.

RESULTS OF THE EXPORT BASE MODEL

In order to test the export base model as defined in Chapter 4, regressions were fitted to each of the specified equations with these statistically significant results:

$$\frac{dTPY}{dt} = \underset{}{6.551} + \underset{(.014)}{.049}\,(\Delta EB) - \underset{(.018)}{.031}\,(CC) \qquad R^2 = .533 \qquad (8.1)$$

$$\Delta EB = -19.72 + \underset{(1.49)}{11.096}\,(IGI) \qquad R^2 = .581 \qquad (8.2)$$

where: $\frac{dTPY}{dt}$ = Average Annual Rate of Growth in Total Personal Income, 1950–60.

ΔEB = The Percentage of Change in the Economic Base Over the Period 1950–67.

IGI = The Index of the Composition of Growth Industries, 1960.

CC = Coefficient of Concentration, 1950.

The measure of infrastructure (non-education government expenditures per capita) was rejected because of non-significance when added as the second independent variable to equation 8.2. Therefore, the *a priori* expectations concerning the importance of this variable must be rejected.

Fifty-three percent of the variance in the rates of growth of total personal income of the OBE Economic Areas in this regional grouping is explained by the variances in the percentage of change of the economic base and the degree of economic diversity. Based on this equation it may be argued that a 1.0 percent average annual increase in the economic base was associated with a .4 percent annual average rate of increase in total personal income between 1950 and 1966. In addition, it appears that the more diversified the economic structure in 1950, the greater the growth in total personal income over the period 1950–66. The results of these tests are consistent with the model specified in Chapter 4. This was stated as the greater the growth in the economic base and the greater the degree of economic diversity of the productive structure, the greater would be the growth in total personal income. This was based on the hypotheses that:

1. Growth in export earnings relative to non-basic earnings relative to non-basic earnings provides a primary stimulus to the total income growth in the area.
2. The greater the degree of economic diversity, the greater would be the internalization of the initial income multipliers.

The second specified relationship made the change in the economic base a function of the OBE Area's composition of growth industries and the development of the area's infrastructure. The coefficient for the measure of infrastructure was insignificant, and that leaves the equation 8.2. From this equation it may be stated that 55.5 percent of the variance in the economic base is accounted for by the variance in the index of the composition of growth industries. The high positive beta coefficient in the index of the composition of growth industries and the amount of variance explained by this variable highlights the importance of the consideration given to the actual industry sectors that determine the growth in the economic base. The dominance of the agricultural sector on the relative size of the economic base in 1950 and the continual decreasing importance of this sector on the relative size of the economic base emphasizes the importance of dealing with the change in the base rather than static value of the base. In addition, it demonstrates the importance of viewing the change in the economic base in terms of the absorption of these decreases in agricultural exports by more viable export sectors.

The results of these tests suggest that the growth in the economic base was a leading force in the growth of the total economic activity in this regional grouping. This must be qualified in the sense that what is being dealt with is a relatively smaller decrease in the economic base rather than a percentage increase in the economic base. The analysis also demonstrates the importance of viewing the increases in the economic base from the viewpoint of the more rapidly growing export oriented industries. In addition, the results also are consistent with the two specified functions of the diversification of economic structure: first in terms of the internalization of income multipliers; and second in terms of inter-industry substitution of productive factors.

However, equation 8.1 explains only about half of the variance of the growth rates of total personal income of the OBE Economic Areas in this regional grouping. This demonstrates the need for the more complete analysis.

LONG TERM ECONOMIC DEVELOPMENT OF THE CENTRAL REGIONAL GROUPING

The results of the factor analysis, using the 1959 level of per capita income as the variable to be explained, are presented in Table 8–4. Three factors are used which explain 90.2 percent of the variance in the level of per capita income of the OBE Economic Areas in this regional grouping. Increasing or decreasing the number of factors did not appreciably affect the total explained variance. Virtually all of the explained variance is explained by the first factor. The components of this factor remained unchanged as the number of factors were increased.

The First Factor

The first factor includes seven variables. Virtually all of the 90.2 percent of explained variance is explained by this factor; in addition, all of the signs on the factor loadings are as expected:

1. Index of the composition of growth industries (+).
2. Coefficient of concentration (–).
3. Manufacturing productivity (+).
4. Ratio of families that earned $10,000 or more to families that earned $3,000 or less (+).
5. Demand, time and savings capital deposits per capita (+).
6. Percentage of high school graduates (+).
7. Percentage of white collar employment (+).

This factor includes variables that generally describe the economic structure and the relative abundance of human resources, private savings, and capital stock available in the higher per capita income areas of the Central Regional Grouping. The first two variables show that the higher per capita income OBE Economic Areas are characterized as having a relatively greater part of the labor force employed in national growth industries and an industrial mix that is relatively more diversified. The remaining variables are interpreted as representing the underlying forces behind the long term structural development of this type of economic structure. The positive relationship between the measure of manufacturing productivity and the level of per capita income may be interpreted as representing the relationship between a larger accumulation of capital in the manufacturing sector and the level of per capita income. The next two variables represent the relatively greater source and stock of financial capital available in the higher per capita income areas. Positively related to these forces is the relative size of the stock of human resources, as measured by the percentage of persons

Table 8–4. Rotated Factor Matrix for the Level of Per Capita Personal Income in 1959: Central Regional Grouping

	Factor 1	*Factor 2*	*Factor 3*	h^2
Per Capita Personal Income, 1959	*.950*	*.013*	*−.013*	*.902*
Index of the Composition of Growth Industries, 1960	.710	−.386	.448	.853
Index of Economic Diversity, 1960	−.719	.256	−.515	.847
Demand, Time, and Savings Capital Deposits Per Capita, 1960	.683	.032	.153	.491
Manufacturing Productivity, 1958	.622	.195	−.336	.538
Ratio of Families that Earned $10,000 to Families that Earned $3,000, 1960	.869	.227	−.001	.806
Percent White Collar Employment, 1960	.859	−.281	.097	.825
Percent High School Graduates, 1960	.817	.310	−.295	.851
Average Local Govt. Bonds Outstanding Per Local Govt. Revenue, 1957 and 1962	.589	−.582	−.120	.700
Local Govt. Revenue Per Capita, 1962	.212	.910	.115	.886
Property Tax Per Capita, 1962	.139	.825	−.285	.781
Non-education Local Govt. Expenditures Per Capita, 1962	.132	.836	.361	.848
Local Govt. Expenditures Per Capita, 1962	.171	.880	.207	.847
Percent Voting in 1960	−.347	.759	.043	.698
Percent Non-White Population, 1960	.248	−.812	.013	.721
Percent of Persons 21 Years of Age and Over that Completed Less than 5 Years of School, 1960	−.228	−.675	.189	.543
Value of Land and Buildings Per Farm, 1959	.514	.052	−.755	.837
Output Per Worker in Agriculture, 1960	.581	.143	−.624	.748
Value of Crops Per Total Agricultural Output, 1959	.184	−.306	−.568	.450

Ratio of Farms of 1000 Acres to 10 Acres, 1959	−.193	−.001	.559	.350
Percent Tenant Farms, 1959	.208	−.035	−.584	.385
Local Govt. Transfers Per Capita, 1962	−.004	.419	.586	.519
Average Manufacturing Capital Investment, 1958 and 1963	−.103	.226	−.484	.296
Population Density, 1960	.369	−.265	.581	.545
Percent Earnings from Manufacturing, 1960	.161	.153	.800	.690
Economic Base, 1959	−.200	.009	.022	.040
Index of Voting Change, 1960–64	−.166	.158	−.066	.057
Percent College Students, 1960	.294	−.384	.131	.251

21 years of age and over that completed high school. The last variable listed above, the percentage of white collar employment, is also positively related to the level of per capita income. Since it is employment in these sectors that is most likely to yield higher levels of income, the percentage of white collar employment is also closely related to the income distribution ratio and the level of financial deposits per capita.

Therefore, the variations in the levels of per capita income are explained by the variations in the measures of the abundance of the stock of financial capital, the stock of human resources, and the stock of capital in the manufacturing sector. Also, there is an indication of the source of the demand for these resources—the relatively greater importance of national growth industries in the industrial mix of these areas. It is these industries that would be expected to have a greater rate of capital investment because of the greater rate of expansion of final output. Therefore, the long term structural development of the higher per capita income areas in the Central Regional Grouping is explained in terms of these basic resources and the demand exerted by the rapid growth rate industries located in these areas.

The Second Factor

The second factor includes eight variables and explains less than one tenth of one percent of the variance in the levels of per capita income of the OBE Areas in this regional grouping:

1. Local government revenue per capita, (+).
2. Local government expenditures per capita, (+).
3. Non-education local government expenditures per capita, (+).
4. Property tax per capita, (+).
5. Average local government bonds outstanding per total local government revenue, (−).
6. Percentage of non-white population, (−).
7. Percentage of persons 21 years of age and over that completed less than five years of school, (−).
8. The percentage voting, (+).

The first four variables are measures of local government revenue and expenditures, or local government services provided. Each is directly associated with the other. The average value of local government bonds outstanding per total local government revenue is negatively associated with the other government variables. A possible explanation for this is that local governments which are able to raise relatively greater per capita revenue need not contract a relatively high level of debt. The percentage of non-white population and the percentage of persons 21 years of age and over that completed less than 5 years of school are directly associated as expected. They are inversely related to the government revenue variables, thus indicating the lower potential tax revenue available from minority family members characterized by a low level of educational achievement. The final variable, the percent voting, used as an indicator of community involvement, is directly associated with the government revenue variables. This most likely reflects the existence of higher income members of the population base having relatively more taxable property; it is thus directly associated with the local government service variables included in the factor.

Therefore, this factor is interpreted as representing the accumulated stock of and provisions for the current supply of local government services and infrastructure. The level of these services is positively related to the level of community involvement. This level of government services is negatively related to measures indicating lower levels of educational achievement and the relative importance of non-white persons in the population base. The variations in the level of local government services provided is not, however, consistent with the variability in the levels of per capita income of the OBE Economic Areas in the Central Regional Grouping.

The Third Factor

There are nine variables included in the third factor; however, the factor does not explain any of the variance in the levels of per capita income of the OBE Areas in the Central Regional Grouping:

1. Value of land and buildings per farm, 1959 (–).
2. Output per worker in agriculture, 1960 (–).
3. Value of crops per total agricultural output; 1959 (–).
4. Ratio of farms of 1,000 acres to ten acres, 1959 (+).
5. Percentage of tenant farms; 1959 (–).
6. Local government transfers per capita, 1962 (+).
7. Average manufacturing capital investment, 1958 and 1963 (–).
8. Population density, 1960 (+).
9. Percentage of earnings from manufacturing, 1960 (+).

The first three variables are positively related to each other. They are measures of the capital investment in agriculture, agricultural productivity, and the orientation toward specialization in the most rapidly growing sector of agriculture.[1]

The measure of local government transfers per capita varies positively with these agricultural variables. This likely reflects the relatively greater local government needs in the more agricultural areas of this regional grouping. This conclusion differs from the trends found in the other regional groupings. The measure of intergovernmental transfers is generally more closely related to the more urban areas. The relatively smaller importance of such urban areas in this regional grouping is most likely responsible for this atypical finding.

The last three variables are representative of the more urban, industrialized areas of this regional grouping. The measure of the degree of industrialization, the percentage of total income earned by the manufacturing sector, and the measure of urbanization (population density) are positively related. The estimate of the rate of capital investment in manufacturing, however, is negatively related to the measures of urbanization and industrialization. From these relationships, it can be summarized that the areas with a longer tradition of urbanization and industrialization do not have the more dynamic manufacturing industries. (This interpretation is partially supported by the much higher factor loading of the index of the composition of growth industries with the first factor than on this factor).

Therefore, this factor represents the higher productivity, capital intensive agricultural sectors. It shows that it is those areas in which there is more investment and productivity in agriculture that are less industrialized and less urban. This should be expected, but it is somewhat surprising that variations in these characteristics are not related to variations in the levels of per capita income. It may be that the greater efficiency of the agricultural sector in the Central Regional Grouping has, in general, obtained an average level of per capita income commensurate with the urban industrial areas also represented in the factor. Therefore, reliance must be placed on the measure of the quality of input sources and the dynamism of the industry sectors which were included in the levels of per capita income in this regional grouping.

LONG TERM ECONOMIC DEVELOPMENT: SUMMARY

The three factors of Table 8–4 explained 90 percent of the variance in the levels of per capita income of the OBE Economic Areas located in the Central Regional Grouping. Virtually all of this variance was explained by the first factor. This factor highlighted the importance of coupling the abundance of financial capital, the stock of human capital, and the stock of capital in the manufacturing sector with a relatively dynamic and diversified economic structure. It is hypothesized that input demand, originating in the more rapidly growing industry sectors located in the higher per capita income areas, was met by the stock of resource characteristics mentioned earlier. The interaction of these forces have, therefore, accounted for the variations in the levels of income of the OBE Areas in this regional grouping.

GROWTH IN TOTAL PERSONAL INCOME: 1950–66

The results of the factor analysis used to describe regional variations in patterns of economic growth, using the rate of growth of total personal income as the variable to be explained, are presented in Table 8–5. Three factors explain 67 percent of the variance in the rates of growth of total personal income of the OBE Economic Areas located in this regional grouping. Virtually all of the explained variance is explained by the first factor.

The First Factor

The first factor explains over 98 percent of the total variance in the rates of growth of total personal income and includes 13 variables:

1. Economic base (−).
2. Index of the composition of growth industries (+).
3. Coefficient of concentration (−).
4. Percentage of earnings from manufacturing (+).
5. Net migration rate (+).
6. Population density (+).
7. Percentage of white collar employment (+).
8. Demand, time and savings capital deposits per capita (+).
9. Ratio of families that earned \$10,000 or more to families that earned \$3,000 or less (+).
10. Rate of growth of financial deposits (+).
11. Percentage of change in the economic base (−).
12. Rate of growth of residentiary employment (+).
13. Percentage of change in the coefficient of concentration (+).

This set of variables represents the more rapid increases in the labor and capital supplies and characteristics of structural change in the more rapidly growing OBE Areas in the Central Regional Grouping. The first four variables characterize the economic structure of these OBE Areas. The negative association of the economic base implies that the percentage of total income earned by the residentiary sectors is directly associated with the factor. Similarly, the negative association of the coefficient of concentration implies that a relatively higher level of economic diversification is also directly associated with the factor. The inclusion of the index of the composition of growth industries and the percentage of earnings from manufacturing also add to the description of the economic structure. It appears that the more rapidly growing OBE Economic Areas in this regional grouping are characterized by a relatively diversified structure that is weighted toward residentiary activities, manufacturing, and national growth industries.

The source and type of labor force available to the industry of this regional grouping is characterized by the next three variables. All three variables are directly associated with the factor. The positive association of the net migration rate implies that the in-migration into these areas is a source of labor supply. Similarly, population density is directly associated with a large potential labor supply. Finally, the percentage of white collar employment characterizes the

Table 8–5. Rotated Factor Matrix for the Rate of Growth of Total Personal Income, 1950–66: Central Regional Grouping

	Factor 1	*Factor 2*	*Factor 3*	h^2
Rate of Growth of Total Personal Income, 1950–66	*.811*	*–.092*	*.028*	*.667*
Economic Base, 1950	–.827	.017	–.057	.688
Percent Change in the Economic Base, 1950–67	.781	–.135	.223	.678
Rate of Growth of Residentiary Employment, 1950–60	.508	–.044	–.513	.522
Index of the Composition of Growth Industries, 1960	.910	–.169	–.090	.865
Coefficient of Concentration, 1950	–.899	.026	.107	.821
Percent Change in the Coefficient of Concentration, 1950–60	.666	.018	–.166	.471
Demand, Time & Savings Capital Deposits per Capita, 1960	.550	.187	–.304	.430
Rate of Growth of Financial Deposits, 1950–64	.769	–.093	.055	.604
Ratio of Families that Earned $10,000 to Families that Earned $3,000, 1960	.608	.382	–.557	.826
Percent White Collar Employment, 1960	.801	–.102	–.452	.856
Population Density, 1960	.648	–.088	.223	.478
Migration Rate, 1950–60	.835	.125	–.404	.877
Percent Earnings from Manufacturing, 1960	.516	.316	.492	.609
Total Local Government Revenue per Capita, 1962	.032	.938	–.067	.884
Property Tax per Capita, 1962	–.260	.777	–.327	.779
Local Government Transfers per Capita, 1962	.295	.508	.444	.543
Non-education Government Expenditures per Capita, 1962	.133	.895	.171	.847
Total Local Government Expenditures per Capita, 1962	.067	.918	.034	.848
Percent Voting, 1960	–.435	.685	.217	.705
Percent Non-white Population, 1960	.431	–.722	–.097	.716
Percent of Persons Completing Less than 5 Years of School, 1960	.178	–.653	.323	.562
Manufacturing Productivity, 1958	.183	.245	–.633	.494
Value of Land and Buildings per Farm, 1959	–.070	.002	–.915	.842
Value of Crops per Total Agric. Output, 1959	–.097	–.367	–.519	.414
Percent Tenant Farms, 1960	–.205	–.126	–.600	.417
Percent Change in Bond Investment, 1957–62	–.263	.250	.503	.385
Percent High School Graduates, 1960	.341	.382	–.761	.841

Output per Worker in Agriculture, 1959	.012	.110	−.878	.784
Percent Change in the Labor Force Participation Rate, 1950–60	.207	−.360	−.145	.193
Percent Change in Mfg. Productivity, 1958–63	.009	.093	−.027	.009
Percent Change in Total Agric. Output, 1950–64	−.242	.129	−.131	.090
Average Bonds per Total Gov. Revenue, 1957 and 1962	.487	−.492	−.450	.681
Index of Voting Change, 1960–64	−.200	.106	.043	.053
Percent College Students	.369	−.299	−.103	.234
Average Mfg. Capital Investment, 1958 and 1963	−.412	.116	−.308	.278
Ratio of Farms of 1000 Acres to 10 Acres or Less, 1959	−.415	−.111	−.277	.261

relatively greater importance of this type of occupational employment in these areas.

Variables 8, 9, and 10 represent the level, source, and growth of financial capital. It is to be expected that the level and growth of financial deposits are directly associated with the income distribution ratio. The two financial variables, discussed in Chapter 3, were designed to measure availability of capital funds in the more rapidly growing OBE Economic Areas in this regional grouping.

Variables 11, 12, and 13 characterize the actual growth pattern. Each of these variables is directly associated with the rates of growth of total personal income of the OBE Areas in the Central Regional Grouping. This growth pattern is characterized as relative increases in the economic base, relatively greater rates of growth in residentiary employment, and relative increases in the degree of economic concentration. Two of these are subject to qualification: first, relative increases in the economic base should be interpreted as relatively smaller declines in the base; secondly, 41 of the 42 OBE Economic Areas in this regional grouping experienced an increase in the degree of diversification of economic activity between 1950 and 1960. Therefore, the positive association of the coefficient of concentration with this factor implies that relatively smaller increases in diversification are directly associated with higher rates of growth of total personal income.

Therefore, this factor represents influences contributing to economic growth and provides indications of the pattern of growth that resulted. The underlying forces included in the factor are characteristics of the economic structure, labor supply, and capital supply. The resulting pattern of growth, as described by this factor, is consistent with the economic base model presented earlier, but is substantially more complete and brings into the model more of the underlying forces of growth.

This factor is interpreted as representing the stock of labor, financial capital, and their sources. In addition, the economic structures of the more rapidly growing areas are characterized as being relatively more diversified and consisting of relatively more residentiary, national growth, and manufacturing industries. Finally, the pattern of economic growth of the higher growth rate areas over the period 1950–66 is closely related to the growth of the economic base and growth of the residentiary sectors. It is this relationship between the growth of the economic base and the growth of the residentiary sectors that are stressed throughout this study. On the basis of this factor, it is concluded that the variability in the rates of growth of the OBE Economic Areas in the Central Regional Groupings is associated with variability in the growth of economic base and residentiary sectors and the availability and growth of the stock of labor and financial resources.

The Second Factor

The second factor, shown in Table 8–5, includes eight variables, but does not explain any of the variance in the rates of growth of total personal income. This factor is very similar to the second factor of Table 8–4. The only difference between the two is that the measure of local government transfers per capita is included in Table 8–5 rather than the average value of local government bonds outstanding to local government revenue. This change does not significantly affect the earlier interpretation of this set of variables:

1. Total local government revenue per capita, 1962.
2. Property tax per capita, 1962.
3. Local government transfers per capita, 1962.
4. Non-education government expenditures per capita, 1962.
5. Total local government expenditures per capita, 1962.
6. Percentage of voting, 1960.
7. Percentage of non-white population, 1960.
8. Percentage of persons completing less than five years of school, 1960.

This factor is interpreted as representing the accumulated stock of, and current provisions for, local government services and infrastructure. The level of these stocks are positively related to the level of community involvement, but negatively related to the measure of the relative importance of the non-white population in the total population and the measure of the lower levels of educational achievement. However, the variability in the level of accumulation of these services and public infrastructure is not associated with the variability in the rates of growth of the OBE Economic Areas in this regional grouping.

The Third Factor

The third factor is not associated with the rate of increase in total personal income. It includes seven variables, six of which have negative factor loadings:

1. Output per worker in agriculture, 1959.
2. Value of land and buildings per farm, 1959.
3. Value of crops per total agricultural output, 1959.
4. Percentage of tenant farms, 1960.
5. Manufacturing productivity, 1958.
6. Percentage of high school graduates, 1960.
7. The percentage of change in bond investment, 1957–62.

The first six variables are positively related. The first four are measures of agricultural productivity, capital investment in the agricultural sector, production orientation toward the most rapidly growing sector of agriculture, and the ownership characteristic of the agricultural sector.[2] Positively related to these variables is the measure of manufacturing productivity, or capital stock invested in the manufacturing sector, and the percent of persons 21 years of age and over that completed high school.[3]

Therefore, this factor is interpreted as representing the variations in capital stock in agriculture and manufacturing and the orientation toward the commercial production of crops in the agricultural sector. The inclusion of the measure of educational achievement, a measure of the stock of human capital, appears to be related to levels of productivity in agriculture and manufacturing. It is somewhat surprising that the variation in capital stock invested in people, agriculture and manufacturing, and levels of productivity is not associated with the variation in the rates of growth of total personal income. The declining nature of the agricultural sector throughout the nation, and the relatively smaller importance of manufacturing in this regional grouping, may be the primary reasons for the lack of influence exerted by these forces on the rates of growth of total personal income.

SHORT TERM ECONOMIC GROWTH: SUMMARY

The first factor of Table 8–5 is the only one of the three that assumes any importance in explaining the variance in the rates of growth of total personal income of the OBE Economic Areas in the Central Regional Grouping. The interpretation of this factor stresses the related aspects of growth in the economic base and growth of the residentiary sectors. Coupled with these components of the growth of total economic activity are the relatively greater stocks and sources of labor and financial capital. In addition, the economic structure of the more rapidly growing OBE Areas in this regional grouping is characterized as more diversified and consisting of more residentiary and national growth industries. In addition, the applicability of the economic base model to the variables included in the factor is stressed. Although no causal relationships between the variables included in the first factor may be assumed, it should be pointed out that the interrelationships stressed between the growth in the economic base and the growth of the residentiary sector by the economic base model are consistent with the cluster of variables found in this factor. It is the variations in these forces that are most closely related to the variations in the rates of growth of total personal income of the OBE Economic Areas in the Central Regional Grouping.

GROWTH IN PER CAPITA INCOME: 1950–66

The factor analysis employed to describe the changes in the average level of welfare, using the average annual rate of growth of per capita income as the dependent variable, is presented in Table 8–6. The three factors included in this table explain 54 percent of the variance in the rates of growth of per capita income of the OBE Economic Areas in the Central Regional Grouping. Increasing the number of factors is rejected because the most important factor, the third factor of Table 8–6, remains the same as the number of factors increase. Also, increasing the number of factors reduces the factor loadings for most of the variables other than those included in the third factor. In other words, the additional factor takes some of the variables now included in the first two factors, yet most of these variables are then explained by both the new factor and either factor one or factor two of Table 8–6.

The only difference in factor components between Tables 8–5 and 8–6 is that the percentages of total income earned accounted for by the manufacturing sector is included in the third factor of Table 8–6 rather than in the first factor as it was in Table 8–5. It is the third factor of Table 8–6 that explains 99 percent of the total explained variance in the rates of growth of per capita income. The addition of the new variable to this factor affects the interpretation presented. This interpretation stresses the variations in manufacturing, agricultural and human capital investment, and the orientation of the agricultural sector toward production of crops, the most rapidly growing segment of all agricultural products. Variations in the extent of these forces are negatively associated with the rates of growth of per capita income. Only two variables included in this factor are positively related to the dependent variable. These are the percentage of change in local government bond investment and the percentage of total income earned accounted for by the manufacturing sector. Each of these, however, has a low factor loading. Given this, the positive relationship between these two variables and the rate of growth of per capita income is interpreted as indicating that per capita incomes grew more rapidly in the industrial OBE Areas. This interpretation is strengthened by the negative relationship between the measures of the extent of capital intensive agricultural sector and the rates of growth of per capita income. In summary, it has been the industrial areas, as opposed to the agricultural or urban areas, that achieved the most rapid rates of growth of per capita income in the Central Regional Grouping.

Table 8–6. Rotated Factor Matrix for the Rate of Growth of Per Capita Income, 1950–66: Central Regional Grouping

	Factor 1	*Factor 2*	*Factor 3*	h^2
Rate of Growth of Per Capita Income, 1950–66	*.088*	*.072*	*.731*	*.540*
Economic Base, 1950	–.810	–.010	–.204	.698
Percent Change in the Economic Base, 1950–67	.734	.134	.335	.669
Rate of Growth of Residentiary Employment, 1950–60	.561	.014	–.471	.536
Index of the Composition of Growth Industries, 1960	.919	.153	.049	.870
Coefficient of Concentration, 1950	–.915	–.009	–.029	.838
Percent Change in the Coefficient of Concentration, 1950–60	.694	–.035	–.076	.489
Demand, Time and Savings Capital Deposits per Capita, 1960	.592	–.206	–.184	.426
Rate of Growth of Financial Deposits, 1950–64	.741	.086	.171	.586
Ratio of Families that Earned $10,000 to Families that Earned $3,000, 1960	.682	–.414	–.470	.857
Percent White Collar Employment, 1960	.870	.073	–.324	.866
Average Bonds per Total Government Revenue, 1957 and 1962	.560	.466	–.390	.683
Population Density, 1960	.607	.091	.359	.505
Migration Rate, 1950–60	.879	–.153	–.278	.873
Total Local Government Revenue per Capita, 1962	.022	–.940	–.035	.885
Property Tax per Capita, 1962	–.221	–.786	–.316	.767
Local Government Transfers per Capita, 1962	.201	–.493	.471	.505
Non-education Government Expenditures per Capita, 1962	.082	–.888	.216	.843
Total Local Government Expenditures per Capita, 1962	.041	–.917	.061	.846
Percent Voting, 1960	–.474	–.669	.194	.711
Percent Non-White Population, 1960	.454	.710	–.085	.718
Percent of Persons Completing Less than 5 Years of School, 1960	.127	.662	.281	.533
Manufacturing Productivity, 1958	.270	–.274	–.595	.501
Value of Land and Buildings per Farm, 1959	.069	–.040	–.929	.870
Value of Crops per Total Agric. Output, 1959	–.022	–.347	–.548	.422
Percent Tenant Farms, 1960	–.106	.106	–.560	.336
Percent Earnings from Manufacturing, 1960	.426	–.301	.594	.626
Output per Worker in Agriculture, 1959	.143	–.145	–.830	.731
Percent Change in Bond Investment, 1957–62	–.344	–.227	.433	.358

Percent High School Graduates, 1960	.458	−.417	−.660	.819
Percent Change in the Labor Force Participation Rate, 1950–60	.242	.354	−.061	.188
Percent Change in Mfg. Productivity, 1958–63	.026	−.094	−.012	.010
Percent Change in Total Agric. Output, 1950–64	−.237	−.127	−.075	.078
Index of Voting Change, 1960–64	−.211	−.099	.067	.059
Percent College Students	.387	.290	−.035	.235
Average Mfg. Capital Investment, 1958 and 1963	−.370	−.124	−.385	.300
Ratio of Farms of 1000 acres to 10 acres or less, 1959	−.378	.102	−.401	.314

Chapter Nine

Economic Growth and Development of the Far West Regional Grouping

INTRODUCTION

By 1966 the Far West Regional Grouping accounted for 16.6 percent of the total personal income earned in the continental United States. Although this share was below the Northeastern and Southeastern Regional Groupings, the Far West Regional Grouping exhibited the highest average annual rate of increase in total personal income over the period 1950–66. In addition, population growth over the same period was the highest of any of the regional groupings. The population increase of 206.5 percent over the period 1950–66 must be considered as the leading force in the high rate of growth of total personal income.

The mean 1959 per capita personal income for the OBE Economic Area in the Far West Regional Grouping was $2,188, the highest of all the regional groupings. However, the mean growth rate of per capita income of the OBE Areas over the period 1950–66 was 3.8 percent per year, the lowest of all the regional groupings. The fact that high per capita income areas achieved the lowest growth rates of per capita income is not unusual and results from the statistical properties of percentage growth rates. What is unusual about this trend in the per capita income levels of this regional grouping is that migration is positively associated with the growth rates of per capita income. In every other case, high per capita income OBE Areas experienced high in-migration which tends to lower the growth rate of per capita income. The non-negative relationship between the migration rate of per capita personal income for this regional grouping reflects the generally higher income, higher educated migrant that is likely to make the relatively longer move to the Far West.

The boundaries of the Far West Regional Grouping, are defined in Chapter 2. The regional grouping is bounded on the north by Canada, on the east by the Rocky Mountains, on the south by Mexico, and the west by the Pacific Ocean. There are 26 OBE Economic Areas in this regional grouping. In many cases the OBE Areas are larger in terms of geographical space than those included in the other regional groupings, because those located west of the Rocky Mountains and east of California are sparsely populated. Since a minimum population criteria of 200,000 was applied by the Office of Business Economics to its Economic Areas, the more sparsely populated areas necessarily have greater geographical space.

EMPLOYMENT GROWTH AND DISTRIBUTION, 1950–60

Total employment grew by 40.1 percent between 1950 and 1960. This was the largest percentage increase in employment for any of the regional groupings over the same period. It compares with a 14.9 percent increase in employment for the continental United States over the same decade. This relatively high increase cannot be attributed to the growth of any one sector. All major sectors, except the primary, had significant increases in employment. Tables 9–1 and 9–2 present the employment growth and distribution by sectors and major sectors.

Because of an 11 percent increase in employment in the mining sector, the primary sector decreased by only 13.9 percent over the 1950s. All other major sectors increased in employment by at least 18 percent. The service sector accounted for the largest share of total employment in 1950 and 1960. In addition, the percentage increase in service employment was 61.3 percent between 1950 and 1960, second only to the increase in manufacturing employment.

With the exception of the primary sector, the manufacturing sector was the only major sector that constituted a share of regional employment less than the share of manufacturing employment in the continental United States. This was true for both 1950 and 1960 (Columns 4 and 7 of Table 9–2). The manufacturing sector exhibited the highest percentage increase in employment of any major sector, 73.6 percent. Because of this increase, the relative share of manufacturing employment increased from 17.5 percent in 1950 to 21.7 in 1960. All of the manufacturing employment sectors, with the exception of textile mill products, increased in terms of employment between 1950 and 1960. The highest percentage increases in manufacturing employment were in the manufacturing sectors that accounted for a relatively small share of total employment in 1950 (see Table 9–1).

The major sectors of services and wholesale and retail trade maintained a relatively large share of total employment. However, the shares accounted for by these two major sectors are not significantly different from the share of these sectors in the national economy.

In general, both the growth of employment by sector and the relative share of employment by sector did not differ significantly from those of the national economy.

INTRODUCTION TO THE ECONOMIC BASE MODEL

Before presenting results of the export base model for this regional grouping, the basic underlying relationships of the model must be explored. Table 9–3 presents the rates of growth of the OBE Economic Areas included in the Far West Regional Grouping ranked by the percentage of change in the economic base between 1950 and 1967. Twenty-one of the 26 OBE Economic Areas in this regional grouping experienced a decline in the export base over the period. However, there was a significant difference in the mean rate of growth of total personal income between those ranked at the top of Table 9–3 and those OBE Areas ranked at the bottom. The mean rate of growth of total personal income by quartile ranking was:

Quartile Rank	*Number of Areas*	*Mean Rate of Growth*
1	6	8.531
2	7	6.142
3	7	6.345
4	6	5.211

The mean rate of growth in total personal income for the second and third quartile ranks are not significantly different. There is significant difference between the first and fourth quartiles. This direct association between these two variables is confirmed by the simple correlation of .682.

An explanation for the decline in the economic base for most of the OBE Economic Areas in this Regional Grouping is less apparent than for the other regional groupings in which this has occurred. The relative importance of agriculture declined, as it did in all regional groupings, but the decline had less of an impact because the sector's share of total employment is relatively small. It appears, as analysis of the short term growth indicates, that increases in the residentiary employment was a dominant force in the growth of this regional grouping. This growth of residentiary employment is a strong indicator of the rise in income generated by these sectors. This income growth is the most likely explanation for the decline in the economic base for this regional grouping. However, this fact alone is not ground for the rejection of the economic base arguments.

RESULTS OF THE EXPORT BASE MODEL

In order to analyze the export base model as defined in Chapter 4, regressions are fitted to each of the specified equations, with these statistically significant results:

Table 9–1. Employment Growth and Distribution by Sector, 1950–60:

	(1) Employment 1950 (000)	(2) Percent of Total 1950
Agriculture	659	9.63
Forestry and Fisheries	25	.36
Mining	109	1.59
Contract Construction	524	7.66
Manufacturing		
Food and Kindred Products	174	2.54
Textile Mill Products	15	0.21
Apparel and Other Textile Products	57	0.83
Printing and Publishing	94	1.37
Chemicals	46	0.67
Lumber and Furniture	236	3.45
Non-electrical Machinery	65	0.95
Electrical Machinery	28	0.40
Transport Equipment	164	2.39
Paper and Allied Products	35	0.49
Petroleum Refining	43	0.62
Primary Metals Industry	68	0.99
Fabricated Metals and Ordinance	65	0.95
Misc.	107	1.56
Transport Services	363	5.30
Communications	105	1.53
Utilities	110	1.60
Wholesale Trade	285	4.16
Eating and Drinking Establishments	253	3.69
Other Retail Trade	896	13.10
Finance, Insurance and Real Estate	267	3.90
Lodging Places	261	3.81
Business and Repair Services	191	2.79
Amusements and Recreation Services	99	1.44
Private Households	168	2.45
Educational, Medical and Professional Services	654	9.56
Public Administration	396	5.79
Armed Forces	278	4.06
Totals	*6,840*	*100.00*

Source: Calculated from basic data not reported.

Far West Regional Grouping

(3) Share of Industry Less Share of Industry in U.S. 1950	(4) Employment 1960 (000)	(5) Percent of Total 1960	(6) Share of Industry Less Share of Industry in U.S. 1960	(7) Percent Change in Employment 1950–60
−2.62	538	5.61	−1.01	−18.36
.11	24	0.25	.11	−4.00
−.05	121	1.26	.24	11.00
1.56	634	6.61	.62	20.99
.14	259	2.70	.15	48.85
−1.98	14	0.14	−1.30	−6.66
−.85	76	0.79	−1.05	33.33
−.14	147	1.53	−.28	56.38
−.49	71	0.74	−.63	54.34
1.34	243	2.53	.86	2.96
−1.34	132	1.37	−1.11	103.07
−1.00	172	1.79	−.57	514.28
.01	361	3.76	.89	120.12
.16	55	0.57	−.34	57.14
.11	51	0.53	.11	18.60
−1.08	92	0.96	−.97	35.29
−.54	218	2.27	.23	235.38
−1.93	187	1.95	−1.62	74.76
.08	398	4.15	−.17	9.64
.28	144	1.50	.21	37.14
.22	140	1.46	.05	27.27
.66	363	3.78	.69	27.36
.70	305	3.18	.34	20.55
.87	1,159	12.09	−.18	29.35
.50	446	4.65	.38	67.04
.52	320	3.33	.27	22.60
.47	305	3.18	.34	20.55
.57	121	1.26	.47	22.22
−.45	246	2.56	−.46	46.42
1.08	1,207	12.59	.63	84.55
1.37	581	6.06	1.03	46.71
2.32	455	4.74	2.15	63.66
–	*9,585*	*100.00*	–	*40.13*

Table 9–2. Employment Growth and Distribution by Major Sector, 1950–60: Far West Regional Grouping

Major Sector	*(1) Employment 1950 (000)*	*(2) Percent of Total 1950*	*(3) Share of Major Sector Less Share of Major Sector in U.S. 1950*	*(4) Employment 1960 (000)*	*(5) Percent of Total 1960*	*(6) Share of Major Sector Less Share of Major Sector in U.S. 1960*	*(7) Percent Change in Employment 1950–60*
Primary	793	11.59	–2.53	683	7.12	–.67	–13.87
Construction	524	7.66	1.56	634	6.61	.62	20.99
Manufacturing	1,197	17.50	–8.32	2,078	21.67	–5.98	73.60
Transportation Communications and Utilities	578	8.45	.60	682	7.11	.08	17.99
Wholesale and Retail Trade	1,434	20.96	2.26	1,827	19.06	.85	27.40
Services	1,640	23.97	2.73	2,645	27.59	1.92	61.28
Government and Armed Forces	674	9.85	3.70	1,036	10.80	3.17	53.70
Totals	*6,840*	*100.00*	–	*9,585*	*100.00*	–	*40.13*

Source: Calculated from Table 9–1 and Table 5–7.

Table 9–3. OBE Economic Areas Located in the Far West Regional Grouping Ranked by the Percent Change in the Economic Base

OBE Economic Area	*Percent Change Economic Base 1950–67*	*Rate of Increase TPY 50–66*
165.0	16.64	8.347
161.0	14.27	11.961
164.0	6.27	8.847
155.0	3.79	6.119
171.0	3.01	7.230
163.0	–.49	8.681
168.0	–2.24	7.817
152.0	–2.56	5.545
160.0	–2.84	7.483
151.0	–4.10	6.126
157.0	–6.04	5.569
153.0	–6.31	3.951
145.0	–7.87	6.500
146.0	–9.37	7.501
149.0	–9.98	6.590
162.0	–10.14	9.297
167.0	–10.19	6.086
156.0	–10.82	4.354
158.0	–10.93	5.169
159.0	–12.35	5.418
166.0	–13.79	5.700
124.0	–15.27	6.696
154.0	–17.31	4.817
169.0	–19.51	4.535
126.0	–21.88	3.507
170.0	–22.74	6.013

$$\frac{dTPY}{dt} = 7.39 + .129\,(\Delta EB) \qquad R^2 = .417 \tag{9.1}$$
$$(.028)$$

$$\Delta EB = -19.49 + 9.306\,(IGI) \qquad R^2 = .44 \tag{9.2}$$
$$(2.13)$$

where: $\frac{dTPY}{dt}$ = Average Annual Rate of Growth in Total Personal Income, 1950–66.

ΔEB = Percent Change in the Economic Base over the Period, 1950–67.

IGI = The Index of the Composition of Growth Industries, 1960.

In each case the second specified independent variable, the coefficient of concentration in equation 9.1 and the measure of infrastructure in equation 9.2 are not statistically significant and the simple regressions listed are used. The signs of each of the beta coefficients are as expected. Also, in comparison with the respective beta coefficients found in the estimation of this model for the other regional groupings, they are relatively large.

Based on equation 9.1 it appears that a 1.0 percent average annual increase in the economic base over the period 1950–67 is associated with a .75 percent annual average rate of increase in total personal income. However, only 46.5 percent of the variance in the rates of growth of total personal income of the OBE Economic Areas in this Regional Grouping is explained by the variance in the percent change in the economic base.

The second specified relationship makes the change in the economic base a function of the index of the composition of growth industries and the development of the region's infrastructure. Again, it is necessary to return to the simple form of the relationship because of the non-significance of the second independent variable. In this case, 44.3 percent of the variance in the percent change in the economic base is explained by the variance of the index of the composition of growth industries. Although the coefficient of determination is low, the result is not inconsistent with the model.

The results obtained in testing the export base relationships force acceptance of a reduced form for each of the specified equations. What remains in the basic framework of the original export base model. The most important of the relationships remain consistent with the specified relationships. However, it cannot be alleged that any form of the synthesis between the export base and sector approaches is accomplished for this regional grouping. The rejection of the coefficient of concentration from the first equation provides only the export base approach as still consistent with the model.

Similar statements must be made concerning the second equation. The importance of the measure of the region's infrastructure has been rejected. However, the results are still consistent with the specified association between the change in the economic base and the index of the composition of growth industries.

The results do suggest that the explanatory power of the two equations need additional information. For this we must turn to the more complete analysis that follows.

LONG TERM ECONOMIC DEVELOPMENT OF THE FAR WEST REGIONAL GROUPING

The factor analysis using the 1959 per capita personal income as the variable to be explained is presented in Table 9–4. The four factors are used to explain 79 percent of the variance of the 1959 per capita income levels of the OBE Economic

Areas in the Far West Regional Grouping. Increasing the number of factors does not significantly change the factor components of those included in Table 9–4.

The First Factor

The first factor contains six variables and explains 57 percent of the total explained variance in the levels of per capita income of the OBE Areas in this regional grouping:

1. Local government revenue per capita.
2. Property tax per capita.
3. Local government transfers per capita.
4. Non-education government transfers per capita.
5. Total local government expenditures per capita.
6. Average bonds per total local government revenue.

All the variables, except number six, are positively related to each other and to the level of per capita income. Each of these variables represent variations among the OBE Economic Areas of the Far West Regional Grouping in the extent of public investment and accumulated social overhead capital. Included in the factor indications of the source of local governments funds as well as the level of local government expenditures. The only variable that varies inversely with the others, and with the level of per capita income, is the ratio of average local government bonds outstanding to local government revenue. It is expected that those areas experiencing greater fiscal capacity have a lower ratio of average bonds outstanding to total local government revenue. This could result either from the relatively larger denominator of the ratio or from the likelihood that areas with a greater tax base need less deficit financing to maintain a sufficient level of social overhead capital.

This factor may be interpreted as representing variations in the stock of infrastructure and social overhead capital between the OBE Areas. The variations in these measures are positively related to the variations in the level of per capita income.

The Second Factor

The second factor consists of nine variables and explains thirty-two percent of the total explained variance:

1. The economic base in 1959 (−).
2. Index of the composition of growth industries, 1960 (+).
3. Coefficient of economic concentration, 1960 (−).
4. Demand, time and savings capital deposits per capita, 1960 (+).
5. Ratio of families that earned $10,000 or more to families that earned $3,000 or less in 1960, (+).

Table 9–4. Rotated Factor Matrix for the Level of Per Capita Personal Income in 1959: Far West Regional Grouping

	Factor 1	*Factor 2*	*Factor 3*	*Factor 4*	h^2
Per Capita Personal Income, 1959	*.672*	*.504*	*.166*	*.242*	*.792*
Local Government Revenue per Capita, 1962	.972	–.005	–.015	.135	.963
Property Tax per Capita, Average, 1957 and 1962	.792	.034	.053	.381	.777
Local Government Transfers per Capita, 1962	.830	–.125	–.098	–.288	.797
Non-education Government Expenditures, per Capita, 1962	.953	.051	–.050	.141	.934
Total Local Government Expenditures per Capita, 1962	.965	.095	–.057	.141	.963
Average Bonds per Total Local Government Revenue, 1957 and 1962	–.580	.183	–.003	.350	.493
Economic Base, 1959	.274	–.684	.000	.238	.600
Index of the Composition of Growth Industries, 1960	.102	.821	–.175	–.284	.795
Coefficient of Concentration, 1960	.224	–.688	.163	–.165	.577
Demand, Time, and Savings Capital Deposits per Capita, 1960	.414	.663	.212	.227	.708
Ratio of Families that Earned $10,000 to Families that Earned $3,000, 1960	.523	.702	.151	.143	.810
Percent White Collar Employment	–.002	.857	–.194	–.135	.790
Estimate of the Percent College Students, 1960	–.042	.730	.226	–.102	.806
Percent of Persons 21 Years of Age and Over that Completed High School, 1960	–.082	.779	.439	–.012	.806
Population Density, 1960	.460	.624	.024	–.052	.604
Value of Land and Buildings per Farm, 1959	.185	.210	–.613	.506	.710
Percent Voting, 1960	.072	.166	.792	–.294	.746
Percent Non-White Population, 1960	.306	.418	–.710	–.032	.774
Percent of Persons who Completed Less than 5 Years of School, 1960	–.113	–.258	–.892	.034	.877
Percent Earnings from Manufacturing, 1960	.428	–.037	.525	–.265	.530
Manufacturing Productivity, 1958	.130	.452	.005	.613	.597
Output per Worker in Agriculture, 1959	.145	–.115	–.277	.616	.491

Value of Crops per Total Agriculture Output, 1959	.128	.064	−.081	.568	.350
Farms of 1000 Acres to 10 Acres	.373	−.314	−.282	.504	.571
Percent Tenant Farms, 1959	−121	−.392	−.213	.697	.700
Average Manufacturing Capital Investment, 1958 and 1963	.010	−.453	.006	.573	.534
Index of Voting Change	.103	.403	−.343	.100	.300

6. Percentage of white collar employment, 1960 (+).
7. Estimate of the percentage of high school students going on to college, 1960 (+).
8. The percentage of persons 21 years of age and over that completed high school or more in 1960 (+).
9. Population density, 1960 (+).

These variables represent variations in the production orientation of the higher income OBE Areas, the actual and potential savings, the abundance of skilled human resources, and the degree of urbanization. The first three variables show that variations in the relative importance of non-basic industries (based on the negative factor loading on the economic base in 1959), variations in the degree of economic diversity (based on the negative factor loading on the coefficient of concentration) are positively associated with differences in the level of per capita income. These measures are positively related, as is expected, to the degree of urbanization. Urban economies are generally more economically diversified and generally contain relatively larger service, or non-basic, industries.

Variables four and six show that differences in the actual and potential savings capacity are positively associated with the level of per capita income. The measure of financial deposits per capita is representative of the greater abundance of savings available in these higher income areas. The ratio of families that earned $10,000 or more to families that earned $3,000 or less, and the percentage of white collar employment, are related to the stock of savings because each of these variables represents a source for greater savings.

Finally, the two measures of educational achievement indicate that variations in the stock and quality of human capital resources are positively related to differences in the other variables and to variations in the level of per capita income. Variations in the quality of human capital are obviously related to the variations in the actual and potential savings.

In summary, variation in the levels of per capita income, not explained by variations in the stock of social capital, is explained to a significant extent by actual and potential savings, variations in the level of human resources, and variations in the relative importance of residentiary industries. This includes greater concentration of production in national growth industries and the degree of economic diversity of production. It is noted that the type of production orientation highlighted by these measures is associated with the relative importance of urbanization.

The Third Factor

The third factor explains approximately 3.4 percent of the total explained variance in the levels of per capita income and consists of five variables:

1. Percentage of total earnings from manufacturing.

2. Percentage voting.
3. Value of land and buildings per farm.
4. Percentage of non-white population.
5. Percentage of persons 21 years of age and over that completed less than five years of school.

The first two variables are positively related to each other and to the level of per capita income, while the last three are negatively related to the level of per capita income.

The positive relationship between the first two variables is interpreted as representing the greater level of community involvement in the more industrialized areas of the Far West Regional Grouping. The signs of the factor loadings on the remaining variables are consistent with this interpretation. It should not be expected that agricultural investment would be very high in the relatively industrialized areas, as the negative relationship between these variables and the value of land and buildings per farm shows. It should be expected, as the interrelationships between the last two variables and measures of industrialization and community involvement show, that the level of community involvement would vary inversely with the proportion of non-white and uneducated persons in the total population.

The relative independence of the level of industrialization (Factor 3) and the level of urbanization (Factor 2) is not surprising. It is only at the very low levels of development that one finds them closely associated. The present trends indicate that industry will locate almost anywhere except in central cities. Therefore, the close relationship between industrialization and urbanization cannot be found. This lack of strong relationship is noted in most of the regional groupings.

This factor is interpreted as representing variability in industrialization and community involvement in the OBE Economic Areas located in the Far West Regional Grouping. However, the variability of these measures is not associated with the variability in the levels of per capita income.

The Fourth Factor

The fourth factor consists of six variables, all of which are positively associated with the level of per capita income, and explains 7.3 percent of the total explained variance in the levels of per capita income:

1. Manufacturing productivity.
2. Average manufacturing capital investment.
3. Output per worker in agriculture.
4. Value of crops per total agricultural output.
5. Ratio of farms of 1,000 acres or more to farms of ten acres or less.
6. Percentage of tenant farms.

The combination of these variables from a dimension that may be defined in terms of the productivity of the labor force. The first three variables represent manufacturing capital investment, the associated advances in productivity, and the productivity of the agricultural sector. The value of crops per total agricultural output is a measure of the growth sub-sector in agriculture. The remaining two variables are indicators of the size and ownership characteristics. It is to be expected that the measure of the large scale character of the agricultural sector be associated with measures of agriculture productivity because of the potential for economies of scale. As noted in earlier chapters, the measure of the ownership characteristic of agriculture most likely indicates the existence of commercial rather than tenant farms.

This association is found between capital investment and productivity of the manufacturing and agricultural sectors in previous regional groupings. It was not expected that these measures would cluster. However, the OBE Economic Areas are large enough, particularly in the Far West Regional Grouping, that significant investment in both rural agriculture and industrial centers is found in the same area. This is even more reasonable when the relatively close proximity of the agricultural and urban areas west of the Rocky Mountains is taken into account.

Therefore, this factor is interpreted as representing the variations in the stock of capital and the associated higher levels of agricultural and manufacturing productivity. The variations in these measures explain an additional 7.3 percent of the variations in the levels of per capita income.

LONG TERM ECONOMIC DEVELOPMENT: SUMMARY

The four factors included in Table 9–4 explain 79 percent of the variance in the levels of per capita income of the OBE Economic Areas located in the Far West Regional Grouping. The first factor is interpreted as representing the inter-OBE Economic Area variability in the level of infrastructure and social capital provided by local governments. This factor explained 57 percent of the total explained variance in the levels of per capita income. The second factor, interpreted as representing variation in the stock of human resources, actual and potential savings, the relative importance of non-basic activities, the degree of economic diversity, and the concentration of production in national growth industries explained 32 percent of the total explained variance in the levels of per capita income. Also positively related to this factor is the degree of urbanization. The first two factors highlight separated aspects of urban economic development. The first factor emphasizes the relative importance of the accumulated stock of social capital, while the second factor emphasizes the residentiary orientation and related forces common to most urban areas. Therefore, it appears that it is the urban areas that are the higher per capita income areas in the Far West

Regional Grouping, because of their greater accumulation of social capital, diversity of economic activities (including greater relative shares of national growth industries), greater actual and potential savings, and a greater stock of human capital.

GROWTH IN TOTAL PERSONAL INCOME: 1950–66

Four factors are used in the rotated factor matrix presented in Table 9–5, which has the rate of growth in total personal income as the dependent variable. The four factors used explain 95.4 percent of the variance in the rates of growth of total personal income of the OBE Economic Areas in the Far West Regional Grouping.

The First Factor

The first factor contains 13 variables and explains 10.2 percent of the total explained variance in the rates of growth of total personal income:

1. Economic base, 1950 (–).
2. Percentage of change in the economic base, 1950–67 (+).
3. Index of the composition of growth industries, 1960 (+).
4. Index of economic diversity, 1950 (–).
5. Percentage of change in the index of economic diversity 1950–60 (+).
6. Demand, time and savings capital deposits per capita, 1960 (+).
7. Ratio of farms of 1,000 acres to farms of 10 acres, 1959 (–).
8. Ratio of families that earned $10,000 to families that earned $3,000, 1960 (+).
9. Percentage of white collar employment (+).
10. Estimate of the percentage of college students (+).
11. Percentage of persons 21 years of age and over that completed high school, 1960 (+).
12. Average manufacturing capital investment, 1958 and 1963 (–).
13. Population density, 1960 (+).

The components of this factor are very similar to those included in the second factor of Table 9–4. That discussion is summarized and modified to account for the addition of four new variables. Earlier discussion emphasized the positive relationship between the variability in the level of per capita income and the variability in the actual and potential savings, human capital, the relative importance of a diversified economic structure consisting of a relatively greater share of national growth industries, and the degree of urbanization. The first factor of Table 9–5 includes four additional variables, two of which add a component of change to the earlier interpretation. These two variables are the

Table 9–5. Rotated Factor Matrix for the Rate of Growth of Total Personal Income, 1950–66: Far West Regional Grouping

	Factor 1	*Factor 2*	*Factor 3*	*Factor 4*	h^2
Rate of Growth of Total Personal Income, 1950–66	*.331*	*–.127*	*.910*	*.025*	*.954*
Economic Base, 1950	–.788	–.134	–.151	.164	.688
Percent Change in the Economic Base, 1950–67	.682	–.009	.496	–.198	.760
Index of the Composition of Growth Industries, 1960	.819	.013	.323	–.011	.776
Coefficient of Concentration, 1950	–.742	–.171	–.271	–.118	.667
Percent Change in the Coefficient of Concentration, 1950–60	.592	.072	.380	–.141	.520
Demand, Time and Savings Capital Deposits per Capita, 1960	.713	–.364	–.143	.187	.695
Ratio of Farms of 1000 Acres to Farms of 10 Acres, 1959	–.478	.393	.087	.361	.521
Ratio of Families that Earned $10,000 to Families that Earned $3,000, 1960	.661	–.454	.339	–.013	.758
Percent White Collar Employment	.786	.097	.293	.074	.719
Estimate of the Percent College Students	.828	.061	–.110	–.027	.702
Percent of Persons 21 Years of Age and Over that Completed High School, 1960	.720	.091	.240	–.327	.691
Average Manufacturing Capital Investment, 1958 and 1963	–.523	–.047	.010	.263	.345
Population Density, 1960	.720	–.381	–.001	.140	.683
Local Government Revenue per Capita, 1962	.040	–.951	.048	.177	.940
Property Tax per Capita, Average 1957 and 1962	.062	–.809	.013	.299	.748
Local Government Transfers per Capita	–.039	–.790	–.022	–.041	.629
Non-education Local Government Expenditures per Capita, 1962	.054	–.933	.160	.150	.922
Total Local Government Expenditures, per Capita, 1962	.099	–.940	.172	.173	.952
Average Local Government Bonds per Total Revenue, 1957 and 1962	.137	.638	–.030	.298	.516
Percent Change in Bond Investment, 1957–62	–.048	–.563	.206	–.177	.393
Rate of Increase in Residentiary Employment, 1950–60	.013	–.137	.921	.062	.871
Percent Change in the Labor Force Participation Rate, 1950–60	–.013	.429	.639	–.185	.627
Rate of Increase in Financial Deposits, 1950–64	.207	–.048	.946	–.042	.942

Manufacturing Productivity, 1958	.305	−.078	.495	.282	.424
Index of Voting Change, 1960–64	.143	−.027	.883	.012	.801
Percent Non-White Population, 1960	.189	−.213	.633	.325	.588
Net Migration Rate, 1950–60	.279	−.345	.785	.094	.822
Value of Land and Buildings per Farms, 1959	.085	−.123	.312	.810	.775
Output per Worker in Agriculture, 1959	−.152	−.162	−.017	.710	.554
Percent Change in Agriculture Output, 1950–64	.349	−.295	.095	.431	.388
Value of Crops per Total Agriculture Output, 1959	.186	−.104	−.241	.728	.634
Percent Tenant Farms, 1959	−.403	.128	−.152	.675	.657
Percent Voting, 1960	.309	−.178	−.402	−.612	.664
Percent of Persons 21 Years of Age and Over that Completed Less than 5 Years of School, 1960	−.367	.189	.174	.567	.522
Percent Change in Manufacturing Productivity, 1958–63	.213	−.034	.063	.188	.086
Percent Earnings from Manufacturing, 1960	.235	−.420	−.377	−.331	.483

percentage change in the economic base and the percentage change in the coefficient of concentration. Each of these variables is positively associated with the variables summarized earlier. Of the 26 OBE Economic Areas located in this regional grouping, only five have a positive change in the economic base between 1950 and 1967. The same thing can be said for changes in the degree of economic concentration, only five of the 26 areas experienced an increase in the degree of economic concentration between 1950 and 1960. Four OBE Areas (Seattle-Everett, Washington; Las Vegas, Nevada; San Diego, California, and San Francisco-Oakland, California) experienced an increase in both the economic base and the degree of economic concentration. In other words, four out of five areas that had an increase in one had an increase in the other. The reason for this should be apparent. Areas that expanded their exporting sectors become relatively more concentrated in these sectors. However, each of these measures must be addressed by considering the extent to which areas experienced a rise or a fall in either measure. In general, the greater the increase or the lesser the decrease in the economic base, the greater the increase or the smaller the decrease in the degree of economic concentration.[1]

Therefore, this factor is interpreted as representing the variability in the growth of the economic base and those related forces. Associated to the growth (or small decline) in the economic base is the relative importance of national growth industries, relatively greater stock of social overhead capital, actual and potential savings, and human capital. It is also noted that such areas are likely to have an increase or a smaller decrease in the degree of economic concentration.[2]

The Second Factor

The second factor of Table 9–5 includes seven variables and explains 1.7 percent of the total explained variance in the rates of growth of total personal income:

1. Local government revenue per capita, 1962.
2. Property tax per capita, average 1957 and 1962.
3. Local government transfers per capita, 1962.
4. Non-education local government expenditures per capita, 1962.
5. Total local government expenditures per capita, 1962.
6. Average bonds per total local government revenue, 1957 and 1962.
7. Percentage of change in local government bond investment, 1957–62.

All variables, except the ratio of local government bonds to total local government revenue, are positively related to each other and to the rate of growth of total personal income. The variables included in this factor are nearly identical to those included in the first factor of Table 9–4. The only variable added to those included in the first factor of Table 9–4 is the percentage change in bond investment.[3]

The interpretation assigned to these variables in the discussion above emphasized the relatively high association between the level of per capita income (the dependent variable of Table 9–4) and the variations in the stock of social overhead capital provided by the local governments. However, this variation is not related to the variations in the rates of growth of total personal income of the OBE Economic Areas in the Far West Regional Grouping.

The Third Factor

The third factor consists of seven variables which are positively related to each other and the rate of growth of total personal income and explain 87 percent of the total explained variance in the rate of growth of total personal income:

1. Rate of increase in residentiary employment, 1950–60.
2. Rate of increase in financial deposits, 1950–64.
3. Manufacturing productivity, 1958.
4. Net migration rate, 1950–60.
5. Percentage of change in the labor force participation rate, 1950–60.
6. Percentage of non-white population, 1960.
7. Index of voting change, 1960–64.

This factor is interpreted as representing the high association between the growth of total economic activity and growth in the supplies of labor and financial capital. In addition, these areas are characterized as having a relatively greater stock of capital in the manufacturing sector. The primary interpretation of this factor focuses on the rate of increase in residentiary employment.[4] In-migration and relative increases in the labor force participation rate acted to increase the supply of labor. Most likely the percentage of non-white population is associated with the net in-migration of black or Spanish-speaking persons from other areas of the United States. The inclusion of manufacturing productivity in the factor is interpreted as representing the positive relationship between the rates of growth of total personal income and the stock of manufacturing capital investment. Finally, the rate of increase in financial deposits per capita represents the increase in financial capital available.[5]

Therefore, this factor is interpreted as representing the high degree of positive association between the variations in the growth rates of residentiary employment and the variations in the growth of total economic activity of the OBE Economic Areas in the Far West Regional Grouping. Associated with the growth of the residentiary sector are increases in the labor supply and financial capital, and a greater stock of manufacturing investment.

The Fourth Factor

The fourth factor contains seven variables; however, it is not related to the rates of growth of total personal income:

1. Value of land and buildings per farms, 1959.
2. Output per worker in agriculture, 1959.
3. Percentage of change in agricultural output, 1950–64.
4. Value of crops per total agricultural output, 1959.
5. Percentage of tenant farms, 1959.
6. Percentage voting, 1960.
7. Percentage of persons 21 years of age and over that completed less than five years of school.

All of the variables, except the percent voting, are positively related to each other. The first five variables are measures of the capital investment in agriculture, agricultural productivity, growth in agricultural output, production orientation toward the most rapidly growing agricultural sector and the ownership characteristic of the agricultural sector. In short, these measures are representative of large scale, capital intensive, commercial agriculture. The variability in these measures across the OBE Economic Areas is not, however, associated with the rates of growth of total personal income.

Also positively associated with these variables is the percent of persons 21 years of age and over that completed less than five years of school. Negatively associated with agricultural variables is the measure of community involvement. Therefore, this factor is interpreted as representing the generally lower level of educational achievement and community involvement in the capital intensive, commercial agricultural OBE Economic Areas in this regional grouping. The variations of these measures is not, however, associated with the variations in the rates of growth of total personal income.

SHORT TERM ECONOMIC GROWTH: SUMMARY

The four factors of Table 9–5 explain 95.4 percent of the variance in the rates of growth of total personal income of the OBE Economic Areas of the Far West Regional Grouping. However, 98 percent of the explained variance is explained by the first and third factors. The first factor summarizes the contribution made to increasing the rates of growth of total personal income by the growth of the economic base, while the third factor summarizes the contributions made by the growth of the residentiary sector. Related to the growth in the economic base is a relatively greater abundance of skilled human capital actual and potential savings, the relative importance of a diversified economic structure consisting of a greater share of national growth industries and a greater degree of urbanization. Associated with the growth of the residentiary sector are increases in the labor supply and financial capital and a greater stock of manufacturing investment.

GROWTH IN PER CAPITA INCOME: 1950–66

The factor analysis accepted to describe changes in the average level of welfare, using the average annual rate of growth of per capita income as the dependent variable, is presented in Table 9–6. Only 37.7 percent of the variance in the rate of growth of per capita income is explained by the four factors. Increasing the number of factors to explain the variance in the rates of growth of per capita personal income increases the explained variance by 14 percent. The use of this rotated factor matrix is rejected because most variables are equally related to more than one factor. In addition, the factor that explains the greatest part of the variance in the rates of growth of per capita income cannot be defined in terms of a meaningful dimension. This factor, which explained 26.2 percent of the variance included the following variables:

1. The economic base in 1950 (negatively related to the dependent variable.
2. The percentage of change in agricultural output, 1950–64 (positively related).
3. The ratio of farms of 1,000 acres to farms of 10 acres, 1964 (negatively related.
4. The average manufacturing capital investment (negatively related).

Based on this, the rotated matrix with four factors was accepted rather than the five factor matrix at the cost of a much lower level of explained variance.

As stated above, the four factors of Table 9–6 explain only 37.7 percent of the variance in the rates of growth of per capita income of the OBE Economic Areas in the Far West Regional Grouping over the period 1950–66. Each of the first three factors explain roughly one-third of the total explained variance. Although the amount of explained variance is very low, a trend unique to this regional grouping is found: The two factors that explain the variance in the rates of growth of total personal income are related in the same direction to the rates of growth of per capita income. In other words, forces associated with the pattern of economic growth are also related in the same way to changes in the average level of welfare. In no other regional grouping is this found to be true.

The first factor, discussed above as reflecting the variations in the percentage of change in the economic base and related forces across the OBE Economic Areas in the Far West Regional Grouping, explains roughly one-third of the explained variance in the rates of growth of per capita income. The third factor, representing the variations in the rates of growth of the residentiary sectors and related forces, also explains roughly one-third of the total explained variance in the rates of growth of per capita income.

The second factor of Table 9–6 also explains roughly one-third of the variance in the rates of growth of per capita income. However, this factor is

Table 9–6. Rotated Factor Matrix for the Rate of Growth of Per Capita Personal Income, 1950–66: Far West Regional Grouping

	Factor 1	Factor 2	Factor 3	Factor 4	h^2
Rate of Growth of Per Capita Personal Income	.379	.331	.351	–.001	.377
Economic Base, 1950	–.812	–.162	–.142	.145	.727
Percent Change in the Economic Base, 1950–67	.700	–.102	.480	–.189	.767
Index of the Composition of Growth Industries, 1960	.826	.008	.298	.001	.771
Coefficient of Concentration, 1950	–.732	–.152	–.261	–.118	.641
Percent Change in the Coefficient of Concentration, 1950–60	.580	–.112	.354	–.145	.495
Demand, Time and Savings Capital Deposits per Capita, 1960	.702	–.360	–.153	.195	.684
Ratio of Farms of 1000 Acres to Farms of 10 Acres, 1959	–.503	.368	.122	.333	.514
Ratio of Families that Earned $10,000 to Families that Earned $3,000, 1960	.659	–.472	.318	–.010	.759
Percent White Collar Employment	.792	.098	.281	.083	.723
Estimate of the Percent College Students	.821	.059	–.135	–.014	.696
Percent of Persons 21 Years of Age and Over that Completed High School, 1960	.725	.080	.221	–.323	.685
Local Government Revenue per Capita, 1962	–.536	–.057	.035	.245	.352
Property Tax per Capita, Average 1957 and 1962	.722	–.371	–.018	.156	.683
Local Government Transfers per Capita	.046	–.946	.037	.187	.933
Property Tax per Capita, Average 1957 and 1962	.058	–.809	.003	.304	.751
Local Government Transfers per Capita	–.026	–.778	–.034	–.027	.609
Non-education Local Government Expenditures per Capita, 1962	.062	–.931	.149	.158	.917
Total Local Government Expenditures, per Capita, 1962	.106	–.938	.159	.181	.950
Average Local Government Bonds per Total Revenue, 1957 and 1962	.127	.641	–.019	.292	.513
Percent Change in Bond Investment, 1957–62	–.038	–.569	.196	–.174	.394
Rate of Increase in Residentiary Employment, 1950–60	.038	–.152	.908	.059	.853
Percent Change in the Labor Force Participation Rate, 1950–60	.010	.424	.655	–.191	.646
Rate of Increase in Financial Deposits, 1950–64	.232	–.066	.936	–.045	.935

Manufacturing Productivity, 1958	.306	−.090	.498	.275	.425
Index of Voting Change, 1960–64	.155	−.058	.871	.005	.785
Percent Non-White Population, 1960	.220	−.193	.639	.335	.606
Net Migration Rate, 1950–60	.294	−.364	.759	.095	.804
Value of Land and Buildings per Farms, 1959	.076	−.128	.305	.811	.772
Output per Worker in Agriculture, 1959	−.165	.162	−.021	.711	.559
Percent Change in Agriculture Output, 1950–64	.363	−.272	.067	.437	.401
Value of Crops per Total Agriculture Output, 1959	.175	−.085	−.250	.739	.646
Percent Tenant Farms, 1959	−.420	.184	−.130	.662	.650
Percent Voting, 1960	.321	−.158	−.414	−.597	.656
Percent of Persons 21 Years of Age and Over that Completed Less than 5 Years of School, 1960	−.360	.205	.198	.566	.531
Percent Change in Manufacturing Productivity, 1958–63	.205	−.041	.063	−.186	.082
Percent Earnings from Manufacturing, 1960	.218	−.436	−.409	.325	.510

not related to the rates of growth of total personal income. It is interpreted as representative of the variations in the stock of social overhead capital provided by local governments. These measures are, as is shown in Table 9–6, negatively related to the rates of growth of per capita income. However, it appears that the relationship described by this factor is much weaker than is evident. The simple correlations between each of the variables included in this factor and the rate of growth in per capita income is statistically insignificant at the 90 percent confidence interval. It cannot, therefore be argued that the cluster of variables included in the second factor is truely related to the rate of growth of per capita income.

The forces described by the first and third factors must be relied upon in explaining the change in the average level of welfare. The reason for the similarity between the pattern of economic growth and pattern of change in the average level of welfare appears to result from the ability of the OBE Economic Areas in this regional grouping to attract migrants of higher socioeconomic levels. The result of the in-migration does not act to lower the average level of per capita income while increasing the level of total personal income, as was found to be the case elsewhere. This conclusion needs more indepth analysis than is possible here before it can be stated with any great degree of certainty.

In summary, the results of this analysis explain a very small part of the variance in the rates of growth of per capita income. Two sets of forces, growth in the economic base and growth in residentiary employment, contribute equally in explaining this variance.

Chapter Ten

Findings: Comparative Analysis of Important Variables

INTRODUCTION

This chapter discusses the findings of this study from a comparative viewpoint. The results obtained in the analysis of the regional grouping are reorganized so that comparisons of the patterns of economic change can be discussed. Along with the analysis presented earlier for each regional grouping, this chapter serves as the basis for conclusions presented in Chapter 11. It defines the pattern of growth and development in terms of the components that are common to all regional groupings and, similarly, distinguishes the forces that are relatively more critical in selective regional groupings.

There is little doubt that this study leaves many questions unanswered. However, much like Morris and Adelman's *Society, Politics and Economic Development,* the study provides a new way in which to view the broad and complicated patterns of economic growth and development. From this viewpoint, an attempt is made to include as many components of the patterns of growth and development as this study and the literature deem important. There are a number of important omissions. These resulted either from data limitation or failure to recognize these forces; however, these omissions have been minimized to the extent possible.

The findings of this study are discussed in terms of the four major analyses completed for each of the regional groupings:

1. The export base model.
2. The long term pattern of economic development.
3. Short term economic growth (growth in total personal income), 1950–66.
4. Short term growth in the average level of economic welfare (growth in per capita income), 1950–60.

FINDINGS: EXPORT BASE MODEL

The results are consistent with the major hypotheses of the export base model for three of the four regional groupings. Only the results of testing the model for the Northeastern Regional Grouping proved inconsistent with the model. It is difficult to compare the strengths of the model for the three regions in which the model was not rejected. However, only in the Central Regional Grouping were both the change in the export base and the coefficient of concentration statistically significant independent variables when regressed on the rate of growth of total personal income. The equation including these two variables (8.1) explained 53 percent of the variance in the rates of growth of total personal income of the OBE Economic Areas in the Central Regional Grouping. This was the highest explained variance for the first equation (4.1) for any of the regional groupings.

The coefficient of concentration included in the first equation is intended to be a measure of the potential income multiplier effects initiated by the growth in export income. This hypothesis is rejected for each of the regional groupings except the Central Regional Grouping. However, when this variable is eliminated in the models for the Southeastern and Far West Regional Groupings, the beta coefficient on the change in the export base assumes a relatively high value.[1] It is concluded from this that a percentage increase in the economic base in the Southeastern and Far Western Regional Groupings is associated with a greater increase in the average annual rate of increase in total personal income than would be the case for the Central Regional Grouping.

The equation explaining income growth in the model for the Central Regional Grouping has the higher coefficient of determination but the lower beta coefficient on the change in the economic base. Therefore, comparative conclusions concerning the strength of the economic base hypothesis between these regional groupings cannot be drawn. However, it can be stated that the model, as applied to the Central Regional Grouping, has the best predictive power and is consistent with the specified functional relationship.

A general finding with regard to the association between the change in the economic base and the rate of growth of total personal income must be reiterated. Although there is the expected positive relationship between these two variables, the vast majority of the OBE Economic Areas in the three regional groupings experienced a decline in the economic base, as defined in this study, between 1950 and 1967. In the cases of the Southeastern and Central Regional Groupings this trend is attributed to the large declines in the relative importance of agriculture, an export commodity in all regional groupings. In the case of the Far West it appears that the decline in the economic base likely resulted from rapid increases in residentiary employment. Rapid increases in the residentiary sectors would cause the decline in the ratio of exports to total production, or the decline in the export base. Therefore, further explanation is needed since it is still argued that the results obtained for these three regional groupings are consistent with the specified relationship. For the first two cases the change must be interpreted in the economic base in terms of absorption of less viable primary exports by more viable export sectors, possibly national growth industries. In most cases the positive association between the two variables is an association between a relatively smaller decline in base and a relatively higher rate of growth of total personal income. For the Far West Regional groupings the decline in base cannot be interpreted in the same terms because the same problem of absorption of large declines in the primary sectors does not exist. The Far West Regional Grouping experienced an average annual rate of increase in residentiary employment of 3.8 percent between 1950 and 1960. This compares with a 2.5 percent average annual rate of increase for the Southeastern Regional Grouping which is the next highest in this category. This rapid increase in residentiary employment most likely caused the decline in the economic base in 21 of the 26 OBE Economic Areas in this regional grouping. This cannot be interpreted as refuting the export base hypothesis, for it may very well be that where changes in the export base were positive, or declines relatively small, greater stimulus was generated by increased export income on the residentiary sector. This interpretation is consistent with the results as well as with the concept of the export base as presented in Chapter 4.

The second equation of the economic base mode (4.2) specifies that the change in the economic base is a function of the degree to which the area's productive structure was oriented toward growth industries and the development of the area's social infrastructure. This rejects the importance of the development of the social infrastructure, measured by the non-educational local government expenditures per capita, in all regional groupings except the Southeastern. The reason for the failure is most likely a result of the indirect measure. Although there is precedent for its use as a measure of public infrastructure, the value of non-education local government expenditures per capita appears to be an invalid estimator of public infrastructure as it was used here.

In each of the regional groupings, with the exception of the Northeastern, the expected relationship between the change in the economic base and the index of the composition of growth industries is consistent with the results. However, the amount of the explained variance in the change in the economic base is relatively low. This is not surprising nor inconsistent with the *a priori* reasoning. In Chapter 4 it is argued that, considering the change in the economic base, there must be concern for the industrial mix of the area. An important component in the industrial mix is considered to be national growth industries. It cannot be alleged that the orientation of the industrial mix toward rapid growth industries "explains" the change in the economic base. It can be stated, however, based on the results obtained, that the orientation of an area's productive structure toward national growth industries is positively associated with changes in the economic base.

ECONOMIC BASE MODEL: COMPARATIVE ANALYSIS

In no regional grouping are the results totally consistent with the specified relationships. In the case of the Northeastern Regional Grouping, the model is simply rejected. In the cases of the other three regional groupings, modifications of the specified relationships is necessary to obtain statistically significant regression equations. In each case the modifications are made by eliminating the statistically insignificant variables from the equations and re-estimating the function.

However, once these modifications are made in the model for the Southeastern, Central, and Far West Regional Groupings, the major hypotheses of the model remain consistent with the tests. These relationships are:

1. Growth in total personal income as a function of the growth in the economic base.
2. Growth in the economic base as a function of the index of the composition of growth industries.

FINDINGS: LONG TERM ECONOMIC DEVELOPMENT

The findings are restricted to those groups of variables, or factors, that explain at least 15 percent of the variance in the levels of per capita income in the regional groupings. In other words, those forces are relatively important components of the long term pattern of economic development in each of the regional groupings. Forces found not to be relatively important in explaining the variance of the levels of per capita income are not reported here. Readers are referred to Chapters 6–9 for a discussion of them.

"Relatively important" components of the pattern of long term development, as this term is to be used here, must be defined. This study is based on analysis of variance, and therefore variables, or factors, that are relatively important have been those that have explained the greater part of the explained variance. Thus, variables, or factors, that are critical to the success or failure of long term development cannot be determined solely through the use of regression or factor analysis. The variables must show significant variation between the various OBE Economic Areas within the regional groupings in order for these statistical techniques to identify variables as relatively important components of the pattern of long term development.

The results of the factor analyses, using the level of per capita income for each regional grouping, are summarized in Table 10–1. This table presents the composition of each factor that explains at least 15 percent of the variance of the level of per capita income in each regional grouping. The factor

Table 10–1. Variables Included in Factors That Explain 15 Percent or More of the Variance in the Levels of Per Capita Income by Regional Grouping

Regional Grouping	*Southeastern*		*Northeastern*	*Central*	*Far West*		*Number of Regional Groupings*
Factor Loading on Per Capita Income	*.713*	*.499*	*.875*	*.950*	*.672*	*.504*	
Financial Deposits per Capita, 1960	+		+	+		+	4
Ratio of Families with Income of $10,000 to $3,000, 1960	+		+	+		+	4
Index of the Composition of Growth Industries		+	+	+		+	4
Percent White Collar Employment, 1960		+	+	+		+	4
Local Government Revenue Per Capita, 1962	+		+		+		3
Average Property Tax Per Capita, 1957 and 1962	+		+		+		3
Non-education Gov. Expenditures Per Capita, 1962	+		+		+		3
Total Local Gov. Expenditures Per Capita, 1962	+		+		+		3
Average Bonds Per Total Revenue, 1962	+			+	−		3
Percent High School Graduates, 1960	+			+		+	3
Coefficient of Concentration, 1960		−		−		−	3
Manufacturing Productivity, 1958	+			+			2
Government Transfers Per Capita, 1962			+		+		2
Economic Base, 1959		−				−	2
Population Density			+			+	2
Value of Land and Buildings Per Farm, 1959	+						1
Output Per Worker in Agriculture, 1960	+						1
Value of Crops per Total Agriculture Output, 1959		−					1
Persons Completing Less Than 5 Years of School, 1960		−					1
Percent Tenant Farms, 1959		−					1
Estimate of the Percent College Students						+	1

analyses for the Southeastern and Far West Regional Groupings have two factors that meet this criteria, while the Northeastern and Central Regional Groupings have one factor. The factor loading of each of these factors on the level of per capita income and the sign of the factor loading for each variable is also reported. The final column summarizes the number of regional groupings in which each variable appears in one of these factors.

Of the 27 variables included in each of these runs, 21 variables appear in at least a factor that meets the criteria. Four variables appear in one of these factors in each regional grouping:

1. Financial deposits per capita.
2. Ratio of families that earned $10,000 or more to families that earned $3,000 or less.
3. Index of the composition of growth industries.
4. Percent white collar employment.

Seven of the 27 variables appear in a factor that meets the criteria in three regional groupings. Three additional variables appear in a factor that meets the criteria in two regional groupings.

It is apparent from the summary table that the pattern of long term economic development in each regional grouping must be defined with a separate set of variables. Yet there are similarities. Most noteworthy are the four variables reported above that are included in a relatively important factor for each regional grouping. However, two, and possibly three, of these variables must be interpreted in terms of cause and effect. Financial deposits per capita and the ratio of families that earned $10,000 or more to families that earned $3,000 or less should be highly correlated with the level of per capita income. This might also be expected to be the case for the percentage of white collar employment since these are relatively higher paying occupations. These restrictions are less important in the case of the fourth variable, the index of the composition of growth industries.

Seven of the variables reported in Table 10–1 are included in relatively important factors in three regional groupings. This group of variables include the five variables designed to measure the revenue sources and expenditure pattern of local governments, the percentage of persons 21 years of age and over that completed high school, and the coefficient of concentration. The signs of the factor loadings of each of these variables are as expected for all regional groupings. The variability in the measures of government revenue and expenditures, the measure of the quantity of education, and the measures of the accumulated stocks of social overhead and human capital are positively associated with the level of per capita income. The negative sign on the factor loadings on the coefficient of concentration in each of the three regional groupings is consistent with the hypothesis that economic diversification of production increases with the level of economic development. Only in the Northeastern Regional Grouping is this variable not included in a relatively important factor. However, in 1960, the Northeastern Regional Grouping was, on the average, the most economically diversified of all the regional groupings. This finding demonstrates the importance of an earlier statement. That is, variance analysis, which in this case is factor analysis, does not select a variable as being a relatively important explanatory variable if it does not show significant variation. Therefore, it is likely that the degree of economic diversity is a relatively important force in the long term economic development of each regional grouping, but because most of the OBE Economic Areas in the Northeastern Regional Grouping had achieved a relatively high level of economic diversity by 1960, this variable does not distinguish itself.

The following four variables appeared in relatively important factors in two regional groupings:

1. Manufacturing productivity.
2. Government transfers per capita.
3. Economic base.
4. Population density.

Government transfers per capita and population density appear in factors of the Northeastern and Far West Regional Groupings. These two regional groupings were the most developed (highest levels of per capita income) in 1959. They were also the most urbanized. The flow of Federal Government revenue to urban areas reflects the greater relative need of urban areas for revenue. These two variables, therefore, must be interpreted as representing the relative importance of urbanization. Manufacturing productivity appears in relatively important factors in the long term analysis of the Southeastern and Central Regional Groupings. These two are the lowest in terms of the 1959 level of per capita income. The distinguishing characteristic of this variable in these two regional groupings is likely a result of the same characteristic, as is true for the degree of economic diversity discussed above. The average productivity estimates for the OBE Economic Areas in the Northeastern and Far West Regional Groupings are higher than those for the Southeastern and Central Regional Groupings. This variable is identified for these two regional groupings because it is an identifying characteristic of higher per capita income areas in these regional groupings. Thus, it is likely an equally important characteristic for the more developed Northeastern and Far West Regional Groupings. But, in these cases, it is a more universal characteristic of the OBE Economic Areas in these regional groupings and does not explain a significant part of the variation in the level of per capita incomes in these regional groupings.

Six variables appeared in a relatively important factor in a single regional grouping and are presented in Table 10–1.

Discussion of the long term development patterns presented in the four previous chapters are synthesized in the conclusions. The findings presented here are consistent with the hypothesis that the patterns of economic growth and development are best seen from a regional viewpoint. These results show that the distinguishing characteristics of regional long term development vary—despite some similarities—between the regional groupings. The comparative analysis presented here is merged with the analysis of long term economic growth (Chapters 6 through 10) in the conclusions in Chapter 11.

FINDINGS: SHORT TERM ECONOMIC GROWTH 1950–66

The comparative analysis of the variables entering into important factors explaining the patterns of short term economic growth is subject to the same constraints discussed for the long term development analysis. The 15 percent of explained variance by factors is also used to determine the relatively important factors and factor components, or variables. This criterion requires that variables discussed in this section are included in factors that explain at least 15 percent of the variance in the rates of growth of total personal income of the OBE Economic Areas in the four regional groupings. In this case, only one factor meets this criterion for each regional grouping. Table 10–2 presents these variables and signs of the factor loadings. Of the 36 variables included in each of the factor analysis runs to explain the variance in the rates of growth of total personal income, 18 variables are included in at least one relatively important factor for some regional grouping. Three of the 18 variables appear in the relatively important factor in each regional grouping. Thirteen of the 18 variables, however, appear in a relatively important factor in either one or two regional groupings.

There is significant similarity between the variables included in the factors for the Northeast and Far West Regional Groupings. There is also similarity between those included in the factors for the Central and Southeastern Regional Groupings. The factor of the Central Regional Grouping includes the greater number of variables. Thirteen variables are included in the relatively important factor of the Central Regional Grouping, compared to seven for the Northeastern and six for the Southeastern and Far West Regional Groupings.

The three variables included in the relatively important factor in each regional grouping are:

1. Rate of increase in residentiary employment.
2. Rate of increase in financial deposits.
3. Net migration rate.

Each of these variables are characterized as strongly economic growth oriented. It is to be expected that each of these variables is closely associated with growth

Table 10–2. Variables Included in Factors That Explained 15 Percent or More of the Variance in the Rate of Growth of Total Personal Income by Regional Grouping

Regional Grouping	*Southeastern*	*Northeastern*	*Central*	*Far West*	*Number of Regional Groupings*
Factor Loading on the Rate of Increase in Total Personal Income	*.832*	*.787*	*.811*	*.910*	
Rate of Increase of Residentiary Employment, 1950–60	+	+	+	+	4
Rate of Increase in Financial Deposits, 1950–64	+	+	+	+	4
Net Migration Rate, 1950–60	+	+	+	+	4
Index of the Composition of Growth Industries, 1960	+	+	+		3
Percent Change in the Economic Base, 1950–67	+		+		2
Percent Change in the Labor Force Participation Rate, 1950–60		–		+	2
Manufacturing Productivity, 1958		+		+	2
Percent Non-White Population, 1960		+		+	2
Percent Change in Agricultural Output, 1950–64	+				1
Economic Base, 1950			–		1
Coefficient of Concentration, 1950			–		1
Percent Change in the Coefficient of Concentration, 1950–60			+		1
Financial Deposits per Capita, 1960			+		1
Ratio of Families that Earned $10,000 to $3,000, 1960			+		1
Percent White Collar Employment, 1960			+		1
Population Density, 1960			+		1
Percent Earnings from Manufacturing, 1959			+		1
Index of Voting Change,				+	1

Index of Voting Change, 1960–64

in the total level of economic activity. The rate of growth of residentiary employment measures the average annual rate of employment growth (1950–60) in selected industries that produce goods and services for the local market. The association between employment growth and in-migration has been discussed. Similarly, financial deposits per capita should increase as the total level of economic activity increases. Each variable, therefore, characterizes an important aspect of the pattern of economic growth.

Only one variable appears in the relatively important factor of three regional groupings. This is the index of the composition of growth industries. This variable does not appear in the factor for the Far West Regional Grouping. Yet the average of this index for the Far West Regional Grouping is higher than the average of the index for the Southeastern and Central Regional Groupings. Failure of this index to be included in this factor cannot be attributed to the lack of variation of the variable between the OBE Areas in this regional grouping.[2] Therefore, it must be concluded that the extent of growth industries in the Far West Regional Grouping is not as important as it is in the other regional groupings.

The following four variables are included in the relatively important factors in two regional groupings:

1. Percentage of change in the economic base.
2. Manufacturing productivity.
3. Percentage of non-white population.
4. Percentage of change in the labor force participation rate.

The percentage of change in the economic base is included in the relatively important factors for the Southeastern and Central regional groupings. The three remaining variables are included in the relatively important factor for the Northeastern and Far West Regional Groupings. However, the signs of the factor loadings on the percent change in the labor force participation rate are opposite in the two regional groupings. This reflects a very different type of interaction between this variable and the other variables included in the factors of the two regional groupings. In the Northeastern Regional Grouping, 41 of the 46 (89 percent) of the OBE Areas experienced a decline in the labor force participation rate between 1950 and 1960. This was true for only 12 of the 26 (46 percent) of the OBE Areas located in the Far West Regional Grouping. Therefore, the negative influence evidenced by the negative factor loading on this variable for the Northeastern Regional Grouping results from the general overall decline in this rate. Since this does not occur in the OBE Areas located in the Far West Regional Grouping, the expected positive association with the growth in total personal income is found to be true.

Eight of the 10 variables that are included in only one relatively important factor are included in that factor for the Central Regional Grouping.

The importance of these variables is discussed in Chapter 8 and returned to in the conclusions.

This short comparative analysis demonstrates that there are important similarities between the short term patterns of economic growth of the regional groupings. In addition, it also shows that there are unique components of the pattern for each regional grouping. It is, therefore, consistent with the hypothesis that a better understanding of the growth patterns can be gained from a regional viewpoint. Discussion of the short term growth patterns of the regional groupings are presented in the previous chapters. A synthesis of the comparative approach taken here with the analysis of the patterns for each regional grouping is presented in the conclusions.

FINDINGS: GROWTH IN PER CAPITA INCOME: 1950–66

The percentage of the variance in the rates of increase in per capita income explained by the factor analysis for each regional grouping is relatively low. It is argued in Chapter 4 that growth in per capita income is a function of the interaction of variables that respond primarily to growth in total personal income. In other words, the trends in per capita income growth are basically a function of the trend in total personal income growth. This cannot be stated conversely.

The importance of the above arguments becomes apparent when the components of the relatively important factors that explain at least 15 percent of the variance in the rates of growth of per capita income are analyzed. For the most part, they lack sound economic basis. In fact, in the factor analysis, using the rate of growth of per capita income as the variable to be explained for the Far West Regional Grouping, no factor meets the criterion of 15 percent of variance explained. More dramatically, in the relatively important factor in this analysis for the Southeastern Regional Grouping, all but three of the 16 included variables have factor loadings that are not consistent with the *a priori* reasoning.

This is the case for each of the regional groupings. Table 10–3 presents a summary of the variables included in the factors that meet the criterion of 15 percent of variance explained in each of the regional groupings. One factor meets this criterion for the Southeastern and Central Regional Groupings; two factors for the Northeastern Regional Grouping. As stated above, no factor meets the criterion in the analysis of the Far West Regional Grouping.

The findings of analysis of growth in the average level of per capita income is presented more simply than those of the analysis of long term development and the analysis of short term growth. A comparative analysis of variables is not presented. To do so would result in repeated statements of the general findings that can now be drawn.

The finding that growth in per capita income over the period 1950–66 is negatively associated with the level of per capita income was to be expected.

Table 10–3. Variables Included in Factor That Explained 15 Percent or More of the Variance in the Rates of Growth of Per Capita Income by Regional Grouping

Regional Grouping	*Southeastern*	*Northeastern*		*Central*	*Far West*	*Number of Regional Groupings*
Factor Loading on the Rate of Increase in Per Capita Income	*.686*	*.427*	*–.414*	*.731*	–	
Manufacturing Productivity, 1958	–		+	–		3
Coefficient of Concentration, 1950	–	+				2
Percent Change in the Coefficient of Concentration, 1950–60	–	–				2
Value of Land & Buildings per Farm, 1959	–			–		2
Output per Worker in Agriculture, 1959	–			–		2
Total Local Gov. Expenditures per Capita, 1962	–	–				
Percent of Persons Completing High School, 1960	–	+				2
Economic Base, 1950	+					1
Financial Deposits per Capita, 1960	–					1
Ratio of Farms of 1,000 Acres to 10 Acres, 1959	–					1
Government Revenue Per Capita, 1962	–					1
Property Tax Per Capita, 1962	–					1
Non-education Government Expenditures per Capita, 1962	–					1
Average Bonds Outstanding per Local Government Revenue, 1957 and 1962	–					1
Families with Incomes of $10,000 to $3,000, 1960	–					1
Percent White Collar Employment, 1960	–					1
Estimate of the Percent College Students, 1960		+				1
Percent of Persons Completing Less than 5 Years of School, 1960		–				1
Rate of Increase in Residentiary Employment, 1950–60			+			1
Index of the Composition of Growth Industries, 1960			+			1
Rate of Growth of Financial Deposits, 1950–64			+			1

Percent Non-White Population, 1960	+		1
Percent Change in the Labor Force Participation Rate, 1950–60	–		1
Migration Rate	+		1
Value of Crops Per Total Agricultural Output, 1959		–	1
Percent Tenant Farms, 1959		–	1
Percent Earnings from Manufacturing, 1959		+	1
Percent Change in Bond Investment, 1957–62		+	1

However, the strength of this relationship exerted a much stronger influence on the results of this aspect of the study than was anticipated. This association is very evident in the results of the factor analysis of each regional grouping. This argument is presented in Chapter 4. Relatively high levels of per capita income influence the growth rates of per capita income in two primary ways. First, areas with relatively higher levels of per capita income, which are often the more urban areas, attract in-migrants. The in-migrants, often unemployed and searching for work, generally are characterized as persons in the lower income brackets. They tend to lower the average level of per capita income or the growth rate of per capita income. In-migration positively affects the rate of increase of per capita income only if the income earned by these in-migrants is greater than average per capita income of the area, plus the average increment in income gained by the population over the period in which the rate of increase of per capita income is measured. It is found that this does not generally occur.

Second, the level of per capita income may influence the growth rate of per capita income because of the statistical properties of growth rates involved. Areas with relatively higher levels of per capita income must achieve relatively larger absolute increments of income to maintain equal growth rates of per capita income with areas that have relatively lower levels. This points out the need for another way in which to view short term economic development; by using as the variable to be explained, or as the dependent variable, the absolute increase in per capita income. Unfortunately, this was outside the scope of this study.

The findings of the factor analyses are summarized using the rate of growth of per capita income by emphasizing the critical influence that migration has on the growth of this dependent variable. The variations in the rates of growth of per capita income is negatively related to the variations in the rates of in-migration. The only regional grouping in which it does not appear is the Far West Regional Grouping. As stated in Chapter 9, the Far West Regional Grouping is able to attract more migrants in higher income categories than the other regional groupings.

Chapter Eleven

Summary of Findings and Conclusions

INTRODUCTION

This study attempts to present a balanced view of regional development in the continental United States. The use of the OBE Economic Areas as the spatial units of analysis, the relatively large data file, and the approach enable analysis of regional development from an original and more comprehensive viewpoint than has been accomplished to date.

The conclusions in this chapter result from the synthesis of the analysis completed for each regional grouping and the results of the comparative analysis of variables presented in Chapter 10. Support for the conclusions is presented in detail in the previous five chapters, and therefore it is only summarized in this chapter. The conclusions are organized according to the four major analyses completed for each regional grouping are general in nature and based on the results for the regional groupings used in this study.

SUMMARY OF FINDINGS AND CONCLUSIONS: EXPORT BASE MODEL

Based on the findings presented in Chapter 10, the following conclusions can be drawn:

1. The importance of growth in the export base in determining the rate of growth of total personal income decreases as the level of economic development increases.
2. At higher levels of economic development neither the proportion of, or the change in the proportion of, export income to total income is associated with higher rates of growth. This may imply a form of relatively balanced growth in exporting and residentiary sectors.

The tests of the export base model for the Northeastern Regional Grouping was not consistent with the hypotheses specified in Chapter 4. In the cases of the other three regional groupings most of the statistical tests were consistent with the expected results. However, the percent change in the economic base was included in a relatively important factor in the analyses using the rate of growth of total personal income as the variable to be explained for only the Southeastern and Central Regional Groupings. This provides the basis for the conclusion that the export base theory is most applicable to areas that are lower on the scale of development used in this study. This is, if fact, consistent with the basic logic expressed by export base theory. To restate briefly, export base theory emphasizes the iterative income multipliers that are initiated by increased flows of income from exports. It is the areas that lack the relatively developed economic structure that would conceivably benefit most from export income. On the opposite end of the scale of development, the Northeastern Regional Grouping, the tests of the economic base model were found to be inconsistent with expectations. In this case, no relationship was found between the variability in the rates of growth of total personal income and the variability in the percent change in the economic base.

The Far West Regional Grouping represents what may be considered as an intermediary stage between significant importance and relatively minor importance of the growth in the economic base. In general, this regional grouping is characterized by OBE Economic Areas that are ranked in the upper quartiles of per capita income levels. In terms of the growth in total personal income, this regional grouping has been growing the fastest of all the regional groupings. The tests of the export base model were found to be consistent with the *a priori* hypotheses, yet the change in the export base did not appear in the relatively important factor explaining the variance of the rates of growth of total personal income. However, the percent change in the export base between 1950 and 1967 explained 46 percent of the variance in the average annual rates of growth of total personal income over the period 1950–66. The explanation of this seemingly inconsistent result is that, although not located in this factor, the percent change in the export base is associated with the factor and the influences exerted by export growth do exist in this regional grouping. The partial correlation of this variable on the relatively important factor is approximately .5. In the analysis of the variability in the rates of growth of total personal income in the Far West Regional Grouping, forces associated with both growth in residentiary employment and change in the economic base were found to be important.

From these results it may be summarized that the association between the variability in the rates of growth of total personal income and the variability in the percent change in the economic base were most closely associated in the Southeastern and Central Regional Groupings. It may also be stated that the variability between these variables was associated, but to a lesser extent when other variables were brought into the analysis, in the Far West Regional Grouping. Finally, in the case of the Northeastern Regional Grouping, the variability in the rates of growth of total personal income was not associated with the variability in the percent change in the economic base.

The importance of export base theory has often been questioned in the literature. This has generally been based on empirical results that have not been consistent with the *a priori* logic of export base theory. The conclusions above show, for the most part, why negative results have been obtained. The application of export base theory has been most commonly applied to urban areas, usually Standard Metropolitan Statistical Areas. These urban areas represent the most highly developed geographical areas within sub-regions, or within OBE Economic Areas. The conclusion states that the importance of the arguments expressed by export base theory decreases as the level of development increases may explain why the negative empirical results have been obtained.

SUMMARY AND CONCLUSIONS: LONG TERM ECONOMIC DEVELOPMENT

In order to draw conclusions concerning the long term pattern of economic development from a static analysis it must be assumed (as explained in Chapter 4) that differences among OBE Areas can be interpreted to represent patterns of change over time such as would be found in a relatively constant economic environment. Also, in order to compare characteristics of the pattern of long term development it must also be assumed that differences among the regional groupings represent patterns of change over time. For the purpose of this discussion it is assumed (with support from Chapter 5 and data on the average level of per capita incomes) that the regional groupings may be ranked, from high to low, in terms of the level of development as follows: Northeastern, Far West, Central and Southeastern Regional Groupings. Given this ranking, comparison may be made of the patterns of development and conclusions drawn concerning a more general pattern of long term regional economic development.

The pattern of long term development of the United States may be described by analyzing the changing clusters of variables found to be relatively important in explaining the levels of development of each regional grouping.

The Southeastern Regional Grouping represents the lowest level of development. There are two clusters of variables that explained a significant amount of variance in the levels of per capita income of that regional grouping. The first represents variations in the abundance of factor supplies, including social overhead capital, and variations in the levels of manufacturing and agricultural productivity. The second cluster is interpreted as representing the shift in industrial structure characterized by greater economic diversification and the greater relative importance of national growth industries.

The variations in the levels of per capita income of the OBE Areas in the Central Regional Grouping are explained by one cluster of variables. This cluster of variables is interpreted as representing variations in the stocks of factor supplies and the variations in the relative importance of national growth industries.

The variations in the levels of per capita income of the OBE Areas in the Far West Regional Grouping are also explained by two clusters of variables. The first, and most important, represents variations in the stock of social overhead capital. The second cluster is interpreted as representing variations in the actual and potential savings, the level of human resources, the relative importance of residentiary sectors, the level of economic diversity, and the relative importance of national growth industries.

Finally, the variance in the levels of per capita income of the OBE Areas in the Northeastern Regional Grouping is explained by one cluster of variables. This cluster is interpreted as representing the combined influences of rapid growth industries, greater stocks and sources of financial capital, and greater levels of services and infrastructure provided by local governments.

From these brief summaries it can be pointed out that three variables enter into the interpretation of one of these clusters in each regional grouping:

1. Relative importance of national growth industries.
2. Relative importance of residentiary industries.
3. Stock and potential source of financial capital.

In addition, the relative importance of the degree of economic diversification and the relative abundance of investment in human capital, as measured by the percent high school graduates, can be added to this list. Both of these variables appear in a relatively important factor in the analysis using the level of per capita income as the dependent variable in all regional groupings except the Northeastern. However, it is clear that these forces play an equally important role in affecting the level of per capita income in this regional grouping. On the average, the OBE Economic Areas located in the Northeastern Regional Grouping are more diversified than in any other regional grouping and have a relatively high percentage of high school graduates. Because of uniformly high levels of economic diversity and levels of educational achievement, these variables do not achieve the necessary degree of variation to be associated with the dependent variable.

The forces discussed represent the major similarities in the clusters of variables. There are dissimilarities as well. Focusing attention on both the similarities and dissimilarities provides the description of the long term pattern of development that is the objective of this analysis. It is noted that two separate clusters explain the variance in per capita income of the Southeastern Regional Grouping. The first, which emphasizes the relative importance of the stocks of factor inputs, social overhead capital, and levels of productivity achieved is not too different from the cluster of variables found to explain the level of development in the Central Regional Grouping. However, the second cluster found the shift from an agricultural economy into a diversified industrial economy. This cluster is not found to explain the level of development in any other regional grouping. It may be concluded therefore, that the level of development represented by the Southeastern Regional Grouping represents the level where the stocks of factor inputs advanced sufficiently to enable the shift of the production orientation toward diversified manufacturing.

The presence of only one cluster of variables explaining the level of development of the OBE Areas in the Central Regional Grouping, and the similarity of this cluster to the first cluster of the Southeastern Regional Grouping, implies that OBE Areas in the Central Region passed the threshold where the shifting from agriculture to industrialization is necessary to achieve increases in per capita GNP. However, the continued inclusion of manufacturing productivity in the important cluster suggests that increases in productivity in manufacturing are still important in raising average income. Manufacturing productivity contributes to the interpretation of important clusters only in the two regional groupings considered to be less developed. However, the average levels of manufacturing productivity achieved for the regional grouping on the upper end of the scale are higher than the average for the Southeastern and Central Regional Groupings. Thus, in addition to representing that stage of development where the shift from an agricultural to an industrial economy is achieved, the Central Regional Grouping represents that stage where the interaction of growth in factor supplies and increases in productivity is a major distinguishing characteristic of higher levels of development. At higher levels of development, it can be argued that higher levels of productivity are a uniform characteristic and thus no longer serve as a distinguishing characteristic of variations in per capita GNP.

At the level of development represented by the Far West Regional Grouping the cluster of variables that is similar to that of the Central Regional Grouping (with the omission of manufacturing productivity) is of lesser importance than a cluster representing variations in the levels of physical and social overhead capital provided. Thus, the level of development represented by the Far West Regional Grouping represents a level where variations in the level of social services and infrastructure provide an important means for increasing per capita income. This operates to some extent independently of increases in the quality and supply of factor resources.

At the level of development represented by the Northeastern Regional Grouping it is found that the greater stocks of private and public capital form a highly associated group of influences. The forces that remain associated with higher levels of development are greater abundance of financial resources and physical and social overhead capital. It is these forces that now combine into a single set of influences contributing significantly to the expansion of industries, particularly the higher growth rate industries.

In all regional groupings the stocks of human capital, the stock and sources of financial capital, the level of economic diversification, and the relative importance of non-basic industry sectors are associated with the levels of per capita income. It is argued, therefore, that regardless of the level of economic development, greater stocks of human and financial resources and the greater level of services provided by areas with relatively larger residentiary sectors[1] contributed significantly to long run increases in per capita income. The association of the index of the composition of growth industries with these variables is consistent with this interpretation. It is these industries that require greater supplies of skilled human resources and greater financial capital for investment.

It is shown that in the lesser developed regional grouping that improvements in a wide range of economic and socioeconomic forces are associated with higher levels of per capita income. In addition, it is evident that the variations in the stocks of resources, which may be considered as attracting industry, are statistically independent of forces measuring the transition from agricultural to industrial production. However, the increases in these stocks must be viewed as complementing the trend toward greater industrialization. Moving up the scale of development to that represented by the Central Regional Grouping, closer association is found between growth in factor supplies and measures of industrialization. In this case, these measures are clustered in only one factor. This stage is interpreted as representing the level of development where the transition is made toward industrialization. Here, increases in private capital formation and manufacturing productivity remain associated with higher levels of development. Therefore, it may be argued that important inducements for industrial expansion directly relate to the availability of these factor supplies. Moving to the next level of development, increases in social overhead capital assume a relatively greater independent importance in the level of development. In this case, the level of factor supplies remain important, but it is now augmented by the inducements provided for growth by public capital investment. At the highest level of development, it is found that greater abundance of human and private capital resources are no longer associated with increases in per capita income. Greater availability of financial capital is important at all levels, and continues to be associated with higher per capita income areas.

Therefore, the long term pattern of development is described as a continuum where initially widespread improvements in the socioeconomic environment must be made to raise income levels. As these improvements are made and higher levels of each are obtained, thresholds are reached at which they no longer pose systematic obstacles to achieving higher levels of development.

SUMMARY OF FINDINGS AND CONCLUSIONS: SHORT TERM ECONOMIC GROWTH, 1950–66

The conclusions of the economic growth patterns are presented in the same way as the patterns of long term economic development. In other words comparison is made of the similarities and dissimilarities in the relatively important clusters as the patterns of economic growth of the Southeastern, Central, Far West and Northeastern Regional Groupings are presented in order. There are significant similarities between some of the conclusions to be drawn here and those that are based on the economic base model presented above. In each case, the variance in the rates of growth of total personal income is statistically explained by one factor. In no regional grouping does more than one factor explain over 15 percent of the variance in the rates of growth of total personal income.

As discussed in Chapter 10, three variables appear in the relatively important factor that statistically explains the variance in the growth rates of total personal income for all regional groupings:

1. Rate of growth of residentiary employment.
2. Net migration rate.
3. Rate of increase in financial deposits.

These variables represent the increasing stocks of labor and financial capital. They strongly suggest a major weakness in the specification of the export base model. They point to a dimension of the relatively important clusters not accounted for in the economic base model; that is, the growth of factor supplies. The similarities between regional growth patterns as represented by the relatively important factors are, therefore, the common relative importance of growth in labor and financial resources and the growth of residentiary employment.

The rate of growth of total personal income of the OBE Areas located in the Southeastern Regional Grouping is statistically explained by the interrelationship of increases in the economic base and growth in residentiary employment. In addition, closely related to these forces are increases in the stock of financial capital, in agricultural output, and in the stock of labor.

The factor that explains the greatest part of the variance in the rates of growth of total personal income in the Central Regional Grouping includes 13 variables. It includes all of the variables found in the relatively important factor of the Southeastern Regional Grouping, except the percentage of change in agricultural output. In addition, the factor for the Central Regional Grouping included eight variables that were not found in the relatively important factor in any other regional grouping. These additional eight variables, listed in Table 10–2, are primarily indicators of industrialization, urbanization, and the relative importance of residentiary industries sectors within a diversified economic setting. In general, it was concluded that the variables included in this factor represented the stock of labor, financial capital, and the sources thereof. In addition, the economic structures of the more rapidly growing OBE Areas may be characterized as being relatively more diversified and consisting of more residentiary industries, national growth industries and manufacturing industries. In the Central Regional Grouping variations in the rates of growth of total personal income of the OBE Areas are associated with increases in the economic base and the rate of growth of residentiary employment. These findings suggest that an expanded version of the economic base model proves to be consistent with the patterns suggested by the important cluster of variables.

The short term patterns of economic growth of the Far West and the Northeastern Regional groupings, as suggested by the relatively important factors, are very similar. Two minor differences exist. First, as discussed in Chapter 10, the signs of the factor loadings on the percent change in the labor force participation rate are opposite in the two cases. Secondly, the relatively important factor for the Northeastern Regional Grouping includes the index of the composition of growth industries, whereas the factor for the Far West Regional Grouping does not. For each grouping, the relative importance of growth in the residentiary sectors along with growth in supporting factor resources should be stressed.

The results of these factor analyses for the lesser developed regional groupings are consistent with the results obtained in testing the economic base model for those regional groupings. However, the results obtained explain why the economic base model explains only 50 percent of the variance in the rates of growth of total personal income. In particular, the model, designed to explain the variations in the rates of growth of total economic activity, does not take into consideration the growth of factor supplies. This analysis shows that these omitted forces are critical to explaining the growth pattern.

The general pattern of economic growth may, therefore, be described as one where the influences of growth in the economic base play the primary role in the initial stages of economic growth. As the degree of urbanization increases, the influence of the growth in exports as a percent of total production decrease. From this point, it is the growth of services, or residentiary goods and services, that assumes a primary role.

SUMMARY OF FINDINGS AND CONCLUSIONS: GROWTH IN PER CAPITA INCOME

The cluster of variables that explain the variance in the per capita income are negatively related to the variation in the rates of growth of per capita income. This negative relationship does not meet the *a priori* expectations with regard to the association of these variables. It is shown that in each case, except for the Far Westᵰthe migration flows largely account for this finding. The in-migrants of the higher per capita income areas are generally of lower income and initially unemployed. This tends to reduce the average level of income in these areas while increasing the level of per capita income in the areas of out-migration. It is the mobility of labor and its migration to higher income areas within regional groupings which is the most important influence systematically related to variations among OBE Areas in rates of growth of per capita income.

This study discusses, analyzes, and interprets the patterns of economic change in major regions of the United States. In so doing it is shown that these patterns differ according to the level of development of the region. Three separate measures of economic change are used and show that each is associated with a separate set of forces.

Appendix A

Export Industries by OBE Economic Area

The method by which the Office of Business Economics defined export industries is discussed in Chapter 3. In addition to standard export sectors of agriculture, mining, manufacturing (except food processing and printing and publishing), and federal government activities, other sectors were also classified as export for some OBE Economic Areas. The other sectors, and their respective codes are:

Sector	*OBE Industry Code*
Food Processing (Mfg.)	410
Printing and Publishing (Mfg.)	440
Railroad Services	511
Trucking and Warehousing	512
Other Transportation Services	513
Communications	520
Public Utilities	530
Wholesale and Retail Trade	600
Finance, Insurance & Real Estate	700
Hotels and Personal Services	811
Business and Repair Services	812
Amusements and Recreation Services	813
Professional Services	820
State and Local Government	912

The OBE Economic Areas that considered to be exporting goods and services in these sectors are listed below with the exporting sectors. The OBE Economic Areas that did not have exporting industries other than the standard export sectors are not included below. Therefore OBE Economic Area 2, which exported only the standard products, is not included in the list.

This information was provided by the Office of Business Economics, Regional Economics Division.

OBE Economic Area	*OBE Industry Codes*
1	410, 511, 912
3	811, 820
4	440, 700, 812, 820
5	440, 700
6	520, 811, 820, 912
7	530, 820, 912
8	410, 440
9	511, 912
10	511
11	511, 530, 912
12	511, 912
13	410, 440, 511, 512, 530
14	440, 513, 520, 600, 700, 812, 813, 820
15	440
16	410, 511, 512
17	410
18	520, 811, 812, 820
19	410, 512, 811, 912
20	511, 512
21	511, 512, 520, 700, 912
23	912
25	512
26	512
27	811
29	912
30	511
31	513
33	410, 511, 513
34	511, 520, 600, 700, 811, 912
35	820
36	513, 520, 600, 700, 811, 812, 813
37	410, 520, 530, 600, 700, 811, 813
38	912
40	511, 912
41	410
42	511, 912
44	512, 513, 520, 600, 700
45	511, 512, 530
46	511, 512, 600
47	812
50	511, 912
51	440, 511, 512
52	511, 530, 912
53	530, 912
54	410, 440, 511, 512
55	410, 511, 530
56	410, 511, 512, 530, 600, 912
57	410, 511, 520, 530, 912
58	511, 912
59	440, 511, 912
60	512, 700
62	410, 440, 511, 512
63	440

OBE Economic Area	*OBE Industry Codes*
64	511
65	511, 530, 912
66	511, 530, 820
67	511
68	440, 512
69	511
70	511
71	512, 530
72	530, 912
73	512
74	410, 530, 912
75	410, 511, 512
77	410, 440, 511, 512, 600, 700, 812
78	410, 511
79	410
80	410
81	410
83	410, 912
84	410, 440, 512
85	410, 912
86	512, 912
87	511, 530, 820, 912
88	410, 600, 820, 912
89	410, 511, 512, 820, 912
90	410, 820
91	410, 440, 511, 600, 700, 820
92	511, 912
93	511
94	511, 912
95	511, 512, 520, 600, 811, 912
96	511, 600, 820, 912
97	511, 520, 530, 600, 820, 912
98	410, 600, 912
99	410, 600, 912
100	530, 912
101	511, 600, 912
102	410, 511
103	410, 600
104	410, 600
105	410
106	440, 512, 520, 600, 700, 912
107	410, 511, 520, 600, 700, 820
108	410, 511, 520, 700, 912
109	511, 530, 912
110	511
111	411, 440, 511, 512, 513, 600, 700
112	511, 520, 811, 912
113	410, 511, 820
114	410, 512, 513, 530
115	511, 912
116	410, 511, 512, 520, 530, 600, 912
117	511, 512, 530, 700

OBE Economic Area	*OBE Industry Codes*
118	410, 512, 530
119	512, 513
120	512, 530, 700, 912
122	511, 530
123	512
124	512, 530, 812
125	530, 600, 820, 912
126	520, 912
127	512, 513, 600, 700
129	811, 912
130	511, 530, 912
131	511, 912
132	511, 530, 912
133	511, 530, 912
135	410, 520, 530, 700, 811
136	511, 530, 912
137	513
138	410, 513, 600
139	513, 530
140	513, 530
141	512, 513, 530, 600, 700, 820
142	811
143	530
144	410, 513, 600, 912
145	511, 530, 812, 912
146	511, 520, 820, 912
147	511, 820, 912
148	410, 512, 520, 600, 700, 820, 912
149	530, 811, 912
150	511, 520, 530, 811, 912
151	511, 512, 912
152	410, 511, 812
153	511, 530, 912
154	511, 912
155	513, 700
156	511, 912
157	410, 511, 512, 600, 912
158	511, 811, 912
159	410, 511, 520, 530, 600
160	511, 520, 811, 813, 912
161	811, 812, 813
162	530, 700, 811, 912
163	811, 820, 912
164	520, 811, 812
165	520, 700, 812, 813
166	410, 912
167	410, 512, 912
168	511, 520, 912
169	511, 512, 530, 811, 912
170	512, 530, 912
171	410, 513, 520, 700, 812, 912

Appendix B

Variables by OBE Economic Area

This appendix includes the variables used in the study. The method used in the calculation of each variables is reported in Chapter 3 and is not, therefore, repeated here.

TABLE B-1
VARIABLES BY OBE ECONOMIC AREA

OBE ECON AREA	RATE OF INCREASE TPY 50-66	RATE OF INCREASE PCY 1950-66	PER CAPITA PERSONAL INCOME 1959	RATE OF INCREASE RESID.EM	ECON BASE 1950
1.0	5.628	5.350	1601.86	2.2850	47.27
2.0	5.043	4.380	1928.61	1.7801	44.09
3.0	5.645	5.171	1747.86	1.7883	41.87
4.0	5.402	4.458	2358.97	1.3989	35.67
5.0	6.025	4.054	2517.62	2.3070	43.46
6.0	5.047	4.080	2154.79	1.6631	39.92
7.0	5.390	4.085	2060.74	2.1825	40.32
8.0	6.261	4.493	2527.59	1.8965	42.32
9.0	4.889	3.843	2312.73	1.8155	41.35
10.0	4.707	4.077	1922.85	1.4599	42.98
11.0	4.483	4.009	1811.35	1.7678	51.92
12.0	5.313	4.364	2014.71	1.4783	44.71
13.0	3.545	4.210	1741.61	.2624	47.03
14.0	5.608	4.097	2872.93	1.5651	37.48
15.0	5.635	3.981	2434.32	1.7879	35.96
16.0	5.049	4.064	2008.28	2.0334	44.85
17.0	6.095	4.251	2205.00	1.8396	34.91
18.0	7.221	3.712	2540.69	2.6960	44.65
19.0	5.679	4.662	1559.62	1.8981	53.38
20.0	5.805	4.835	1558.64	2.0063	49.46
21.0	6.228	4.687	1819.05	2.0270	38.47
22.0	6.261	3.981	1758.55	3.6191	55.19
23.0	5.916	4.764	1288.68	2.6821	54.90
24.0	6.926	5.263	1398.54	3.0433	54.36
25.0	6.563	4.870	1765.28	2.6054	52.56
26.0	6.467	4.870	1699.06	2.7597	51.12
27.0	5.529	4.870	1438.00	1.4752	47.93
28.0	6.216	5.100	1543.05	2.1973	55.15
29.0	7.413	5.681	1321.50	2.8280	40.99
30.0	6.052	5.540	1047.98	2.6641	56.20
31.0	7.315	4.595	1327.55	3.3206	52.48
32.0	7.275	5.803	1352.19	2.4489	51.68
33.0	5.706	4.862	1392.29	2.6467	45.49
34.0	7.523	4.921	1774.35	3.6890	37.40
35.0	11.654	4.688	1948.67	7.9984	30.47
36.0	10.424	4.073	2224.38	7.0423	33.45
37.0	9.285	4.113	1870.09	6.8372	35.32
38.0	7.092	5.574	1302.19	4.0507	48.19
39.0	8.695	5.109	1744.83	5.3841	50.84
40.0	5.695	5.279	1281.60	2.0158	46.66
41.0	6.252	5.841	1200.85	3.1602	51.28
42.0	6.571	5.628	1284.51	3.3856	49.25
43.0	5.720	4.459	1419.44	1.9673	57.49
44.0	7.493	5.098	1871.44	2.8753	36.95
45.0	5.645	5.109	1539.86	2.4210	46.01
46.0	5.833	5.187	1399.57	1.8940	42.23
47.0	8.868	6.727	1397.33	4.1720	48.37
48.0	6.475	5.568	1494.10	2.4853	47.68
49.0	6.726	5.681	1502.17	2.4203	39.04
50.0	4.965	4.817	1301.31	1.7007	47.59
51.0	4.838	5.162	1263.95	1.6489	51.58
52.0	3.836	4.447	1454.33	1.0982	55.66
53.0	6.109	5.863	1239.91	2.2778	48.24
54.0	6.311	4.585	1997.59	2.0001	42.49
55.0	5.129	5.155	1638.10	1.3720	43.19
56.0	4.655	4.908	1744.15	.6506	46.40
57.0	5.254	4.493	2047.49	1.7764	42.08
58.0	5.984	4.782	2030.17	2.1739	47.27
59.0	6.166	5.150	1922.36	1.8985	52.08
60.0	6.471	4.428	2260.98	2.6700	34.05
61.0	5.813	4.454	2113.33	2.0850	45.74
62.0	5.706	4.105	2268.82	1.9232	36.28
63.0	6.323	4.076	2278.46	2.9078	38.02
64.0	6.231	4.362	2033.52	2.5466	34.92
65.0	4.071	4.834	1480.34	.5831	51.76
66.0	4.483	4.253	2157.21	1.2045	46.84
67.0	5.231	4.055	2179.92	2.2463	52.41
68.0	5.707	3.869	2407.33	2.0587	40.90

TABLE B-1
VARIABLES BY OBE ECONOMIC AREA

OBE ECON AREA	RATE OF INCREASE TPY 50-66	RATE OF INCREASE PCY 1950-66	PER CAPITA PERSONAL INCOME 1959	RATE OF INCREASE RESID.EM	ECON BASE 1950
69.0	5.669	4.537	1853.60	1.4736	41.51
70.0	5.172	3.752	2174.00	2.1497	43.88
71.0	6.170	4.134	2470.18	2.4543	47.42
72.0	6.610	4.972	1825.62	2.8885	46.86
73.0	5.833	4.300	1950.92	2.5406	44.65
74.0	6.358	4.424	2139.54	3.0790	48.15
75.0	6.366	4.724	2056.23	2.6473	43.66
76.0	5.372	3.739	2271.14	2.7888	51.49
77.0	5.729	4.004	2794.18	1.7351	35.57
78.0	5.111	4.149	2274.63	1.6774	33.61
79.0	5.198	4.039	2212.50	1.5514	39.37
80.0	5.748	4.234	2183.32	2.5386	46.31
81.0	4.373	4.005	1594.88	1.3521	56.24
82.0	6.146	4.083	2320.82	2.4695	48.50
83.0	6.287	4.584	2046.03	2.5960	40.00
84.0	5.729	3.938	2551.95	2.1499	35.99
85.0	5.648	4.685	1829.13	1.7878	45.31
86.0	5.850	5.282	1679.27	1.5464	46.84
87.0	4.440	4.193	1834.08	.9233	45.20
88.0	4.973	5.079	1688.40	1.5221	47.24
89.0	5.044	4.869	1655.49	1.3660	45.58
90.0	5.311	4.278	1949.08	2.2241	48.97
91.0	6.064	4.602	2108.38	2.0764	36.28
92.0	4.672	4.416	1531.72	1.7308	53.89
93.0	4.303	3.716	1511.05	1.9075	54.51
94.0	4.242	2.760	2138.91	2.5446	51.98
95.0	3.703	3.379	2046.60	2.6459	44.20
96.0	4.289	4.338	1324.91	2.0062	49.59
97.0	3.877	3.850	1509.98	1.6889	46.82
98.0	3.832	4.510	1199.43	.8268	50.82
99.0	4.323	4.253	1435.79	1.2574	49.44
100.0	4.865	3.993	1745.81	2.7928	50.92
101.0	2.706	3.165	1980.00	.9428	58.04
102.0	4.044	4.379	1842.78	.7968	54.26
103.0	3.439	3.721	1612.85	.5997	51.45
104.0	4.696	5.009	1590.86	.6880	55.06
105.0	4.461	4.102	1942.36	1.5501	51.75
106.0	5.039	4.830	2001.60	1.3749	39.38
107.0	5.409	4.182	2116.18	1.9352	41.29
108.0	5.208	4.994	1955.25	1.8589	42.31
109.0	4.408	4.540	1901.97	1.8877	49.77
110.0	5.340	3.956	2225.13	2.4169	43.43
111.0	5.632	4.268	2140.30	1.8548	37.23
112.0	4.682	4.443	1611.75	2.0877	54.36
113.0	4.818	4.906	1826.85	1.0084	50.39
114.0	5.489	4.194	2233.47	1.6127	37.02
115.0	4.754	5.345	1388.63	1.5380	51.73
116.0	4.468	4.612	1592.55	1.2522	44.97
117.0	6.475	5.755	1477.26	1.7423	39.63
118.0	5.174	5.277	1342.86	.9283	39.43
119.0	5.639	4.589	1913.60	1.8316	40.66
120.0	5.712	4.944	1803.68	1.8471	31.74
121.0	5.033	4.413	1796.29	1.9541	51.74
122.0	5.041	3.296	2361.00	2.6906	53.85
123.0	6.185	3.655	2160.80	3.6347	49.10
124.0	6.696	3.601	2223.01	5.8415	49.68
125.0	4.152	4.219	1799.72	1.1797	45.98
126.0	3.507	3.407	1824.19	.2542	48.84
127.0	6.795	4.101	2224.76	2.8108	34.66
128.0	5.369	4.479	1676.73	1.4941	45.22
129.0	6.083	4.865	1529.27	2.3231	40.39
130.0	5.626	5.580	1483.31	1.1325	43.74
131.0	5.560	6.169	1240.78	-.1355	45.26
132.0	4.701	3.770	1673.35	3.0423	44.84
133.0	5.812	4.907	1292.27	2.7132	46.05
134.0	4.789	5.284	1206.28	1.4612	53.12
135.0	6.187	5.244	1381.56	2.5142	38.11
136.0	5.378	5.357	1136.78	2.2199	45.94

TABLE B-1
VARIABLES BY OBE ECONOMIC AREA

OBE ECON AREA	RATE OF INCREASE TPY 50-66	RATE OF INCREASE PCY 1950-66	PER CAPITA PERSONAL INCOME 1959	RATE OF INCREASE RESID.EM	ECON BASE 1950
137.0	7.299	5.093	1528.83	3.8289	47.08
138.0	6.680	4.510	1773.84	2.7652	35.22
139.0	7.290	5.133	1421.67	3.9446	44.03
140.0	6.047	4.294	1891.01	2.2311	47.28
141.0	6.828	3.430	2191.51	3.4906	37.26
142.0	6.039	3.743	1580.27	2.7390	41.56
143.0	5.733	4.026	1562.64	2.3318	41.44
144.0	4.942	3.662	1096.85	2.6828	48.40
145.0	6.500	3.632	1878.39	4.4652	48.01
146.0	7.501	4.746	1882.77	4.9639	33.16
147.0	6.487	4.628	1844.54	2.8196	40.48
148.0	7.024	3.921	2375.53	3.8763	34.26
149.0	6.590	4.675	1821.11	5.0517	43.68
150.0	4.013	2.804	2378.03	3.1529	45.78
151.0	6.126	3.863	1940.56	3.5782	38.25
152.0	5.545	4.329	1893.60	2.5529	40.62
153.0	3.951	2.975	1960.23	1.1224	43.56
154.0	4.817	3.924	2082.64	1.7337	44.06
155.0	6.119	4.126	2433.61	2.0877	34.81
156.0	4.354	3.654	2067.29	1.2704	41.68
157.0	5.569	4.051	2218.48	1.5992	34.59
158.0	5.169	2.828	2074.83	2.8934	44.55
159.0	5.418	4.016	1954.28	2.4409	41.59
160.0	7.483	3.546	2780.62	5.1941	42.87
161.0	11.961	4.173	2507.09	9.1538	40.56
162.0	9.297	4.110	1916.63	7.0665	38.92
163.0	8.681	4.165	2030.65	6.4064	38.42
164.0	8.847	3.910	2291.56	5.6536	41.60
165.0	8.347	4.178	2783.69	4.0735	31.18
166.0	5.700	3.545	2180.14	3.1746	45.90
167.0	6.086	3.776	2187.04	2.6387	44.23
168.0	7.817	3.468	2394.31	5.5207	39.21
169.0	4.535	2.519	2387.42	2.8781	54.15
170.0	6.013	3.318	2402.15	4.8170	50.03
171.0	7.230	4.150	2773.77	3.0899	31.81

TABLE B-2
VARIABLES BY OBE ECONOMIC AREA

OBE ECON AREA	ECON BASE 1959	ECON BASE 1967	PCT.CH. EC.BASE 1950-67	PCT.CH. EC.BASE 1950-59	PCT.CH. EC.BASE 1959-67
1.0	42.95	44.73	-5.37	-9.13	4.14
2.0	40.18	38.72	-12.17	-8.86	-3.36
3.0	42.17	39.64	-5.32	-.71	-5.99
4.0	38.63	36.83	3.25	8.29	-4.65
5.0	46.11	43.86	.92	6.09	-4.87
6.0	42.66	39.87	-.12	6.86	-6.54
7.0	40.81	40.63	.76	1.21	-.44
8.0	48.21	47.56	12.38	13.91	-1.34
9.0	42.33	42.02	1.62	2.37	-.73
10.0	48.05	49.21	14.49	11.79	2.41
11.0	52.19	49.01	-5.60	.52	-6.09
12.0	48.31	47.90	7.13	8.05	-.84
13.0	40.90	39.25	-16.54	-13.03	-4.03
14.0	38.50	37.20	-.74	2.72	-3.37
15.0	37.47	36.19	.63	4.19	-3.41
16.0	44.14	41.52	-7.42	-1.58	-5.93
17.0	36.97	36.22	3.75	5.90	-2.03
18.0	43.11	41.17	-7.79	-3.44	-4.50
19.0	47.12	43.06	-19.33	-11.72	-8.61
20.0	45.95	45.39	-8.22	-7.09	-1.21
21.0	36.12	35.64	-7.35	-6.10	-1.32
22.0	49.04	51.29	-7.06	-11.14	4.58
23.0	46.72	45.09	-17.86	-14.89	-3.48
24.0	53.40	53.50	-1.58	-1.76	.18
25.0	51.93	48.47	-7.78	-1.19	-6.66
26.0	44.37	45.17	-11.63	-13.20	1.80
27.0	47.48	43.47	-9.30	-.93	-8.44
28.0	51.50	49.26	-10.67	-6.61	-4.34
29.0	41.14	40.52	-1.14	.36	-1.50
30.0	51.15	48.57	-13.57	-8.89	-5.04
31.0	46.82	51.16	-2.51	-10.78	9.26
32.0	51.04	55.93	8.22	-1.23	9.58
33.0	41.61	41.56	-8.63	-8.52	-.12
34.0	34.86	36.80	-1.60	-6.79	5.56
35.0	36.70	37.42	22.80	20.44	1.96
36.0	31.62	36.00	7.62	-5.47	13.85
37.0	31.22	33.86	-4.13	-11.60	8.45
38.0	42.24	45.11	-6.39	-12.34	6.79
39.0	50.75	50.55	-.57	-.17	-.39
40.0	42.22	42.47	-8.97	-9.51	.59
41.0	44.51	45.67	-10.93	-13.14	2.53
42.0	46.73	48.71	-1.09	-5.11	4.23
43.0	52.02	52.93	-7.93	-9.51	1.74
44.0	36.28	36.20	-2.02	-1.81	-.22
45.0	42.27	40.52	-11.93	-8.12	-4.14
46.0	40.67	39.62	-6.18	-3.69	-2.58
47.0	45.51	48.89	1.06	-5.91	7.42
48.0	46.06	46.62	-2.22	-3.39	1.21
49.0	36.31	35.90	-8.04	-6.99	-1.12
50.0	43.30	40.50	-14.89	-9.01	-6.46
51.0	47.65	44.37	-13.97	-7.61	-6.88
52.0	47.88	43.55	-21.75	-13.97	-9.04
53.0	40.32	38.47	-20.25	-16.41	-4.58
54.0	40.77	41.58	-2.14	-4.04	1.98
55.0	43.56	42.17	-2.36	.85	-3.19
56.0	41.34	41.27	-11.05	-10.90	-.16
57.0	38.72	40.59	-3.54	-7.98	4.82
58.0	41.64	44.96	-4.88	-11.91	7.97
59.0	48.35	50.09	-3.82	-7.16	3.59
60.0	38.08	39.26	15.30	11.83	3.09
61.0	54.55	54.90	20.02	19.26	.64
62.0	40.43	38.00	4.74	11.43	-6.01

TABLE B-2
VARIABLES BY OBE ECONOMIC AREA

OBE ECON AREA	ECON BASE 1959	ECON BASE 1967	PCT.CH. EC.BASE 1950-67	PCT.CH. EC.BASE 1950-59	PCT.CH. EC.BASE 1959-67
63.0	48.25	49.10	29.14	26.90	1.76
64.0	37.48	35.84	2.63	7.33	-4.37
65.0	47.73	44.54	-13.94	-7.78	-6.68
66.0	45.99	43.50	-7.13	-1.81	-5.41
67.0	53.47	52.85	.83	2.02	-1.15
68.0	45.94	44.24	8.16	12.32	-3.70
69.0	45.44	48.20	16.11	9.46	6.07
70.0	44.31	42.80	-2.46	.97	-3.40
71.0	45.38	44.07	-7.06	-4.30	-2.88
72.0	47.81	48.21	2.88	2.02	.83
73.0	45.34	43.21	-3.22	1.54	-4.69
74.0	48.62	46.62	-3.17	.97	-4.11
75.0	46.95	47.08	7.83	7.53	.27
76.0	53.47	49.42	-4.02	3.84	-7.57
77.0	39.39	38.52	8.29	10.73	2.20
78.0	43.00	42.00	24.96	27.93	-2.32
79.0	45.02	43.52	10.54	14.35	-3.33
80.0	42.08	42.17	-8.93	-9.13	.21
81.0	45.51	42.02	-25.28	-19.07	-7.66
82.0	50.92	51.42	6.02	-4.98	.98
83.0	38.46	39.30	-1.75	-3.85	2.18
84.0	45.36	42.71	18.67	26.03	-5.84
85.0	43.64	44.43	-1.94	-3.68	1.81
86.0	43.88	42.01	-10.31	-6.31	-4.26
87.0	44.51	44.30	-1.99	-1.52	-.47
88.0	44.64	42.46	-10.11	-5.50	-4.88
89.0	41.70	41.27	-9.45	-8.51	-1.03
90.0	43.71	46.31	-5.43	-10.74	5.94
91.0	33.71	35.08	-3.30	-7.08	4.06
92.0	41.78	46.26	-14.15	-22.47	10.72
93.0	28.71	43.71	-19.81	-47.33	52.24
94.0	37.71	41.09	-20.95	-27.45	8.96
95.0	37.44	34.97	-20.88	-15.29	-6.59
96.0	40.34	37.42	-24.54	-18.65	-7.23
97.0	34.82	39.00	-16.70	-25.63	12.00
98.0	33.62	42.54	-16.29	-33.84	26.53
99.0	37.56	40.03	-19.03	-24.02	6.57
100.0	42.25	47.96	-5.81	-17.02	13.51
101.0	44.79	42.47	-26.82	-22.82	5.17
102.0	41.90	44.12	-18.68	-22.77	5.29
103.0	40.65	41.03	-20.25	-20.99	.93
104.0	42.23	45.50	-17.36	-23.30	7.74
105.0	46.18	46.26	-10.60	-10.76	.17
106.0	35.39	35.00	-11.12	-10.13	-1.10
107.0	37.35	37.46	-9.27	-9.54	.29
108.0	35.77	35.51	-16.07	-15.45	-.72
109.0	44.02	41.87	-15.87	-11.55	-4.88
110.0	42.04	41.72	-3.93	-3.20	-.76
111.0	34.98	35.10	-5.72	-6.04	.34
112.0	43.47	41.27	-24.08	-20.03	-5.06
113.0	46.66	46.56	-7.60	-7.40	-.21
114.0	36.71	36.41	-1.64	-.83	-.81
115.0	42.19	43.31	-16.27	-18.44	2.65
116.0	41.77	38.71	-13.92	-7.11	-7.32
117.0	37.67	36.24	-8.55	-4.94	-3.79
118.0	40.20	33.77	-14.35	1.95	-15.99
119.0	38.29	36.72	-9.69	-5.82	-4.10
120.0	33.37	35.59	12.12	5.13	6.65
121.0	47.62	51.75	.01	-7.96	8.67
122.0	50.00	43.42	-19.36	-7.14	-13.16
123.0	46.84	42.66	-13.11	-4.60	-8.92

TABLE B-2
VARIABLES BY OBE ECONOMIC AREA

OBE ECON AREA	ECON BASE 1959	ECON BASE 1967	PCT.CH. EC.BASE 1950-67	PCT.CH. EC.BASE 1950-59	PCT.CH. EC.BASE 1959-67
124.0	46.44	42.09	-15.27	-6.52	-9.36
125.0	41.54	39.45	-14.20	-9.65	-5.03
126.0	43.55	38.15	-21.88	-10.83	-12.39
127.0	35.65	37.40	7.90	2.85	4.90
128.0	44.16	50.32	11.27	-2.34	13.94
129.0	36.56	36.67	-9.21	-9.48	.30
130.0	40.53	39.55	-9.57	-7.33	-2.41
131.0	41.46	42.80	-5.43	-8.39	3.23
132.0	35.31	37.06	-17.35	-21.25	4.95
133.0	41.73	41.32	-10.27	-9.38	-.98
134.0	51.33	50.38	-5.15	-3.36	-1.85
135.0	32.20	33.64	-11.72	-15.50	4.47
136.0	41.68	40.24	-12.40	-9.27	-3.45
137.0	44.22	42.13	-10.51	-6.07	-4.72
138.0	33.72	35.58	1.02	-4.25	5.51
139.0	40.63	46.29	5.01	-7.72	13.93
140.0	48.65	49.23	4.12	2.89	1.19
141.0	39.03	39.47	5.93	4.75	1.12
142.0	37.96	37.90	-8.80	-8.66	-.15
143.0	41.65	38.41	-7.31	.50	-7.77
144.0	41.85	40.18	-16.98	-13.53	-3.99
145.0	43.91	44.23	-7.87	-8.53	.72
146.0	35.87	30.05	-9.37	8.17	-16.22
147.0	40.68	44.14	9.04	.49	8.50
148.0	32.42	33.60	-1.92	-5.37	3.63
149.0	34.53	39.32	-9.98	-20.69	13.87
150.0	38.73	41.74	-8.82	-15.39	7.77
151.0	34.88	36.68	-4.10	-8.81	5.16
152.0	38.25	39.58	-2.56	-5.83	3.47
153.0	40.27	40.81	-6.31	-7.55	1.34
154.0	39.18	36.43	-17.31	-11.07	-7.01
155.0	34.42	36.13	3.79	-1.12	4.96
156.0	42.14	37.17	-10.82	1.10	-11.79
157.0	34.13	32.50	-6.04	-1.32	-4.77
158.0	44.50	39.68	-10.93	-.11	-10.83
159.0	37.36	36.45	-12.35	-10.17	-2.43
160.0	37.33	41.65	-2.84	-12.92	-11.57
161.0	42.66	46.35	14.27	5.17	8.64
162.0	32.28	34.97	-10.14	-17.06	8.33
163.0	38.25	38.23	-.49	-.44	-.05
164.0	40.90	44.21	6.27	-1.68	8.09
165.0	36.62	36.37	16.64	17.44	-.68
166.0	42.11	39.57	-13.79	-8.25	-6.03
167.0	44.28	39.72	-10.19	.11	-10.29
168.0	40.13	38.33	-2.24	2.34	-4.48
169.0	47.44	43.58	-19.51	-12.39	-8.13
170.0	47.91	44.34	-22.74	-4.23	-7.45
171.0	32.69	32.77	3.01	2.76	.24

TABLE B-3
VARIABLES BY OBE ECONOMIC AREA

OBE ECON AREA	INDEX OF GROWTH INDUSTRIES	COEF OF CONTCENTR 1950	COEF OF CONTCENTR 1960	PERCENT CHANGE CC	PERCENT CHANGE LFPR
1.0	1.63	27.40	25.47	-7.07	8.638
2.0	1.73	25.07	25.03	-.15	2.340
3.0	1.33	26.98	26.27	-2.63	1.313
4.0	2.35	24.48	24.71	.94	1.110
5.0	2.38	23.25	24.29	4.44	-3.391
6.0	2.20	24.00	24.96	3.99	-5.154
7.0	2.12	24.18	25.12	3.87	-3.323
8.0	2.12	27.08	27.70	2.27	-3.316
9.0	2.08	22.83	23.83	4.36	-5.405
10.0	2.04	24.24	24.70	1.91	-6.222
11.0	1.94	24.17	25.01	3.48	-2.224
12.0	1.69	27.73	26.98	-2.68	-2.233
13.0	1.54	27.84	25.25	-9.30	.191
14.0	2.25	23.73	24.08	1.49	-1.637
15.0	2.18	22.17	22.59	1.87	-2.955
16.0	1.57	23.49	23.74	1.05	-1.019
17.0	2.23	23.55	24.14	2.52	-5.842
18.0	2.62	34.01	33.80	-.63	-6.281
19.0	.93	30.82	26.41	-14.31	-.728
20.0	.82	29.03	25.59	-11.85	1.111
21.0	1.53	26.32	25.05	-4.82	-3.662
22.0	2.00	29.59	27.42	-7.35	.840
23.0	.74	39.91	30.09	-24.59	-2.688
24.0	1.59	37.94	33.27	-12.32	-.899
25.0	.60	31.60	28.85	-8.72	1.130
26.0	.50	35.52	31.16	-12.28	-.256
27.0	.58	33.04	29.55	-10.58	.330
28.0	.44	40.07	35.57	-11.24	1.224
29.0	1.47	34.84	27.72	-20.44	2.512
30.0	-.15	51.85	34.96	-32.58	-6.592
31.0	2.29	29.04	29.23	.65	-.989
32.0	1.13	34.98	26.44	-24.43	-4.141
33.0	1.18	32.94	25.59	-22.33	-2.587
34.0	1.83	26.00	25.59	-1.57	-.999
35.0	1.95	29.02	26.19	-9.74	-2.754
36.0	1.67	27.34	26.48	-3.15	-6.970
37.0	1.62	26.81	27.05	.90	-7.670
38.0	1.48	32.65	28.14	-13.83	-.204
39.0	2.24	30.72	28.49	-7.27	1.906
40.0	.98	37.24	27.03	-27.42	-2.077
41.0	.59	44.14	30.10	-31.81	-2.749
42.0	1.01	34.51	27.29	-20.93	-2.884
43.0	1.37	32.13	30.11	-6.29	-4.625
44.0	1.47	26.45	24.15	-8.70	-1.022
45.0	1.22	30.04	24.52	-18.35	-1.451
46.0	.72	39.84	28.98	-27.25	-3.727
47.0	1.14	43.55	26.10	-40.08	4.780
48.0	.90	28.69	25.33	-11.73	.735
49.0	1.22	34.40	26.06	-24.24	1.923
50.0	.98	28.65	25.22	-11.99	1.219
51.0	.62	32.43	26.84	-17.24	-3.639
52.0	1.03	31.53	26.59	-15.65	-9.063
53.0	.50	41.84	30.86	-26.25	-1.373
54.0	2.00	25.34	24.00	-5.28	-6.130
55.0	1.15	28.37	25.65	-9.59	-2.911
56.0	1.40	27.07	25.11	-7.26	-3.174
57.0	1.58	27.63	26.65	-3.56	-1.948
58.0	1.91	29.29	28.45	-2.84	-.940
59.0	1.60	30.48	28.77	-5.59	-.620
60.0	2.19	23.85	24.07	.92	-3.013
61.0	2.38	25.11	25.89	3.11	-2.757
62.0	1.98	23.55	23.31	-1.03	-5.547
63.0	2.38	25.58	25.01	-2.24	-4.819

TABLE B-3
VARIABLES BY OBE ECONOMIC AREA

OBE ECON AREA	INDEX OF GROWTH INDUSTRIES	COEF OF CONTCENTR 1950	COEF OF CONTCENTR 1960	PERCENT CHANGE CC	PERCENT CHANGE LFPR
64.0	2.05	25.07	24.76	-1.22	-2.568
65.0	1.11	31.11	28.07	-9.80	-4.098
66.0	1.79	27.02	26.99	-.15	-4.675
67.0	1.93	31.88	30.96	-2.89	-8.276
68.0	2.15	23.62	23.99	1.57	-7.415
69.0	1.69	27.99	25.32	-9.54	-6.024
70.0	1.96	24.06	24.19	.55	-6.336
71.0	2.48	34.37	29.86	-13.12	-9.854
72.0	1.72	27.91	25.28	-9.44	-3.534
73.0	1.79	25.46	27.57	-3.49	-3.947
74.0	2.11	25.59	26.18	2.32	-2.805
75.0	1.95	26.49	25.09	-5.28	-4.241
76.0	1.94	26.69	24.98	-6.41	-5.419
77.0	2.30	22.90	23.48	2.54	-6.324
78.0	1.57	28.49	28.25	-.83	-3.606
79.0	1.44	28.40	26.66	-6.11	-4.500
80.0	1.67	34.16	30.58	-10.47	-.795
81.0	.10	43.17	37.12	-14.01	-4.740
82.0	1.80	26.82	25.76	-3.94	-5.471
83.0	1.41	34.01	30.19	-11.25	-1.656
84.0	2.28	23.69	24.18	2.05	-7.461
85.0	1.18	28.11	25.01	-11.03	-4.710
86.0	.63	37.42	30.24	-19.20	-5.990
87.0	.99	26.33	27.23	3.40	-11.240
88.0	.51	38.73	32.13	-17.03	-2.284
89.0	.46	38.94	32.78	-15.82	-5.901
90.0	.92	39.46	33.48	-15.15	-6.093
91.0	1.41	29.83	27.09	-9.19	-4.675
92.0	-.07	50.55	40.32	-20.24	-3.430
93.0	.05	49.16	37.57	-23.59	-6.242
94.0	1.01	34.14	29.96	-12.26	-5.952
95.0	.53	35.87	30.72	-14.35	-2.816
96.0	-.53	52.75	43.98	-16.61	-3.148
97.0	-.03	47.54	39.38	-17.16	-6.389
98.0	-.34	50.04	42.63	-14.80	-5.117
99.0	.03	45.16	38.93	-13.80	-5.427
100.0	.51	41.97	33.37	-20.50	-5.187
101.0	.04	41.89	35.96	-14.16	-2.104
102.0	-.10	44.94	39.21	-12.77	-2.352
103.0	-.03	45.00	39.82	-11.51	-4.686
104.0	.10	43.60	37.30	-14.45	-4.627
105.0	.54	37.97	33.68	-11.30	-5.639
106.0	1.24	32.44	28.81	-11.17	-2.121
107.0	1.43	30.40	27.11	-10.81	-2.263
108.0	1.19	36.22	30.45	-15.93	1.408
109.0	.42	42.04	33.68	-19.90	1.287
110.0	1.51	29.76	27.77	-6.71	-.886
111.0	1.68	27.94	25.69	-8.07	-3.145
112.0	.78	39.82	32.33	-18.81	-1.478
113.0	1.06	32.34	28.44	-12.03	-1.749
114.0	1.92	23.42	23.24	-.77	-5.547
115.0	.48	41.27	30.63	-25.78	-2.852
116.0	.84	37.59	28.59	-23.94	-.919
117.0	1.13	34.47	26.45	-23.27	-.052
118.0	1.03	35.64	27.20	-23.68	-.014
119.0	1.31	28.63	25.78	-9.96	-.041
120.0	1.42	30.16	27.83	-7.71	2.029
121.0	1.72	31.68	30.45	-3.85	2.265
122.0	1.07	31.64	27.59	-12.81	3.313
123.0	.52	35.25	32.25	-8.49	-.625
124.0	.60	31.39	29.22	-6.92	-.874

TABLE B-3
VARIABLES BY OBE ECONOMIC AREA

OBE ECON AREA	INDEX OF GROWTH INDUSTRIES	COEF OF CONTCENTR 1950	COEF OF CONTCENTR 1960	PERCENT CHANGE CC	PERCENT CHANGE LFPR
125.0	.95	32.30	28.04	-13.19	3.655
126.0	.82	34.81	30.17	-13.33	1.121
127.0	1.86	25.80	24.75	-4.05	-1.810
128.0	1.91	31.65	30.21	-4.55	3.439
129.0	1.45	33.66	30.69	-8.83	1.387
130.0	1.01	31.50	26.37	-16.29	-1.827
131.0	.95	36.93	26.99	-26.90	-1.378
132.0	1.51	28.37	25.74	-9.25	-3.001
133.0	1.03	35.79	28.37	-20.73	-3.575
134.0	-.03	48.12	33.46	-30.46	-4.124
135.0	.90	39.66	28.71	-27.61	-4.392
136.0	.67	40.14	27.59	-31.26	-6.206
137.0	1.90	26.41	25.27	-4.32	-4.299
138.0	1.45	26.09	25.14	-3.64	-6.865
139.0	.77	33.55	27.01	-19.50	-2.530
140.0	1.49	27.30	27.33	.09	-6.011
141.0	1.55	24.66	25.04	1.57	-5.784
142.0	1.89	28.67	27.85	-2.86	-4.271
143.0	1.16	29.24	26.90	-7.99	-3.803
144.0	.44	40.31	32.97	-18.21	.579
145.0	1.94	28.12	27.87	-.91	-2.193
146.0	2.06	29.59	28.32	-4.30	2.183
147.0	1.87	28.68	27.41	-4.40	1.776
148.0	1.90	26.83	26.07	-2.85	-.285
149.0	.43	37.13	29.83	-19.66	-3.809
150.0	1.09	28.69	27.62	-3.72	-7.569
151.0	1.58	27.47	26.65	-2.99	2.130
152.0	.49	37.87	31.79	-16.05	2.066
153.0	.69	28.39	27.47	-3.25	-7.036
154.0	1.28	28.03	26.89	-4.06	-2.872
155.0	2.15	25.04	25.73	2.73	-2.656
156.0	.87	32.37	29.48	-8.94	-.668
157.0	1.55	26.51	25.86	-2.47	-3.550
158.0	.93	35.25	33.86	-3.95	-4.449
159.0	.91	35.28	29.43	-16.57	3.180
160.0	1.40	27.63	26.33	-4.71	1.037
161.0	1.56	26.95	28.73	6.62	7.001
162.0	1.50	28.34	26.28	-7.25	3.689
163.0	1.98	27.37	27.23	-.50	6.939
164.0	3.23	32.68	33.27	1.81	.529
165.0	2.30	24.16	23.80	-1.48	1.003
166.0	.62	33.39	30.80	-7.76	2.825
167.0	1.16	32.50	28.71	-11.66	-1.668
168.0	1.89	28.37	27.37	-3.53	.046
169.0	.72	32.63	29.42	-9.84	-2.827
170.0	.81	38.42	38.58	.43	-8.830
171.0	2.37	24.49	24.87	1.56	-2.086

TABLE B-4
VARIABLES BY OBE ECONOMIC AREA

OBE ECON AREA	DEMAND AND TIME DEP PER.CAPITA	DEMAND, TIME + SAVINGS K PER.CAPITA	RATE OF CH OF DD + TD + SK 1950-64	MANUF. PRODUCTIVITY 1958	PCT.CH PROD. 6958-63
1.0	786.36	831.91	4.77	4.00	23.01
2.0	1169.04	1288.76	5.50	3.74	21.60
3.0	1206.44	1294.31	5.36	4.72	19.75
4.0	1822.67	2166.47	5.16	4.93	28.01
5.0	1670.93	1901.69	5.40	5.42	29.36
6.0	1531.09	1725.31	5.49	6.37	19.33
7.0	1351.90	1499.63	5.67	6.58	27.42
8.0	1478.48	1737.30	6.17	7.41	43.93
9.0	1515.36	1657.22	5.64	6.69	22.62
10.0	932.72	1093.98	4.62	6.03	21.73
11.0	820.64	910.20	5.11	4.72	20.69
12.0	946.17	1067.74	5.64	5.56	26.88
13.0	1063.74	1184.60	4.56	3.60	19.77
14.0	3071.90	3409.20	5.20	6.49	26.32
15.0	1334.55	1611.13	5.30	6.14	24.65
16.0	961.40	1079.29	5.88	4.88	24.73
17.0	934.07	1351.30	5.68	6.50	24.04
18.0	917.45	1500.88	8.24	7.30	21.49
19.0	684.96	708.89	6.47	5.20	38.40
20.0	722.78	880.60	6.43	4.21	24.08
21.0	901.54	1090.29	6.22	6.84	15.91
22.0	488.94	661.54	6.88	4.71	23.41
23.0	377.76	606.00	6.83	3.69	36.59
24.0	294.59	512.33	8.31	5.16	19.91
25.0	507.32	847.18	8.00	4.90	25.61
26.0	515.81	811.24	7.33	3.20	28.69
27.0	386.24	584.19	8.14	3.84	37.90
28.0	383.11	691.91	7.60	2.87	36.08
29.0	333.56	642.71	7.92	4.11	2.04
30.0	236.51	385.47	7.06	4.01	25.63
31.0	308.02	499.35	8.16	4.50	25.52
32.0	410.23	550.51	7.52	5.18	28.65
33.0	489.25	615.41	6.75	5.76	9.41
34.0	679.93	897.07	8.32	5.47	37.52
35.0	667.12	1269.72	13.88	8.05	50.87
36.0	907.26	1773.09	13.33	5.00	28.88
37.0	838.78	1459.12	13.23	5.12	47.87
38.0	354.84	583.51	9.65	4.60	36.26
39.0	385.87	506.10	9.76	2.80	38.21
40.0	494.73	545.15	6.64	3.02	22.40
41.0	415.38	568.27	7.30	3.36	23.74
42.0	386.76	514.38	7.39	3.71	21.13
43.0	378.71	508.28	6.18	3.24	21.32
44.0	710.36	1054.98	8.07	4.57	31.90
45.0	540.10	700.92	7.00	5.17	34.41
46.0	609.47	747.16	6.62	5.17	13.88
47.0	390.51	525.51	9.30	5.28	21.33
48.0	550.86	704.36	6.59	4.60	18.50
49.0	698.25	887.94	7.75	4.59	23.36
50.0	481.94	606.02	6.87	4.59	13.40
51.0	484.40	632.74	6.27	5.68	25.43
52.0	500.69	619.48	5.53	8.22	44.60
53.0	523.54	644.85	5.57	5.76	30.04
54.0	704.45	1069.78	6.22	8.68	26.60
55.0	719.65	1042.68	5.67	5.80	21.66
56.0	806.73	1048.79	4.26	6.73	17.51
57.0	899.42	1195.35	6.12	7.13	25.33
58.0	726.07	1007.57	5.57	7.91	-5.67
59.0	857.49	1124.67	5.42	5.51	16.13
60.0	882.07	1233.09	5.46	6.64	21.51
61.0	596.35	1058.66	6.08	5.97	31.53
62.0	855.04	1553.85	5.20	7.24	31.92

TABLE B-4
VARIABLES BY OBE ECONOMIC AREA

OBE ECON AREA	DEMAND AND TIME DEP PER.CAPITA	DEMAND, TIME + SAVINGS K PER.CAPITA	RATE OF CH OF DD + TD + SK 1950-64	MANUF. PRODUCTIVITY 1958	PCT.CH PROD. 6958-63
63.0	646.66	1186.06	6.69	6.08	28.88
64.0	731.78	1156.11	6.21	6.91	22.21
65.0	570.79	619.45	4.54	4.75	13.84
66.0	1161.71	1488.30	5.03	6.66	21.60
67.0	775.28	1248.18	5.33	6.93	11.91
68.0	1188.10	1800.61	6.16	6.97	23.37
69.0	715.92	1001.54	5.37	6.54	31.22
70.0	1071.13	1459.02	5.45	7.36	20.42
71.0	1043.77	1249.01	5.99	7.16	30.35
72.0	744.85	906.85	6.79	6.88	21.20
73.0	868.99	993.04	6.71	6.11	19.74
74.0	792.39	1087.24	7.22	7.48	24.11
75.0	912.54	1245.54	6.05	6.16	18.07
76.0	832.96	1089.12	6.41	7.03	4.68
77.0	1505.82	2175.59	6.13	7.35	20.17
78.0	870.27	1490.41	5.98	9.17	11.84
79.0	1009.63	1261.18	5.20	7.30	14.76
80.0	1008.83	1188.24	5.09	8.22	42.97
81.0	939.16	999.96	3.99	5.52	26.56
82.0	1000.87	1158.28	5.74	6.54	31.44
83.0	945.15	1300.57	6.42	5.22	27.88
84.0	1085.95	1660.53	6.62	6.72	22.87
85.0	851.58	1118.62	6.10	5.47	19.89
86.0	725.02	911.43	6.06	4.81	25.85
87.0	802.19	950.06	4.48	5.74	20.82
88.0	776.90	927.68	5.75	5.37	13.88
89.0	832.59	1046.53	5.78	5.98	12.11
90.0	841.40	1200.45	7.00	6.70	-.93
91.0	1074.37	1527.58	6.71	7.20	23.09
92.0	863.74	1054.13	5.62	5.53	41.08
93.0	790.92	997.06	5.42	6.99	11.98
94.0	1020.37	1234.39	4.84	8.67	11.44
95.0	970.76	1107.01	5.23	7.51	36.59
96.0	874.61	960.93	4.08	6.34	4.87
97.0	852.59	1167.85	5.81	5.55	34.83
98.0	798.40	910.78	4.22	4.39	43.75
99.0	902.39	1074.31	5.15	6.01	10.94
100.0	814.08	903.37	5.42	4.21	42.77
101.0	960.24	1096.30	2.97	5.78	28.73
102.0	821.49	923.43	3.44	5.97	25.57
103.0	880.47	1004.05	3.74	5.35	24.58
104.0	920.20	1069.67	4.14	6.79	13.70
105.0	769.47	1019.54	5.66	6.86	21.91
106.0	865.74	1247.05	6.15	7.64	24.20
107.0	902.60	1172.42	5.05	6.47	24.08
108.0	765.17	1180.18	6.42	5.29	25.43
109.0	929.53	1141.95	4.76	6.69	24.21
110.0	786.14	1143.01	6.17	6.21	18.00
111.0	981.93	1310.39	5.91	7.19	26.13
112.0	780.18	943.96	6.29	4.24	22.71
113.0	864.64	1189.49	5.15	7.02	25.01
114.0	1019.28	1352.87	6.08	6.39	26.91
115.0	530.44	647.84	7.06	4.85	36.26
116.0	637.55	1144.54	7.01	5.06	22.10
117.0	567.66	735.12	7.27	4.51	19.26
118.0	520.36	761.91	11.04	3.63	37.04
119.0	1007.76	1366.33	6.19	5.89	22.21
120.0	780.77	1081.06	7.09	5.49	45.22
121.0	807.69	956.11	5.45	4.59	-3.21
122.0	811.16	1041.34	6.40	10.16	10.23
123.0	831.63	1038.43	5.33	6.99	9.38
124.0	756.14	989.24	8.67	10.38	55.95

TABLE B-4
VARIABLES BY OBE ECONOMIC AREA

OBE ECON AREA	DEMAND AND TIME DEP PER.CAPITA	DEMAND, TIME + SAVINGS K PER.CAPITA	RATE OF CH OF DD + TD + SK 1950-64	MANUF. PRODUCTIVITY 1958	PCT.CH PROD. 6958-63
125.0	764.39	938.38	3.93	6.12	12.25
126.0	893.97	1120.11	3.98	4.22	45.71
127.0	1233.89	1504.24	8.80	6.23	23.92
128.0	574.62	822.74	6.65	5.56	18.54
129.0	590.14	906.14	7.62	4.79	9.85
130.0	599.07	939.85	6.86	5.13	14.50
131.0	510.61	636.28	6.14	3.46	31.52
132.0	783.36	952.05	5.14	5.85	3.91
133.0	463.50	648.71	7.20	4.04	36.65
134.0	466.15	526.49	5.22	4.09	22.93
135.0	591.72	800.86	8.24	4.53	30.72
136.0	418.17	598.19	6.98	3.69	35.07
137.0	515.81	637.74	7.39	4.94	32.28
138.0	675.42	953.30	7.47	7.12	28.50
139.0	466.11	715.46	7.80	7.73	17.96
140.0	668.92	884.02	7.83	7.63	79.08
141.0	1116.99	1326.47	7.91	10.71	29.39
142.0	739.35	971.54	6.71	5.64	-1.52
143.0	496.12	716.81	6.54	10.10	-2.15
144.0	344.54	453.14	5.03	3.54	38.10
145.0	561.83	726.85	7.20	5.33	2.56
146.0	589.20	723.71	9.44	5.14	32.41
147.0	614.79	785.96	5.49	6.22	13.14
148.0	1018.16	1538.77	8.61	7.35	35.71
149.0	594.45	777.66	7.23	5.17	22.56
150.0	890.89	1156.01	6.12	6.53	41.91
151.0	863.70	1165.38	7.12	8.00	29.55
152.0	761.36	924.63	6.00	6.08	25.76
153.0	800.84	963.04	4.76	5.21	16.96
154.0	886.91	1304.51	5.51	6.88	14.66
155.0	1061.12	1448.40	6.38	6.71	56.50
156.0	705.13	980.20	4.56	5.51	78.31
157.0	1056.90	1329.31	5.77	6.51	19.96
158.0	737.00	867.72	5.12	5.18	17.86
159.0	822.23	1142.22	6.11	5.61	15.06
160.0	1431.59	1664.59	8.34	6.32	39.06
161.0	879.54	953.71	21.23	10.53	22.52
162.0	781.35	936.56	12.37	5.62	46.29
163.0	718.32	964.81	11.27	6.77	7.40
164.0	745.52	1331.97	11.90	6.35	76.86
165.0	1113.00	1891.76	11.08	7.13	29.37
166.0	900.37	1110.38	6.59	7.49	17.34
167.0	1041.93	1232.08	6.32	6.76	27.26
168.0	1044.25	1223.95	8.54	7.05	67.87
169.0	995.91	1027.47	6.16	4.69	24.75
170.0	962.60	1069.89	6.17	4.94	24.91
171.0	1738.56	2121.84	7.85	8.37	28.46

TABLE B-5
VARIABLES BY OBE ECONOMIC AREA

OBE ECON AREA	AVERAGE CAPITAL INVEST.	PERCENT CH AGRIC.OUTPUT 1650-1964	VALUE OF CROPS PER TOTAL OUTPUT	VALUE CROPS + LIVESTOCK PER TOT OUTP	FARMS OF 1000 TO 10 ACRES
1.0	8.890	110.30	62.18	64.79	.62
2.0	6.397	87.64	17.38	23.31	.22
3.0	5.426	33.45	8.79	19.13	.55
4.0	4.322	.66	31.79	38.84	.03
5.0	5.370	14.61	34.15	39.65	.05
6.0	4.929	30.97	14.87	25.38	.19
7.0	5.184	28.44	12.99	24.46	.16
8.0	5.013	48.54	51.46	61.75	.19
9.0	5.673	49.75	29.05	41.32	.08
10.0	6.022	57.37	27.45	41.37	.07
11.0	5.723	41.79	19.30	35.06	.07
12.0	5.216	30.33	9.98	21.22	.25
13.0	3.961	30.76	19.70	29.59	.06
14.0	4.061	9.21	42.11	47.20	.02
15.0	5.814	20.86	42.86	52.82	.04
16.0	5.213	58.85	23.92	47.70	.04
17.0	4.673	62.70	32.31	43.39	.11
18.0	6.484	13.20	35.04	68.59	.19
19.0	6.461	55.27	22.38	49.65	.42
20.0	6.274	61.67	54.59	76.27	.07
21.0	7.347	65.42	49.20	72.66	.25
22.0	3.661	61.17	74.20	89.51	.18
23.0	6.007	82.51	83.40	91.55	.07
24.0	8.836	121.09	78.03	87.60	.05
25.0	4.011	120.20	52.72	64.37	.03
26.0	6.876	64.41	38.46	52.90	.15
27.0	5.441	73.61	43.86	62.47	.05
28.0	6.271	15.00	50.49	67.38	.31
29.0	6.352	96.74	64.78	78.53	.30
30.0	8.319	58.36	89.87	96.37	.11
31.0	10.258	98.68	65.99	90.25	.22
32.0	4.522	89.59	58.50	77.79	1.00
33.0	7.749	107.12	61.63	86.76	.55
34.0	7.533	156.54	49.66	73.35	.54
35.0	8.635	205.52	88.94	94.61	.15
36.0	6.888	259.51	70.31	81.61	.36
37.0	8.998	153.53	80.12	88.15	.29
38.0	7.168	60.91	50.71	81.73	.53
39.0	16.406	106.54	43.71	77.99	.32
40.0	5.682	52.85	47.21	81.35	.60
41.0	15.458	87.45	68.85	92.92	.80
42.0	5.547	91.71	58.24	81.60	1.40
43.0	6.106	107.45	38.74	71.28	1.07
44.0	5.480	173.32	19.17	30.00	.18
45.0	6.085	134.66	39.26	59.23	.24
46.0	6.506	77.41	85.88	95.95	.28
47.0	6.091	65.64	57.12	78.63	.20
48.0	5.298	188.39	29.70	47.50	.13
49.0	7.576	44.53	39.60	80.07	.06
50.0	5.724	75.10	39.61	66.20	.03
51.0	7.148	49.22	44.83	75.77	.02
52.0	10.268	9.59	28.45	66.77	.13
53.0	7.856	33.94	52.76	88.82	.03
54.0	4.404	44.43	36.66	73.90	.04
55.0	1.829	85.63	47.90	87.58	.17
56.0	11.512	63.27	54.11	92.52	.38
57.0	7.795	46.76	63.48	95.79	.29
58.0	5.989	53.27	68.25	95.40	.24
59.0	8.944	42.59	44.71	93.82	.15
60.0	5.968	39.14	33.98	88.01	.08
61.0	4.457	34.25	38.52	83.80	.06

TABLE B-5
VARIABLES BY OBE ECONOMIC AREA

OBE ECON AREA	AVERAGE CAPITAL INVEST.	PERCENT CH AGRIC.OUTPUT 1650-1964	VALUE OF CROPS PER TOTAL OUTPUT	VALUE CROPS + LIVESTOCK PER TOT OUTP	FARMS OF 1000 TO 10 ACRES
62.0	5.487	22.92	37.95	77.14	.03
63.0	4.552	46.81	36.32	75.53	.05
64.0	7.198	24.92	29.32	76.96	.24
65.0	5.718	19.28	9.10	56.70	.59
66.0	9.200	38.77	23.35	46.59	.08
67.0	6.885	25.68	22.72	43.01	.06
68.0	5.814	46.27	37.91	63.48	.05
69.0	4.250	60.62	42.59	75.44	.03
70.0	5.926	67.82	53.69	85.08	.04
71.0	5.331	45.69	41.18	61.77	.03
72.0	7.472	80.74	52.27	71.93	.18
73.0	4.902	64.07	43.69	62.22	.09
74.0	5.227	65.13	40.02	67.70	.09
75.0	5.406	55.89	38.80	74.08	.03
76.0	4.749	66.88	41.77	72.97	.03
77.0	6.617	44.34	49.48	87.96	.18
78.0	4.580	57.23	38.10	94.70	.23
79.0	7.634	55.38	17.01	92.90	.11
80.0	3.631	47.16	12.43	90.32	.13
81.0	6.601	51.38	7.18	69.40	.15
82.0	4.555	58.01	21.60	73.15	.13
83.0	5.355	41.99	13.77	49.16	.20
84.0	4.411	30.30	18.54	42.92	.04
85.0	6.938	38.56	12.39	35.18	.10
86.0	7.338	70.31	15.29	34.74	.25
87.0	4.697	-11.39	16.56	38.62	.48
88.0	6.278	48.86	9.78	29.06	.28
89.0	5.655	50.50	12.31	41.60	.25
90.0	8.220	39.06	29.16	69.94	.17
91.0	4.663	42.85	27.50	65.43	.21
92.0	7.347	50.08	76.08	90.12	12.68
93.0	8.301	36.21	64.54	93.97	48.36
94.0	6.972	38.67	57.43	97.07	33.10
95.0	14.135	40.70	28.80	96.11	16.14
96.0	10.007	47.30	31.44	90.18	69.89
97.0	6.920	45.23	51.89	82.66	9.07
98.0	7.444	36.05	18.48	84.97	7.89
99.0	5.162	51.34	18.02	87.90	1.37
100.0	7.503	42.46	14.83	96.18	42.37
101.0	8.149	34.14	45.22	98.54	14.14
102.0	10.348	77.56	36.34	95.23	5.41
103.0	6.019	63.54	16.04	92.70	1.41
104.0	5.735	78.96	33.42	91.51	.10
105.0	5.361	64.53	25.62	85.43	.07
106.0	4.950	51.35	22.82	90.64	.18
107.0	7.666	65.88	23.18	94.51	.20
108.0	4.883	69.27	45.15	91.07	.43
109.0	9.397	65.36	49.76	95.25	8.74
110.0	4.822	55.76	46.27	95.53	6.44
111.0	5.543	36.72	30.13	89.54	1.03
112.0	4.842	58.39	28.97	87.52	.99
113.0	4.769	63.11	31.89	92.42	.34
114.0	5.882	60.20	41.49	86.42	.30
115.0	8.473	45.79	73.39	94.74	.37
116.0	4.937	55.01	23.54	68.11	.96
117.0	5.109	126.26	71.33	83.08	1.03
118.0	4.609	145.73	19.21	65.72	1.14
119.0	7.289	84.86	19.02	59.73	1.22
120.0	6.686	32.31	45.90	90.37	3.45
121.0	5.723	4.97	52.82	96.04	7.05
122.0	10.455	30.57	55.50	99.08	19.16

TABLE B-5
VARIABLES BY OBE ECONOMIC AREA

OBE ECON AREA	AVERAGE CAPITAL INVEST.	PERCENT CH AGRIC.OUTPUT 1650-1964	VALUE OF CROPS PER TOTAL OUTPUT	VALUE CROPS + LIVESTOCK PER TOT OUTP	FARMS OF 1000 TO 10 ACRES
123.0	6.775	57.66	85.24	98.82	9.12
124.0	21.839	7.45	73.35	98.58	11.52
125.0	3.554	-11.05	52.34	93.90	6.91
126.0	6.050	4.49	25.30	93.39	12.86
127.0	5.490	9.62	35.68	78.90	1.54
128.0	4.613	27.68	39.84	85.34	2.38
129.0	5.708	24.61	37.80	84.84	2.73
130.0	13.805	76.00	18.89	57.50	.64
131.0	5.311	73.41	27.32	70.13	.92
132.0	7.035	13.24	47.05	77.93	.46
133.0	8.361	82.74	66.42	90.62	.34
134.0	10.663	100.05	86.07	96.11	.68
135.0	5.388	229.79	37.34	58.90	.53
136.0	5.709	109.52	31.22	68.28	.38
137.0	13.914	68.59	53.26	85.75	.37
138.0	8.625	70.86	45.54	70.42	.30
139.0	14.263	69.78	76.56	93.09	.39
140.0	22.128	102.47	55.58	76.44	.98
141.0	10.052	68.43	54.11	85.77	1.18
142.0	4.926	36.36	30.07	84.06	4.16
143.0	11.339	17.24	54.58	93.80	10.15
144.0	6.538	-12.63	87.76	96.87	.63
145.0	6.012	57.87	53.74	94.54	3.57
146.0	8.993	30.14	13.38	85.84	1.28
147.0	5.331	4.65	39.23	93.21	7.04
148.0	5.636	70.22	34.99	92.64	6.55
149.0	9.169	15.07	27.85	93.68	2.91
150.0	5.354	13.87	13.25	97.53	20.08
151.0	5.651	23.77	23.63	73.61	1.04
152.0	11.051	77.63	59.67	91.61	1.74
153.0	12.547	28.16	21.10	89.58	3.84
154.0	6.509	68.99	76.50	94.31	2.49
155.0	6.366	47.03	26.32	40.84	.04
156.0	5.516	77.53	64.17	94.63	1.25
157.0	7.436	47.59	57.95	75.84	.32
158.0	9.578	29.59	40.56	80.28	.60
159.0	6.672	78.68	39.68	82.35	.91
160.0	6.912	42.97	10.89	93.79	6.68
161.0	8.403	38.59	20.58	82.46	2.84
162.0	7.484	131.97	57.43	93.99	1.13
163.0	3.321	114.49	46.10	92.93	2.57
164.0	3.224	113.71	46.29	57.69	.05
165.0	5.252	91.72	46.80	75.15	.19
166.0	12.198	136.74	74.39	90.15	.65
167.0	7.586	102.89	55.16	72.45	.37
168.0	6.847	104.04	73.50	89.91	.66
169.0	10.864	36.38	36.90	91.92	2.39
170.0	8.525	40.60	22.11	50.05	1.21
171.0	7.141	69.73	64.87	79.35	.34

TABLE B-6
VARIABLES BY OBE ECONOMIC AREA

OBE ECON AREA	VALUE OF LAND + BLDG PER FARM	TENANT FARMS PER TOTAL FARMS	LOCAL GOV. REVENUE PER CAPITA 1960	PROPERTY TAX PER CAPITA	GOVERNMENT TRANSFERS PER CAPITA
1.0	15.69	2.25	141.55	54.14	30.23
2.0	14.10	2.14	138.95	57.01	22.00
3.0	18.49	3.19	146.59	58.28	25.67
4.0	28.52	3.42	236.74	83.67	58.95
5.0	36.70	4.15	201.73	76.44	41.91
6.0	21.27	4.06	236.78	69.10	93.85
7.0	18.10	4.01	264.68	62.04	119.21
8.0	25.85	5.85	259.33	64.27	90.74
9.0	21.03	4.32	247.94	67.45	90.06
10.0	15.33	2.86	155.24	35.59	53.55
11.0	15.33	6.72	141.03	23.76	59.4C
12.0	16.26	3.74	243.31	49.96	117.11
13.0	16.43	4.79	121.30	28.76	47.88
14.0	53.92	9.75	304.20	59.51	68.01
15.0	38.52	9.84	186.07	49.92	38.43
16.0	22.64	14.04	146.27	28.37	55.81
17.0	34.41	14.93	213.10	47.57	92.89
18.0	45.93	15.16	238.15	46.65	71.39
19.0	19.47	6.13	99.83	21.28	39.62
20.0	13.15	23.07	116.33	22.85	47.95
21.0	18.28	17.56	132.37	31.53	45.40
22.0	23.34	31.22	145.84	20.94	54.59
23.0	16.28	48.68	127.68	19.18	71.45
24.0	15.34	28.17	119.61	16.39	73.49
25.0	13.01	16.81	151.04	28.00	69.10
26.0	14.17	15.47	136.53	25.78	68.23
27.0	11.30	13.00	125.20	21.11	66.13
28.0	13.96	21.75	109.23	20.77	46.62
29.0	14.54	31.65	101.57	16.28	46.31
30.0	14.11	45.51	88.93	14.14	47.35
31.0	15.50	12.62	101.46	17.76	49.41
32.0	14.95	31.53	120.68	19.21	51.70
33.0	17.81	28.15	129.37	24.16	51.43
34.0	33.43	8.29	150.91	28.90	55.72
35.0	84.37	2.61	176.95	39.58	56.93
36.0	137.60	10.87	213.60	61.13	39.82
37.0	82.83	3.66	178.49	43.95	33.59
38.0	19.06	10.25	162.31	20.42	75.69
39.0	17.00	7.74	149.60	20.94	66.63
40.0	11.62	34.63	112.86	8.25	62.85
41.0	20.02	32.93	131.10	17.78	63.74
42.0	19.18	25.90	131.43	19.46	58.80
43.0	12.72	30.12	123.91	17.23	52.24
44.0	13.32	19.09	154.05	34.17	49.48
45.0	9.88	26.85	124.57	15.09	52.07
46.0	17.06	48.05	128.17	25.72	48.77
47.0	12.08	26.98	126.54	11.33	53.23
48.0	11.50	16.87	131.20	23.43	52.93
49.0	12.68	16.43	125.46	22.97	54.19
50.0	9.95	9.13	114.74	21.01	52.82
51.0	12.14	10.26	100.35	19.13	48.46
52.0	8.83	7.56	120.37	23.86	51.84
53.0	15.82	18.92	107.81	19.69	47.81
54.0	17.04	14.05	148.91	32.35	38.7C
55.0	25.85	14.60	156.33	38.77	52.0(
56.0	32.42	12.54	191.35	51.94	64.61
57.0	89.52	42.52	188.05	61.11	39.76
58.0	96.39	42.74	179.39	56.98	38.09
59.0	67.16	32.67	175.98	56.27	48.70
60.0	43.57	17.92	193.96	64.11	47.20
61.0	44.60	19.94	185.99	57.69	55.31
62.0	23.39	19.26	204.33	49.61	55.50

TABLE B-6
VARIABLES BY OBE ECONOMIC AREA

OBE ECON AREA	VALUE OF LAND + BLDG PER FARM	TENANT FARMS PER TOTAL FARMS	LOCAL GOV. REVENUE PER CAPITA 1960	PROPERTY TAX PER CAPITA	GOVERNMENT TRANSFERS PER CAPITA
63.0	40.90	23.63	194.17	50.02	56.87
64.0	29.78	13.51	181.50	40.64	63.29
65.0	9.13	4.74	102.42	20.11	37.75
66.0	15.32	5.50	163.90	39.64	46.00
67.0	20.17	4.69	169.33	45.63	48.02
68.0	28.74	9.83	200.18	61.00	50.76
69.0	44.09	22.61	170.75	44.39	56.84
70.0	44.84	22.67	195.99	48.70	58.02
71.0	32.67	8.25	231.01	69.90	65.94
72.0	25.37	6.97	190.66	45.63	79.30
73.0	18.16	4.27	182.17	43.63	76.33
74.0	26.62	7.45	202.99	50.39	72.76
75.0	38.11	18.93	180.89	55.03	48.53
76.0	32.83	13.03	180.36	53.74	57.49
77.0	82.79	38.56	230.54	76.10	46.23
78.0	80.41	42.72	183.13	63.64	33.90
79.0	58.63	41.12	208.07	66.95	37.71
80.0	53.89	32.66	202.66	74.77	38.71
81.0	31.22	28.04	183.07	55.74	55.99
82.0	55.15	37.25	201.29	62.61	54.59
83.0	25.54	18.46	251.66	67.28	97.51
84.0	33.00	16.45	267.56	82.33	81.32
85.0	18.88	5.08	207.21	51.17	89.69
86.0	13.91	3.95	223.60	51.68	104.77
87.0	9.38	1.88	303.35	82.14	111.67
88.0	14.13	6.81	252.81	49.62	139.72
89.0	17.00	13.37	234.97	54.95	108.54
90.0	38.35	20.22	246.37	73.83	73.63
91.0	31.89	17.47	237.44	68.07	74.12
92.0	37.31	14.65	224.86	62.74	74.13
93.0	41.62	17.21	184.17	58.17	49.17
94.0	97.22	14.15	214.48	74.68	43.18
95.0	62.64	16.98	225.29	70.20	46.03
96.0	38.27	16.64	172.90	54.30	39.73
97.0	32.19	17.49	205.80	60.01	62.27
98.0	33.12	23.47	188.81	73.12	19.26
99.0	44.90	38.47	200.61	71.16	36.85
100.0	56.81	16.12	185.10	67.94	36.04
101.0	68.40	33.74	227.69	67.88	50.59
102.0	50.40	33.48	208.16	67.66	43.32
103.0	45.19	39.05	186.82	65.35	39.33
104.0	66.62	48.02	225.71	73.25	53.32
105.0	53.36	38.88	213.43	73.13	44.70
106.0	40.86	28.24	218.55	73.44	44.80
107.0	48.50	36.89	195.60	61.23	37.42
108.0	41.28	38.47	188.95	60.91	34.78
109.0	55.78	28.60	234.91	80.64	56.18
110.0	68.65	31.18	241.74	77.03	55.18
111.0	31.50	19.06	181.82	52.84	42.38
112.0	22.83	11.53	137.14	36.66	33.77
113.0	41.88	24.94	172.73	56.58	37.32
114.0	26.67	15.74	167.04	46.89	34.69
115.0	20.67	24.55	138.24	27.85	55.16
116.0	15.03	10.20	148.86	35.68	54.07
117.0	15.75	19.98	106.61	22.55	40.73
118.0	11.63	11.13	105.92	20.45	49.47
119.0	21.27	14.90	136.09	34.00	44.03
120.0	35.58	21.48	152.02	34.60	54.54
121.0	48.35	26.08	143.80	31.84	54.43
122.0	98.24	27.82	208.21	50.27	63.44
123.0	106.27	43.54	166.86	48.23	51.47

TABLE B-6
VARIABLES BY OBE ECONOMIC AREA

OBE ECON AREA	VALUE OF LAND + BLDG PER FARM	TENANT FARMS PER TOTAL FARMS	LOCAL GOV. REVENUE PER CAPITA 1960	PROPERTY TAX PER CAPITA	GOVERNMENT TRANSFERS PER CAPITA
124.0	140.18	33.79	232.88	72.68	42.73
125.0	46.21	25.33	162.20	41.89	47.94
126.0	79.54	21.73	158.78	41.34	53.34
127.0	34.53	21.71	158.90	44.17	42.67
128.0	29.73	21.66	124.17	25.40	55.29
129.0	32.83	19.89	134.91	29.76	49.10
130.0	15.73	11.50	154.80	35.76	58.63
131.0	14.08	12.99	124.44	21.15	60.64
132.0	17.64	20.52	151.88	28.56	78.21
133.0	16.46	24.27	144.12	19.43	91.08
134.0	19.83	41.09	118.94	22.87	47.38
135.0	11.81	30.84	136.43	29.13	49.88
136.0	10.75	19.28	135.07	19.11	64.38
137.0	15.56	14.77	131.12	17.89	51.26
138.0	18.88	15.86	155.33	24.55	63.74
139.0	26.00	32.81	137.49	22.59	68.06
140.0	31.97	10.44	181.63	57.88	45.89
141.0	45.76	20.34	186.88	58.63	40.18
142.0	46.02	18.75	133.48	32.16	48.25
143.0	96.22	26.88	178.34	46.67	50.42
144.0	62.07	14.43	156.66	31.88	55.35
145.0	92.85	15.53	165.55	28.26	73.32
146.0	33.78	5.26	158.43	18.69	90.03
147.0	53.55	17.32	237.61	56.38	103.79
148.0	68.76	28.44	240.62	70.14	72.04
149.0	42.28	9.53	275.25	64.56	113.39
150.0	88.61	14.04	227.20	52.31	78.41
151.0	42.19	5.17	188.53	47.63	68.87
152.0	53.18	17.85	184.16	51.12	51.94
153.0	44.32	7.70	172.37	59.94	34.70
154.0	67.40	13.03	210.20	41.30	85.60
155.0	27.14	6.19	226.19	37.85	91.09
156.0	59.91	10.84	209.16	38.60	92.73
157.0	33.53	6.34	211.46	59.14	61.80
158.0	35.37	5.53	222.05	54.70	89.49
159.0	44.11	14.82	177.84	49.41	47.14
160.0	116.71	8.41	245.79	52.30	82.96
161.0	41.32	2.93	246.71	55.51	77.96
162.0	186.80	11.85	195.13	49.91	70.40
163.0	127.32	11.60	202.50	56.68	71.31
164.0	80.13	5.20	265.44	65.59	92.64
165.0	132.93	11.91	302.57	84.94	96.01
166.0	126.52	11.38	336.63	85.25	125.10
167.0	75.07	13.27	331.26	76.08	123.57
168.0	96.73	10.75	286.06	71.29	106.66
169.0	73.24	8.12	329.78	76.98	138.59
170.0	55.91	19.12	312.04	67.29	136.67
171.0	99.57	11.88	309.59	84.46	101.35

TABLE B-7
VARIABLES BY OBE ECONOMIC AREA

OBE ECON AREA	NON EDUC GOV.EXP PER.CAP.	TOT.GOV. EXPEND PER.CAP.	AVERAGE BONDS PER TOT.REV.	PERCENT CHANGE BOND INV.	RESIDUAL FROM EXP GOV.REV
1.0	65.12	145.64	62.33	-16.68	-15.99
2.0	63.60	143.58	79.48	-23.92	-50.03
3.0	65.77	147.49	73.97	-32.80	-25.00
4.0	139.37	227.82	119.85	-34.72	6.35
5.0	111.68	215.51	146.76	-6.04	-43.93
6.0	123.30	238.21	104.82	-10.01	26.03
7.0	146.79	277.94	112.40	10.39	62.98
8.0	155.07	276.80	116.26	33.07	12.72
9.0	150.23	262.22	132.66	-3.32	22.00
10.0	62.39	161.74	116.31	-4.70	-33.19
11.0	45.06	142.39	125.03	-3.76	-36.67
12.0	114.84	261.72	91.94	6.81	46.04
13.0	59.21	137.40	87.90	22.43	-49.69
14.0	200.44	307.79	187.29	-30.29	24.35
15.0	107.10	191.19	182.53	-15.58	-51.58
16.0	53.55	163.85	169.26	-16.02	-50.38
17.0	126.24	221.44	181.17	-35.63	-2.47
18.0	165.14	266.31	123.95	-1.49	-9.73
19.0	35.95	108.41	89.00	-7.66	-53.64
20.0	49.98	122.17	130.11	-30.25	-37.06
21.0	68.99	144.24	149.27	-8.94	-46.07
22.0	137.70	208.80	244.36	42.49	-26.78
23.0	61.56	136.73	135.57	-51.19	.28
24.0	53.16	122.54	124.47	-59.49	-18.37
25.0	79.28	161.59	130.95	-43.76	-22.23
26.0	66.00	145.08	153.19	-57.39	-30.36
27.0	53.73	124.17	148.31	-50.20	-16.58
28.0	46.10	106.74	110.80	-39.02	-42.65
29.0	44.26	103.90	76.96	-36.17	-28.99
30.0	28.38	87.15	33.53	-34.97	-15.31
31.0	36.98	101.05	63.55	-53.84	-29.69
32.0	62.84	124.25	97.02	-17.42	-12.84
33.0	65.37	125.38	166.15	-21.04	-8.01
34.0	91.00	170.35	152.23	-37.52	-23.23
35.0	96.17	189.92	160.00	-50.66	-13.96
36.0	132.25	213.63	144.71	-40.57	-3.85
37.0	118.03	199.37	159.11	-26.35	-4.86
38.0	73.52	164.33	132.58	-36.12	33.59
39.0	74.22	169.52	123.96	-24.46	-21.70
40.0	61.47	117.49	129.28	-38.41	-13.87
41.0	63.21	134.48	106.49	-30.89	12.14
42.0	69.09	134.31	92.75	-29.16	4.42
43.0	63.09	126.80	131.21	-20.40	-16.08
44.0	97.09	166.96	165.70	-14.49	-29.44
45.0	71.42	128.24	152.03	-19.31	-27.01
46.0	82.30	144.57	230.62	-39.06	-9.91
47.0	72.35	134.58	189.23	-13.41	-11.32
48.0	79.44	145.24	157.73	-14.82	-15.97
49.0	71.42	135.83	197.55	-21.70	-22.49
50.0	48.29	117.91	172.73	-27.04	-13.88
51.0	36.62	100.62	126.03	-19.26	-24.67
52.0	45.21	124.66	82.81	-11.14	-22.97
53.0	44.20	111.18	116.39	-3.93	-14.91
54.0	67.95	154.23	156.55	-14.57	-46.71
55.0	75.20	157.28	113.55	-35.70	-4.70
56.0	111.75	221.46	71.67	45.51	20.11
57.0	81.14	177.63	120.39	-36.50	-12.37
58.0	76.55	180.64	109.08	-15.75	-19.36
59.0	75.07	169.58	63.11	-2.63	-12.40
60.0	98.31	205.26	100.08	15.96	-27.00
61.0	81.42	198.59	68.70	-22.98	-20.77

TABLE B-7
VARIABLES BY OBE ECONOMIC AREA

OBE ECON AREA	NON EDUC GOV.EXP PER.CAP.	TOT.GOV. EXPEND PER.CAP.	AVERAGE BONDS PER TOT.REV.	PERCENT CHANGE BOND INV.	RESIDUAL FROM EXP GOV.REV
62.0	125.48	216.47	158.16	-13.53	-17.39
63.0	103.60	198.43	126.55	-21.16	-28.47
64.0	102.44	188.79	135.68	-12.98	-17.58
65.0	39.49	98.69	56.58	-19.80	-43.43
66.0	85.20	174.39	172.49	-3.94	-47.07
67.0	82.60	174.77	118.42	1.31	-43.84
68.0	114.78	208.43	135.16	-20.93	-33.87
69.0	83.85	174.56	96.06	7.40	-11.01
70.0	99.53	204.73	105.75	-4.65	-16.60
71.0	136.53	246.74	115.66	17.70	-10.08
72.0	101.34	208.70	90.48	-5.74	11.59
73.0	99.02	196.66	76.18	41.80	-8.95
74.0	104.63	220.25	82.42	20.27	-6.29
75.0	90.41	182.56	64.89	-10.26	-20.37
76.0	86.52	193.11	89.58	8.51	-41.58
77.0	146.32	242.65	165.76	-10.18	-41.72
78.0	73.83	182.75	115.72	-8.21	-39.15
79.0	96.05	200.79	113.65	-16.31	-8.22
80.0	100.03	211.69	84.91	-3.09	-10.83
81.0	102.28	183.79	62.92	-3.23	26.20
82.0	101.43	205.87	111.63	-11.64	-25.43
83.0	170.80	283.28	107.11	14.69	51.38
84.0	182.42	277.32	103.31	3.64	18.60
85.0	132.00	221.76	77.74	-.03	27.80
86.0	137.30	227.79	51.65	1.00	58.61
87.0	165.41	293.19	67.41	-19.01	123.46
88.0	152.56	275.71	61.11	8.97	86.94
89.0	149.27	247.02	55.85	17.67	72.27
90.0	143.00	264.49	127.80	-8.98	55.42
91.0	139.63	249.77	122.65	11.27	31.16
92.0	118.47	232.79	97.69	-2.57	74.06
93.0	96.27	201.56	92.75	-1.38	35.37
94.0	90.71	190.82	116.71	-20.24	5.25
95.0	110.19	225.74	106.17	-9.18	24.96
96.0	79.36	176.94	78.32	24.15	42.01
97.0	108.08	213.43	100.68	19.87	57.10
98.0	86.24	185.52	34.31	-10.84	69.99
99.0	98.59	195.27	67.40	-22.17	59.05
100.0	72.58	174.45	57.48	-23.35	13.71
101.0	115.42	226.61	114.21	-18.82	33.77
102.0	109.70	205.28	147.17	-66.36	27.44
103.0	106.92	196.49	70.25	.94	28.22
104.0	102.11	203.83	64.18	-18.39	69.23
105.0	101.96	211.94	76.43	-2.23	23.12
106.0	104.46	209.84	68.89	-2.31	22.53
107.0	108.85	194.23	195.33	-71.93	-11.43
108.0	97.59	175.03	101.82	-53.93	-2.60
109.0	128.88	240.09	93.14	-8.63	48.49
110.0	118.03	234.21	139.85	-33.87	24.23
111.0	89.54	181.74	156.57	-20.74	-27.53
112.0	64.41	144.57	103.62	3.50	-21.35
113.0	80.10	174.21	90.80	-13.04	-6.46
114.0	86.98	170.32	138.26	-3.07	-51.28
115.0	53.97	136.99	107.20	-22.76	1.21
116.0	67.83	146.91	90.30	-33.96	-7.78
117.0	49.86	109.00	138.20	-21.01	-38.93
118.0	40.63	103.71	85.90	-17.86	-26.71
119.0	65.14	140.49	154.14	-20.56	-51.45
120.0	72.05	151.99	135.81	-22.44	-24.94
121.0	66.86	146.14	119.91	-34.39	-32.45
122.0	89.16	201.29	144.36	-36.49	-22.38

TABLE B-7
VARIABLES BY OBE ECONOMIC AREA

OBE ECON AREA	NON EDUC GOV.EXP PER.CAP.	TOT.GOV. EXPEND PER.CAP.	AVERAGE BONDS PER TOT.REV.	PERCENT CHANGE BOND INV.	RESIDUAL FROM EXP GOV.REV
123.0	81.85	177.69	217.17	-39.68	-44.46
124.0	108.73	234.72	177.42	-39.29	15.57
125.0	71.61	156.00	177.40	-37.40	-14.39
126.0	67.18	153.45	160.67	-45.22	-20.15
127.0	90.32	171.60	231.68	-27.06	-58.57
128.0	50.85	127.22	156.27	-19.49	-40.58
129.0	76.82	153.19	268.03	-47.38	-15.64
130.0	56.27	155.43	127.79	-37.15	8.66
131.0	48.55	126.08	126.17	-31.14	1.64
132.0	68.31	163.29	153.96	-2.95	-12.54
133.0	64.68	156.46	169.28	-21.77	16.37
134.0	63.20	124.37	107.75	12.95	-.54
135.0	83.81	147.30	142.23	18.36	.08
136.0	72.82	148.80	87.29	-10.45	22.27
137.0	83.00	140.80	175.38	-26.08	-19.39
138.0	94.91	166.04	216.52	-4.19	-18.76
139.0	72.14	152.79	193.02	2.69	-2.72
140.0	99.65	198.13	250.06	-27.44	-3.74
141.0	104.15	204.84	235.52	-24.85	-27.40
142.0	66.08	139.54	213.72	-34.41	-21.98
143.0	88.79	177.47	219.32	-33.39	24.57
144.0	81.36	166.64	237.04	-11.47	47.71
145.0	76.66	173.90	107.87	-35.89	-18.64
146.0	62.19	164.28	122.49	-32.14	-26.14
147.0	131.74	238.74	79.20	-44.42	56.72
148.0	128.45	239.39	131.28	-39.41	8.64
149.0	145.32	277.03	77.71	-16.17	96.61
150.0	113.29	239.03	98.85	-17.71	-5.03
151.0	72.59	194.69	129.85	-22.90	-1.60
152.0	101.94	194.08	89.73	-8.99	-1.45
153.0	82.93	170.12	79.48	4.61	-19.66
154.0	97.34	205.19	302.99	-74.36	6.40
155.0	121.13	237.87	140.40	-44.03	-11.38
156.0	97.19	215.80	173.47	-31.29	6.83
157.0	97.74	213.28	91.84	-32.77	-5.42
158.0	97.86	225.50	82.24	-27.42	19.00
159.0	84.70	176.07	164.18	-30.70	-13.61
160.0	155.35	282.14	99.22	27.39	-25.17
161.0	166.00	279.67	146.93	-14.91	2.07
162.0	95.96	214.69	177.17	-40.78	7.30
163.0	86.11	214.31	89.84	-11.74	3.70
164.0	153.51	281.33	89.69	-12.51	41.54
165.0	182.19	314.46	99.14	-24.89	31.31
166.0	196.38	342.53	66.16	-16.26	123.45
167.0	214.65	335.66	90.74	7.06	117.41
168.0	176.12	317.11	86.87	3.75	52.27
169.0	194.68	335.21	52.54	-30.42	96.65
170.0	174.58	304.30	46.58	-2.55	77.49
171.0	183.26	318.99	94.65	-10.94	39.29

TABLE B-8
VARIABLES BY OBE ECONOMIC AREA

OBE ECON AREA	PERCENT VOTING 1960	INDEX OF CHANGE IN VOTE 60-64	FAMILIES WITH Y OF 10K TO 3K	PERCENT WHITE COL EMPLOYMENT	PERCENT NON-WHITE POPULATION
1.0	65.86	7.40	.23	35.65	1.22
2.0	76.19	6.69	.44	35.07	.29
3.0	73.96	2.43	.39	37.03	.18
4.0	76.50	3.31	1.23	43.06	2.31
5.0	76.18	2.00	1.67	42.71	3.66
6.0	81.33	3.93	.84	43.48	2.08
7.0	76.15	4.58	.97	42.65	1.89
8.0	77.78	1.96	1.57	42.88	3.61
9.0	73.55	3.66	1.13	40.50	5.42
10.0	68.08	2.45	.63	38.50	1.94
11.0	68.64	4.62	.44	35.44	.62
12.0	75.18	4.37	.67	37.67	.86
13.0	78.59	8.08	.33	33.96	.37
14.0	65.50	.53	1.84	48.16	10.46
15.0	70.87	.41	1.24	41.84	12.71
16.0	66.91	3.84	.56	35.61	2.45
17.0	56.25	1.19	.84	40.62	21.24
18.0	30.06	22.32	2.30	56.40	24.50
19.0	45.25	5.02	.22	31.29	5.29
20.0	34.26	10.75	.24	32.17	19.42
21.0	33.33	14.32	.41	39.56	33.20
22.0	28.53	11.04	.37	38.88	32.09
23.0	41.91	5.33	.13	30.98	37.83
24.0	43.94	3.85	.11	31.02	29.18
25.0	58.50	1.25	.30	30.11	16.48
26.0	61.35	.37	.27	30.36	18.27
27.0	62.24	1.09	.16	28.88	13.64
28.0	32.55	7.23	.20	27.90	20.45
29.0	28.30	13.62	.17	34.39	41.84
30.0	28.44	11.66	.09	26.07	44.76
31.0	29.28	13.70	.20	34.73	40.86
32.0	31.51	17.74	.15	31.32	39.86
33.0	34.61	20.91	.17	32.63	33.85
34.0	47.61	13.47	.34	40.52	25.61
35.0	47.81	14.50	.44	44.15	16.17
36.0	51.50	7.30	.53	44.09	16.91
37.0	51.41	8.52	.30	41.05	13.18
38.0	43.14	16.25	.19	37.86	30.83
39.0	45.70	12.18	.35	39.36	17.95
40.0	27.50	7.69	.14	31.58	39.83
41.0	29.80	18.64	.11	29.12	38.77
42.0	32.40	19.16	.18	31.80	39.88
43.0	25.47	10.64	.17	29.94	35.90
44.0	34.81	17.96	.41	39.46	21.48
45.0	30.69	6.74	.20	33.32	28.19
46.0	40.21	9.42	.15	32.51	36.26
47.0	36.07	4.62	.20	33.75	13.26
48.0	46.65	6.34	.20	31.44	10.04
49.0	49.42	3.21	.17	33.44	13.21
50.0	59.27	1.66	.15	34.26	4.80
51.0	53.58	.34	.14	31.15	4.92
52.0	75.37	4.96	.21	36.07	4.01
53.0	64.11	3.96	.14	32.75	6.81
54.0	66.46	3.24	.48	37.40	9.43
55.0	75.91	3.71	.24	33.34	3.74
56.0	80.58	4.99	.30	35.73	2.08
57.0	79.53	2.76	.61	41.12	2.97
58.0	73.44	1.03	.57	41.48	3.80
59.0	82.27	.80	.57	37.88	.66
60.0	73.12	1.11	.99	41.57	7.83
61.0	76.74	2.39	.77	33.03	3.66

TABLE B-8
VARIABLES BY OBE ECONOMIC AREA

OBE ECON AREA	PERCENT VOTING 1960	INDEX OF CHANGE IN VOTE 60-64	FAMILIES WITH Y OF 10K TO 3K	PERCENT WHITE COL EMPLOYMENT	PERCENT NON-WHITE POPULATION
62.0	71.05	4.63	.84	40.24	8.50
63.0	69.28	2.18	1.10	40.17	8.56
64.0	69.59	.12	.67	41.52	6.49
65.0	77.61	5.33	.20	35.29	1.87
66.0	72.25	3.57	.72	39.63	5.11
67.0	71.22	4.71	1.04	35.71	7.33
68.0	71.11	3.55	1.39	40.50	9.16
69.0	77.77	5.46	.47	34.61	3.01
70.0	71.46	3.76	.97	38.22	5.02
71.0	72.46	2.67	1.51	42.05	13.55
72.0	72.28	2.34	.54	36.54	3.30
73.0	74.87	1.69	.68	37.44	3.57
74.0	70.28	2.33	1.00	40.05	4.07
75.0	77.78	1.29	.83	38.05	2.47
76.0	76.64	4.60	.86	37.06	5.06
77.0	74.67	.22	2.19	43.76	13.95
78.0	76.53	2.68	.80	39.69	2.52
79.0	74.78	3.01	.74	36.92	1.42
80.0	74.28	2.06	.60	39.61	.70
81.0	79.55	6.21	.28	29.14	.10
82.0	73.34	2.03	.93	36.52	2.79
83.0	73.07	.31	.66	41.62	.79
84.0	71.44	.14	1.65	40.14	4.02
85.0	74.52	2.72	.49	33.96	1.06
86.0	77.64	3.45	.32	31.00	.51
87.0	79.42	3.75	.43	37.60	1.19
88.0	75.51	4.58	.31	32.51	.64
89.0	75.03	5.35	.31	31.95	.45
90.0	76.30	1.13	.49	36.03	.23
91.0	76.78	1.70	.72	43.00	1.39
92.0	78.32	5.22	.28	32.07	1.23
93.0	74.58	4.29	.27	34.58	5.40
94.0	69.68	1.11	.78	40.31	5.07
95.0	72.70	.92	.56	40.05	2.63
96.0	82.12	5.76	.23	32.64	1.78
97.0	77.29	4.05	.26	33.98	.87
98.0	82.61	5.81	.14	32.14	1.61
99.0	80.17	3.93	.21	32.83	.49
100.0	73.50	1.26	.38	34.86	9.18
101.0	76.32	6.06	.41	34.38	1.82
102.0	75.95	5.12	.21	33.44	.31
103.0	77.71	6.09	.21	31.99	1.42
104.0	79.19	8.29	.30	32.73	.20
105.0	77.22	5.69	.43	34.10	1.31
106.0	76.47	5.43	.47	41.08	1.75
107.0	69.36	1.73	.60	41.59	3.89
108.0	69.73	4.74	.31	40.46	1.10
109.0	73.40	5.92	.33	35.45	.99
110.0	70.29	5.99	.70	42.62	3.73
111.0	70.09	5.60	.57	42.64	7.73
112.0	76.12	5.08	.18	35.91	4.48
113.0	77.78	5.76	.31	33.89	1.83
114.0	73.05	2.65	.66	39.91	10.66
115.0	67.84	4.95	.11	30.58	10.41
116.0	73.93	4.64	.14	35.08	1.70
117.0	40.59	16.10	.15	35.73	19.85
118.0	54.08	7.14	.09	35.72	6.25
119.0	65.67	1.51	.38	43.91	9.64
120.0	63.96	2.70	.37	42.75	8.49
121.0	47.92	1.05	.28	39.45	7.98
122.0	51.43	2.68	.63	37.89	3.51

TABLE B-8
VARIABLES BY OBE ECONOMIC AREA

OBE ECON AREA	PERCENT VOTING 1960	INDEX OF CHANGE IN VOTE 60-64	FAMILIES WITH Y OF 10K TO 3K	PERCENT WHITE COL EMPLOYMENT	PERCENT NON-WHITE POPULATION
123.0	44.27	4.41	.51	37.84	6.78
124.0	43.90	4.10	.89	40.88	5.17
125.0	44.49	.24	.28	37.21	4.06
126.0	45.60	2.09	.25	36.65	3.35
127.0	41.68	8.01	.60	45.47	12.73
128.0	36.69	3.46	.18	37.67	15.76
129.0	40.57	8.57	.24	42.36	17.25
130.0	42.79	6.10	.17	34.72	27.58
131.0	43.76	5.85	.09	32.75	25.86
132.0	35.47	6.42	.26	38.58	37.34
133.0	36.16	10.65	.12	33.04	35.75
134.0	28.03	8.21	.09	26.71	52.20
135.0	26.26	11.57	.16	35.47	46.27
136.0	28.48	10.41	.08	29.16	38.09
137.0	31.18	9.37	.26	37.38	29.92
138.0	44.70	3.97	.34	39.10	33.45
139.0	52.49	4.47	.20	33.13	25.66
140.0	47.37	2.85	.48	37.03	21.06
141.0	44.54	7.09	.65	42.72	20.70
142.0	38.75	5.75	.28	40.21	6.54
143.0	41.64	3.73	.25	37.98	3.06
144.0	34.98	2.60	.13	32.35	.56
145.0	43.11	4.28	.56	43.66	3.44
146.0	65.99	4.31	.65	49.05	9.25
147.0	69.45	.95	.42	40.90	2.34
148.0	71.80	6.47	1.09	49.00	3.47
149.0	68.42	.67	.42	38.21	8.38
150.0	72.68	1.49	1.09	43.09	2.78
151.0	80.41	5.52	.94	44.85	1.59
152.0	82.95	1.11	.57	35.89	1.62
153.0	72.73	1.08	.44	37.94	1.71
154.0	72.07	2.25	.73	41.02	2.12
155.0	73.18	1.86	1.29	47.23	4.23
156.0	69.21	.89	.68	32.79	2.66
157.0	73.74	.87	.87	43.46	2.25
158.0	69.68	2.38	.76	37.24	.97
159.0	76.95	2.26	.45	38.85	1.77
160.0	66.13	5.81	1.67	42.54	6.14
161.0	60.38	22.86	1.44	39.28	7.79
162.0	53.43	12.76	.67	42.26	11.86
163.0	57.04	7.31	.70	44.70	5.81
164.0	65.77	5.13	1.33	49.50	5.50
165.0	68.14	6.17	1.76	47.91	8.12
166.0	61.82	2.76	.64	37.44	6.73
167.0	62.36	2.99	.60	36.63	6.49
168.0	65.32	10.08	1.41	47.64	5.66
169.0	71.61	5.05	.75	37.53	3.01
170.0	64.24	1.34	1.21	34.00	3.03
171.0	68.34	5.21	1.82	49.64	9.89

TABLE B-9
VARIABLES BY OBE ECONOMIC AREA

OBE ECON AREA	EST.OF PER-CENT COLLEGE STUDENTS	PERCENT HIGH SCH GRADUATES	PERCENT COMPLETED 5 YRS OR LESS	POP.DENSITY PER SQ MILE 1960
1.0	26.81	43.45	4.84	17.8
2.0	25.73	43.07	4.53	55.9
3.0	47.44	42.35	4.11	37.7
4.0	40.74	45.48	6.07	570.4
5.0	38.47	42.64	6.47	334.2
6.0	30.48	41.10	5.14	95.3
7.0	55.12	41.75	5.29	97.7
8.0	32.37	41.89	6.00	233.4
9.0	27.03	38.36	5.33	210.7
10.0	22.03	42.27	5.04	115.7
11.0	69.55	39.92	4.72	60.3
12.0	20.29	41.57	3.87	73.2
13.0	21.50	36.27	10.35	196.4
14.0	33.52	41.40	8.22	1641.5
15.0	28.59	38.07	7.14	607.3
16.0	19.22	36.24	4.82	157.5
17.0	26.19	33.73	9.23	271.5
18.0	45.24	55.55	5.62	405.2
19.0	37.05	30.61	12.58	43.9
20.0	27.07	29.78	15.99	73.4
21.0	34.84	35.91	14.65	75.1
22.0	17.08	37.81	12.09	185.2
23.0	36.27	31.76	19.33	86.4
24.0	4.73	33.46	15.96	65.0
25.0	24.77	32.29	14.63	118.3
26.0	17.24	33.07	14.92	141.3
27.0	19.99	30.94	16.16	68.3
28.0	31.77	29.35	18.41	116.3
29.0	35.23	34.32	18.98	81.8
30.0	4.46	25.67	25.69	63.3
31.0	15.50	33.93	19.29	76.6
32.0	9.66	30.07	21.75	50.9
33.0	15.34	30.75	19.32	47.4
34.0	28.76	37.79	13.04	56.3
35.0	16.15	46.94	7.39	98.2
36.0	19.41	46.46	7.70	153.9
37.0	14.76	39.27	8.30	107.5
38.0	54.07	34.25	19.26	33.1
39.0	9.52	40.32	10.82	67.4
40.0	18.69	30.57	19.80	48.1
41.0	10.32	27.32	23.57	41.7
42.0	18.08	26.95	22.90	48.1
43.0	35.74	30.43	20.03	67.4
44.0	32.28	35.66	13.75	117.6
45.0	24.43	30.07	14.83	75.0
46.0	23.53	28.62	18.30	74.5
47.0	18.47	29.60	14.46	61.8
48.0	12.59	26.99	15.61	79.5
49.0	33.33	29.02	15.16	62.8
50.0	25.95	27.33	17.96	81.6
51.0	18.84	24.52	18.53	93.0
52.0	15.04	27.87	13.16	79.0

TABLE B-9
VARIABLES BY OBE ECONOMIC AREA

OBE ECON AREA	EST.OF PER-CENT COLLEGE STUDENTS	PERCENT HIGH SCH GRADUATES	PERCENT COMPLETED 5 YRS OR LESS	POP.DENSITY PER SQ MILE 1960
53.0	47.76	26.01	17.11	60.7
54.0	20.89	33.67	8.46	128.8
55.0	12.89	32.17	8.47	66.7
56.0	30.51	38.33	5.31	72.7
57.0	18.72	40.45	5.55	74.4
58.0	122.36	46.15	4.06	75.1
59.0	108.68	48.81	2.95	65.9
60.0	32.87	44.64	4.30	161.3
61.0	30.39	40.51	4.41	162.4
62.0	30.71	36.15	6.18	201.1
63.0	23.03	44.33	3.95	249.6
64.0	50.47	43.18	4.62	134.7
65.0	45.98	32.89	8.93	70.0
66.0	19.68	38.34	7.43	277.7
67.0	22.55	40.73	7.40	360.7
68.0	21.28	42.89	5.60	365.7
69.0	15.21	42.48	3.57	98.7
70.0	26.56	41.72	4.55	199.8
71.0	29.74	41.18	6.29	677.9
72.0	18.31	37.41	6.25	43.8
73.0	22.14	39.38	4.10	80.3
74.0	61.52	45.63	3.68	149.9
75.0	26.26	46.66	3.04	106.2
76.0	31.20	42.23	4.36	160.7
77.0	29.09	41.56	6.73	584.8
78.0	43.58	43.40	3.80	89.7
79.0	18.52	42.49	3.38	95.2
80.0	80.27	51.66	2.44	65.9
81.0	35.21	38.68	3.34	39.7
82.0	11.31	41.86	4.67	118.4
83.0	82.64	50.13	3.60	60.4
84.0	28.24	42.75	4.94	348.4
85.0	18.18	38.99	6.96	42.1
86.0	12.45	35.36	8.01	31.1
87.0	21.32	41.44	6.93	19.5
88.0	21.52	37.45	5.68	31.2
89.0	28.88	37.75	5.11	39.2
90.0	15.38	43.32	2.48	53.7
91.0	35.96	45.56	3.71	61.2
92.0	26.74	36.67	5.93	11.9
93.0	14.65	39.90	5.09	7.0
94.0	17.34	50.22	3.81	4.3
95.0	32.42	49.76	3.98	3.8
96.0	12.05	33.89	8.93	6.2
97.0	36.37	38.00	5.10	14.9
98.0	17.06	38.20	5.87	11.0
99.0	25.74	41.23	2.76	22.6
100.0	14.01	44.26	3.68	4.5
101.0	16.14	46.83	4.46	7.1
102.0	13.88	45.35	3.33	9.4
103.0	25.54	40.11	4.11	21.1
104.0	7.63	47.83	2.52	34.0
105.0	23.13	46.47	2.97	47.8

TABLE B-9
VARIABLES BY OBE ECONOMIC AREA

OBE ECON AREA	EST.OF PER-CENT COLLEGE STUDENTS	PERCENT HIGH SCH GRADUATES	PERCENT COMPLETED 5 YRS OR LESS	POP.DENSITY PER SQ MILE 1960
106.0	43.21	49.09	3.21	53.9
107.0	24.36	48.64	3.48	68.6
108.0	58.81	50.54	3.40	37.5
109.0	19.92	47.71	2.96	11.7
110.0	23.62	50.26	3.42	24.7
111.0	38.74	46.54	4.32	67.3
112.0	81.56	36.64	5.66	27.6
113.0	20.57	39.46	3.81	43.6
114.0	27.39	33.13	7.12	106.6
115.0	15.86	24.87	16.03	45.1
116.0	22.95	34.11	7.08	30.3
117.0	23.27	32.43	12.89	37.4
118.0	9.64	27.46	13.38	22.2
119.0	42.56	42.27	7.91	56.5
120.0	38.87	42.11	7.50	34.4
121.0	12.45	40.42	7.59	24.5
122.0	23.41	45.87	5.58	9.3
123.0	54.25	41.19	11.30	23.9
124.0	14.50	45.87	9.79	10.0
125.0	38.27	40.00	9.10	18.3
126.0	13.83	37.75	12.00	8.2
127.0	35.44	44.25	7.77	104.8
128.0	29.56	35.37	11.52	40.4
129.0	114.06	37.95	16.39	34.5
130.0	24.42	32.64	13.25	35.5
131.0	7.42	27.60	15.29	27.4
132.0	14.88	36.64	18.93	58.7
133.0	27.22	28.51	22.86	41.6
134.0	13.77	25.35	24.60	38.3
135.0	28.43	35.18	16.68	55.3
136.0	23.97	30.10	17.09	36.6
137.0	9.41	36.11	12.82	61.1
138.0	28.47	33.36	17.93	94.3
139.0	18.58	27.94	30.64	53.7
140.0	20.46	39.12	13.24	74.7
141.0	29.94	41.01	11.08	111.9
142.0	21.13	35.15	20.73	36.8
143.0	22.78	33.54	27.36	25.1
144.0	15.54	27.50	40.32	87.1
145.0	23.53	44.52	14.33	8.8
146.0	24.90	47.48	12.59	12.5
147.0	25.95	45.68	7.41	12.1
148.0	49.93	55.07	3.63	34.1
149.0	16.63	46.02	7.54	4.6
150.0	31.35	53.88	3.23	4.3
151.0	48.13	55.52	2.85	11.6
152.0	19.22	50.40	3.00	7.0
153.0	31.32	45.20	4.17	6.3
154.0	39.22	50.43	3.36	13.1
155.0	32.22	52.46	3.12	89.3
156.0	26.05	47.28	4.86	12.5
157.0	31.59	48.71	3.48	46.0

TABLE B-9
VARIABLES BY OBE ECONOMIC AREA

OBE ECON AREA	EST.OF PER-CENT COLLEGE STUDENTS	PERCENT HIGH SCH GRADUATES	PERCENT COMPLETED 5 YRS OR LESS	POP.DENSITY PER SQ MILE 1960
158.0	29.72	47.35	2.64	14.6
159.0	18.12	49.23	3.71	5.8
160.0	26.84	53.77	4.18	2.2
161.0	16.88	53.10	3.17	2.9
162.0	27.49	44.25	11.02	10.5
163.0	45.31	49.35	7.76	15.4
164.0	31.32	54.60	3.30	242.4
165.0	38.29	52.74	4.98	141.1
166.0	24.20	39.03	11.77	40.7
167.0	18.57	37.76	11.08	49.0
168.0	33.83	51.35	5.29	74.2
169.0	13.23	45.80	4.42	6.1
170.0	21.49	41.55	4.55	17.0
171.0	45.51	53.20	5.88	236.4

TABLE B-10
VARIABLES BY OBE ECONOMIC AREA

OBE ECON AREA	OUTPUT PER WORKER IN AGRIC1960	PCT.EARNINGS FROM MFG. 1950	PCT.EARNINGS FROM MFG. 1959
1.0	10.16	21.1800	21.8400
2.0	8.68	35.1100	32.9200
3.0	6.33	25.7100	28.4700
4.0	5.46	29.2700	31.6700
5.0	7.13	36.0300	40.6800
6.0	6.14	27.6600	32.0100
7.0	6.60	26.0300	31.4600
8.0	7.10	34.5300	43.9600
9.0	6.75	33.9700	37.8800
10.0	6.14	36.2300	43.5200
11.0	5.46	26.2100	39.3700
12.0	6.62	23.9500	38.7700
13.0	5.16	21.1500	30.9400
14.0	4.77	24.1100	26.4900
15.0	6.83	30.3400	33.2400
16.0	7.83	25.7800	31.4700
17.0	7.16	22.8400	26.9700
18.0	4.11	1.4500	2.2400
19.0	6.94	24.5700	28.9200
20.0	3.31	30.8300	33.7900
21.0	4.14	19.1700	20.9900
22.0	4.67	9.8500	12.6200
23.0	3.78	14.3100	16.0900
24.0	3.89	6.4300	11.4600
25.0	3.83	39.1000	43.5900
26.0	4.00	40.6600	38.4700
27.0	2.91	31.4600	37.8400
28.0	3.60	46.8000	45.7300
29.0	3.06	16.7400	14.9500
30.0	3.14	16.6700	22.2600
31.0	2.60	13.8900	13.5100
32.0	3.47	23.4600	28.1900
33.0	4.33	15.5200	19.1100
34.0	5.11	10.3700	12.0800
35.0	9.38	3.3300	12.5900
36.0	4.73	4.5200	7.8500
37.0	7.73	7.7500	9.5100
38.0	2.85	12.3600	11.1600
39.0	4.54	9.9200	20.3500
40.0	3.28	17.1100	13.6000
41.0	4.44	10.8300	13.3300
42.0	4.64	16.9400	16.6500
43.0	4.07	29.5400	25.6900
44.0	6.30	20.9200	23.3500
45.0	3.80	26.1600	30.4700
46.0	5.00	10.9900	14.5600
47.0	4.31	16.7500	20.4000
48.0	5.05	35.9500	37.9100
49.0	3.45	13.5000	20.0400

TABLE B-10
VARIABLES BY OBE ECONOMIC AREA

OBE ECON AREA	OUTPUT PER WORKER IN AGRIC1960	PCT.EARNINGS FROM MFG. 1950	PCT.EARNINGS FROM MFG. 1959
50.0	2.87	24.8500	29.7100
51.0	2.66	15.0900	23.6600
52.0	3.10	17.9500	24.1400
53.0	3.77	5.7500	12.1000
54.0	4.51	21.0600	27.4300
55.0	6.09	14.7400	25.6600
56.0	8.02	16.8100	18.6400
57.0	10.89	8.9400	20.6100
58.0	10.74	8.0800	15.7200
59.0	10.98	18.6500	26.8400
60.0	8.04	22.2800	30.9700
61.0	7.90	32.9000	50.1100
62.0	4.84	27.8400	36.5000
63.0	7.30	23.6900	39.9900
64.0	5.85	19.3400	28.4100
65.0	3.69	14.3200	19.4900
66.0	4.55	32.5700	37.9400
67.0	5.37	47.0600	50.1800
68.0	5.74	36.2500	43.1300
69.0	8.48	16.7800	34.8800
70.0	9.59	32.4100	36.5900
71.0	5.58	44.7800	43.5500
72.0	7.56	30.5500	36.6200
73.0	6.34	32.2900	39.3100
74.0	6.95	34.7900	39.2500
75.0	8.19	24.6100	39.2600
76.0	7.49	41.3400	48.4900
77.0	10.26	26.8800	32.7200
78.0	12.27	9.9500	32.3300
79.0	13.38	15.3700	34.5400
80.0	11.74	10.9200	27.2300
81.0	6.90	8.3400	16.6400
82.0	10.12	30.9600	41.4100
83.0	6.40	9.1000	12.3900
84.0	6.43	29.2700	41.8600
85.0	5.10	25.9600	31.7100
86.0	4.75	24.8600	30.0700
87.0	3.35	15.9200	17.1700
88.0	5.11	18.0600	23.2600
89.0	5.33	14.5600	19.1200
90.0	7.99	13.1300	21.7100
91.0	6.40	13.7000	20.0000
92.0	7.46	.3200	1.0000
93.0	6.38	.1900	1.1600
94.0	11.09	3.4400	3.9400
95.0	9.14	3.9400	4.9000
96.0	5.07	.4400	.8900
97.0	6.30	.9600	1.6300
98.0	5.38	2.0300	7.0500

TABLE B-10
VARIABLES BY OBE ECONOMIC AREA

OBE ECON AREA	OUTPUT PER WORKER IN AGRIC1960	PCT.EARNINGS FROM MFG. 1950	PCT.EARNINGS FROM MFG. 1959
99.0	8.43	1.3500	6.7000
100.0	8.49	2.7600	3.5700
101.0	11.82	.5400	1.2800
102.0	10.24	2.6700	3.5600
103.0	10.75	3.4400	9.9100
104.0	12.35	2.3600	7.8500
105.0	10.50	8.5800	25.4700
106.0	8.88	5.5300	15.1500
107.0	11.87	8.8500	15.7800
108.0	8.76	2.8500	7.1700
109.0	10.67	.5500	2.0700
110.0	13.22	15.1200	23.9100
111.0	8.04	11.7400	17.9100
112.0	6.80	6.1600	9.6300
113.0	9.26	15.0700	25.1600
114.0	6.90	23.7400	27.8900
115.0	6.17	10.0600	14.4000
116.0	5.55	8.5700	18.6700
117.0	6.04	10.0000	14.3700
118.0	5.58	12.4600	18.4900
119.0	7.01	11.4500	16.6900
120.0	8.02	3.4900	5.2900
121.0	8.07	1.9300	5.7400
122.0	14.00	6.3600	7.3300
123.0	13.32	1.0800	2.5600
124.0	11.78	2.2000	4.1000
125.0	7.52	3.4600	6.7800
126.0	8.40	1.7000	2.6800
127.0	5.61	12.5900	21.1900
128.0	5.31	7.2100	9.9400
129.0	5.02	3.2600	5.6000
130.0	4.99	12.7700	19.4100
131.0	4.95	11.4300	19.5600
132.0	4.70	9.3500	10.8300
133.0	4.94	14.5500	13.6300
134.0	4.99	14.4700	17.8900
135.0	3.93	10.5500	12.6900
136.0	3.01	19.7600	22.6800
137.0	3.94	16.8500	20.1100
138.0	3.53	16.7400	16.6500
139.0	4.65	10.9400	10.2500
140.0	7.27	35.4300	34.7100
141.0	5.57	13.9000	20.5800
142.0	5.09	3.9800	5.9700
143.0	5.65	4.8200	8.1300
144.0	4.12	2.8500	3.8700
145.0	11.49	5.8400	6.0200
146.0	6.69	5.4600	5.0600
147.0	10.72	6.8600	10.9800

TABLE B-10
VARIABLES BY OBE ECONOMIC AREA

OBE ECON AREA	OUTPUT PER WORKER IN AGRIC1960	PCT.EARNINGS FROM MFG. 1950	PCT.EARNINGS FROM MFG. 1959
148.0	13.79	9.5300	12.3900
149.0	7.05	1.4900	3.4100
150.0	10.41	4.9600	7.0400
151.0	8.59	7.8800	12.7400
152.0	11.96	1.2200	6.8000
153.0	7.12	10.3900	14.7700
154.0	11.20	11.9600	15.0300
155.0	6.02	18.0700	25.0900
156.0	10.65	13.5200	17.0300
157.0	7.59	21.7300	21.7200
158.0	7.62	33.9000	36.3600
159.0	8.73	5.9200	7.5100
160.0	12.58	3.6700	2.8000
161.0	7.54	3.1100	4.0900
162.0	10.91	4.5900	11.0900
163.0	10.81	2.9500	10.6500
164.0	7.61	6.7300	15.1800
165.0	9.17	18.0500	28.0300
166.0	12.55	3.0700	5.4500
167.0	11.73	8.1400	12.1200
168.0	12.54	3.7200	10.2800
169.0	10.59	25.4200	25.4300
170.0	8.19	37.2800	39.5300
171.0	8.87	11.2600	17.1300

Appendix C

List of OBE Economic Areas

001 Bangor, Maine
002 Portland, Maine
003 Burlington, Vermont
004 Boston, Massachusetts
005 Hartford, Connecticut
006 Albany, Schenectady, Troy, New York
007 Syracuse, New York
008 Rochester, New York
009 Buffalo, New York
010 Erie, Pennsylvania
011 Williamsport, Pennsylvania
012 Binghamton, New York–Pennsylvania
013 Wilkes Barr-Hazelton, Pennsylvania
014 New York, New York
015 Philadelphia, Pennsylvania–New Jersey
016 Harrisburg, Pennsylvania
017 Baltimore, Maryland
018 Washington, D.C.–Maryland–Virginia
019 Stauton, Virginia
020 Roanoke, Virginia
021 Richmond, Virginia
022 Norfolk–Portsmouth, Virginia
023 Raleigh, North Carolina
024 Wilmington, North Carolina
025 Greensboro–Winston Salem–Highpoint, North Carolina
026 Charlotte, North Carolina
027 Asheville, North Carolina
028 Greenville, South Carolina
029 Columbia, South Carolina
030 Florence, South Carolina

031 Charleston, South Carolina
032 Augusta, Georgia
033 Savannah, Georgia
034 Jacksonville, Florida
035 Orlando, Florida
036 Miami, Florida
037 Tampa–St. Petersburg, Florida
038 Tallahassee, Florida
039 Pensacola, Florida
040 Montgomery, Alabama
041 Albany, Georgia
042 Macon, Georgia
043 Columbus, Georgia
044 Atlanta, Georgia
045 Birmingham, Alabama
046 Memphis, Tennessee–Arkansas
047 Huntsville, Alabama
048 Chattanooga, Tennessee–Georgia
049 Nashville, Tennessee
050 Knoxville, Tennessee
051 Bristol, Virginia–Tennessee
052 Huntington–Ashland, West Virginia–Kentucky–Ohio
053 Lexington, Kentucky
054 Louisville, Kentucky–Indiana
055 Evansville, Indiana
056 Terre Haute, Indiana
057 Springfield, Illinois
058 Champaign–Urbana, Illinois
059 Lafayette–West Lafayette, Indiana
060 Indianapolis, Indiana
061 Muncie, Indiana
062 Cincinnati, Ohio–Kentucky–Indiana
063 Dayton, Ohio
064 Columbus, Ohio
065 Clarksburg, West Virginia
066 Pittsburgh, Pennsylvania
067 Youngstown–Warren, Ohio
068 Cleveland, Ohio
069 Lima, Ohio
070 Toledo, Ohio
071 Detroit, Michigan
072 Saginaw, Michigan
073 Grand Rapids, Michigan
074 Lansing, Michigan
075 Fort Wayne, Indiana
076 South Bend, Indiana
077 Chicago, Illinois

078 Peoria, Illinois
079 Davenport–Rock Island–Moline, Iowa–Illinois
080 Cedar Rapids, Iowa
081 Dubuque, Iowa
082 Rockford, Illinois
083 Madison, Wisconsin
084 Milwaukee, Wisconsin
085 Green Bay, Wisconsin
086 Wausau, Wisconsin
087 Duluth–Superior, Minnesota–Wisconsin
088 Eau Claire, Wisconsin
089 La Crosse, Wisconsin
090 Rochester, Minnesota
091 Minneapolis, St. Paul, Minnesota
092 Grand Forks, North Dakota
093 Minot, North Dakota
094 Great Falls, Montana
095 Billings, Montana
096 Bismarck, North Dakota
097 Fargo–Moorhead, North Dakota–Minnesota
098 Aberdeen, South Dakota
099 Sioux Falls, South Dakota
100 Rapid City, South Dakota
101 Scotts Bluff, Nebraska
102 Grand Island, Nebraska
103 Sioux City, Iowa–Nebraska
104 Fort Dodge, Iowa
105 Waterloo, Iowa
106 Des Moines, Iowa
107 Omaha, Nebraska–Iowa
108 Lincoln, Nebraska
109 Salina, Kansas
110 Wichita, Kansas
111 Kansas City, Missouri–Kansas
112 Columbia, Missouri
113 Quincy, Illinois
114 St. Louis, Missouri–Illinois
115 Paducah, Kentucky
116 Springfield, Missouri
117 Little Rock–North Little Rock, Arkansas
118 Fort Smith, Arkansas–Oklahoma
119 Tulsa, Oklahoma
120 Oklahoma City, Oklahoma
121 Witchita Falls, Texas
122 Amarillo, Texas
123 Lubbock, Texas
124 Odessa, Texas

125 Abilene, Texas
126 San Angelo, Texas
127 Dallas, Texas
128 Waco, Texas
129 Austin, Texas
130 Tyler, Texas
131 Texarkana, Texas
132 Shreveport, Louisiana
133 Monroe, Louisiana
134 Greenville, Mississippi
135 Jackson, Mississippi
136 Meridian, Mississippi
137 Mobile, Alabama
138 New Orleans, Louisiana
139 Lake Charles, Louisiana
140 Beaumont–Port Arthur–Orange, Texas
141 Houston, Texas
142 San Antonio, Texas
143 Corpus Christi, Texas
144 Brownsville–Harlingen–San Benito, Texas
145 El Paso, Texas
146 Albuquerque, New Mexico
147 Pueblo, Colorado
148 Denver, Colorado
149 Grand Junction, Colorado
150 Cheyenne, Wyoming
151 Salt Lake City, Utah
152 Idaho Falls, Idaho
153 Butte, Montana
154 Spokane, Washington
155 Seattle–Everett, Washington
156 Yakima, Washington
157 Portland, Oregon–Washington
158 Eugene, Oregon
159 Boise City, Idaho
160 Reno, Nevada
161 Las Vegas, Nevada
162 Phoenix, Arizona
163 Tucson, Arizona
164 San Diego, California
165 Los Angeles–Long Beach, California
166 Fresno, California
167 Stockton, California
168 Sacramento, California
169 Redding, California
170 Eureka, California
171 San Francisco, Oakland, California

Appendix D

Correlation Matrices

This appendix reports correlation matrices for the 171 OBE Economic Areas and for the OBE Economic Areas grouped into each of the regional groupings. The variables of each matrix are as follows:

Variable

1. Rate of Increase in Total Personal Income, 1950–66.
2. Rate of Increase in Per Capita Income, 1950–66.
3. Per Capita Personal Income, 1959.
4. Economic Base, 1950.
5. Economic Base, 1959.
6. Economic Base, 1967.
7. Percent Change in the Economic Base, 1950–67.
8. Percent Change in the Economic Base, 1950–59.
9. Percent Change in the Economic Base, 1959–67.
10. Rate of Increase in Residentiary Employment, 1950–60.
11. Index of Growth Industries, 1960.
12. Coefficient of Concentration, 1950.
13. Coefficient of Concentration, 1960.
14. Percent Change Coefficient of Concentration, 1950–60.
15. Percent Change in the Civilian LFPR, 1950–60.
16. Demand Deposits + Time Deposits Per Capita, 1960.
17. Demand Deposits + Time Deposits + Savings Capital Per Capita, 1960.
18. Rate of Change in Demand, Time and Savings Capital Deposits Per Capita, 1950–64.
19. Manufacturing Productivity, 1958.
20. Percent Change Mfg. Productivity, 1958–63.
21. Value of Land and Buildings Per Farm, 1959.

22. Output Per Worker in Agriculture, 1960.
23. Percent Change Agriculture Output, 1950–64.
24. Value of Land and Building Per Farm, 1959.
25. Value of Crops and Livestock Per Total Output, 1959.
26. Farms of 1000 to 10 Acres, 1959.
27. Percent Tenant Farms, 1959.
28. Local Government Revenue Per Capita, 1962.
29. Property Tax Per Capita, Average 1957 and 1962.
30. Government Transfers Per Capita, 1962.
31. Non-Education Government Expenditures Per Capita, 1962.
32. Total Government Expenditures Per Capita, 1962.
33. Average Bonds Per Total Revenue, 1957–62.
34. Percent Change in Bond Investment, 1957–62.
35. Percent Voting, 1960.
36. Index of Change in Voting, 1960–64.
37. Families with income of 10K or more to Families with income of 3K or less, 1960.
38. Percent White Collar Employment, 1960.
39. Percent Non-White Population, 1960.
40. Estimate of Percent College Students.
41. Percent High School Graduates, 1960.
42. Percent Persons 21 and over that completed 5 years of school or less, 1960.
43. Percent Change in Employment/Population Ratio, 1950–60.
44. Average Manufacturing Capital Investment, 1958 and 1963.
45. Population Density, 1960.
46. Residual From Expected Government Revenue, 1962.
47. Net Migration Rate, 1950–60.
48. Percent Earnings from Manufacturing, 1950.
49. Percent Earnings from Manufacturing, 1960.

TABLE D-1
CORRELATION COEFFICIENTS (171 OBE AREAS)

CORRELATION MATRIX

VARIABLE NUMBER	1	2	3	4	5	6	7	8	9	10
1	1.000	.232	.166	-.413	-.150	-.039	.494	.346	.133	.847
2		1.000	-.630	.073	.096	.164	.061	-.010	.072	-.115
3			1.000	-.473	-.125	-.196	.420	.477	-.145	.218
4				1.000	.654	.676	-.582	-.563	.036	-.247
5					1.000	.848	.053	.243	-.341	-.162
6						1.000	.192	.060	.180	-.061
7							1.000	.819	.167	.252
8								1.000	-.383	.127
9									1.000	.139
10										1.000

TABLE D-1 (CONT.)

VARIABLE NUMBER	11	12	13	14	15	16	17	18	19	20
1	.438	-.284	-.301	.166	.077	-.109	.028	.867	.112	.200
2	-.136	.236	-.087	-.547	.238	-.449	-.435	.154	-.437	-.057
3	.586	-.594	-.329	.723	-.094	.739	.810	.074	.580	.102
4	-.546	.575	.546	-.417	-.037	-.384	-.534	-.326	-.305	-.115
5	-.016	.049	.062	-.020	-.062	-.255	-.317	-.180	-.151	-.080
6	-.030	.148	.164	-.062	-.158	-.307	-.353	-.097	-.156	-.085
7	.670	-.581	-.526	.478	-.129	.183	.342	.325	.265	.073
8	.662	-.651	-.591	.510	-.043	.226	.360	.209	.247	.061
9	-.081	.221	.231	-.093	-.167	-.087	-.051	.118	.014	-.017
10	.262	-.162	-.104	.176	.070	-.102	-.017	.814	.186	.221
11	1.000	-.824	-.695	.694	-.119	.353	.470	.265	.262	.056
12		1.000	.868	-.781	-.000	-.396	-.467	-.162	-.321	-.014
13			1.000	-.384	-.061	-.210	-.277	-.187	-.159	.002
14				1.000	-.111	.529	.579	.072	.411	.038
15					1.000	-.092	-.146	.213	-.167	.069
16						1.000	.929	-.183	.361	.019
17							1.000	-.051	.425	.052
18								1.000	.090	.249
19									1.000	-.046
20										1.000

TABLE D-1 (CONT.)

VARIABLE NUMBER	21	22	23	24	25	26	27	28	29	30
1	.247	-.072	.471	.293	.050	-.245	-.150	.031	-.141	.136
2	-.530	-.514	.315	.126	-.115	-.276	.156	-.564	-.569	-.182
3	.493	.542	-.197	-.203	-.126	-.058	-.222	.720	.676	.254
4	-.201	-.113	-.128	.089	.129	.218	.247	-.262	-.217	-.092
5	-.256	-.129	-.115	.030	-.140	-.149	.094	-.178	-.207	.047
6	-.225	-.138	-.071	.092	-.023	-.031	.164	-.184	-.176	-.018
7	.049	.022	.087	-.000	-.163	-.293	-.126	.150	.118	.071
8	-.007	.019	.019	-.067	-.293	-.400	-.198	.160	.082	.160
9	.059	-.020	.080	.143	.207	.280	.132	.005	.095	-.138
10	.466	.134	.352	.302	.223	-.010	-.157	.179	.002	.209
11	.081	.029	-.008	-.081	-.288	-.360	-.342	.169	.087	.104
12	-.105	-.095	.030	.169	.339	.378	.414	-.163	-.105	-.083
13	.062	.087	-.090	.041	.295	.425	.303	.082	.157	-.004
14	.265	.267	-.188	-.243	-.287	-.160	-.394	.424	.414	.145
15	-.021	.071	.008	-.195	-.026	-.098	-.066	-.180	-.203	-.039
16	.255	.326	-.267	-.284	-.310	.026	-.249	.601	.629	.122
17	.328	.321	-.168	-.214	-.256	-.034	-.217	.609	.637	.091
18	.234	-.103	.460	.219	.088	-.162	-.190	-.004	-.170	.120
19	.448	.458	-.192	.015	.192	.131	.033	.465	.513	.038
20	.098	.031	.188	.073	-.003	-.077	-.203	.116	.030	.100
21	1.000	.714	.083	.246	.464	.218	.138	.505	.520	.098
22		1.000	-.042	.005	.386	.166	.222	.526	.643	.056
23			1.000	.312	.027	-.167	.043	-.178	-.212	-.073
24				1.000	.541	.007	.310	-.177	-.237	-.081
25					1.000	.283	.547	-.078	.008	-.262
26						1.000	.040	.072	.182	-.126
27							1.000	-.196	-.041	-.342
28								1.000	.845	.631
29									1.000	.200
30										1.000

TABLE D-1 (CONT.)

VARIABLE NUMBER	31	32	33	34	35	36	37	38	39	40
1	.155	.102	.207	-.156	-.367	.424	.228	.352	.314	.019
2	-.461	-.554	-.038	-.101	-.357	.330	-.500	-.437	.453	-.021
3	.684	.728	.037	.131	.457	-.315	.892	.743	-.443	.192
4	-.305	-.280	-.267	.038	-.103	.058	-.435	-.671	.074	-.166
5	-.195	-.174	-.192	.070	-.097	-.021	-.078	-.463	.065	-.144
6	-.186	-.168	-.228	.105	-.106	.061	-.129	-.460	.142	-.176
7	.203	.189	.097	.057	.043	-.010	.439	.387	.041	.025
8	.194	.184	.111	.029	.053	-.102	.488	.353	-.039	.049
9	.015	.014	-.054	.027	.016	.117	-.121	.005	.105	-.058
10	.230	.241	.144	-.115	-.271	.340	.235	.360	.170	-.031
11	.220	.218	.183	.049	.027	-.017	.613	.697	-.019	.240
12	-.181	-.196	-.253	.003	-.107	.143	-.505	-.586	.147	-.175
13	.019	.045	-.309	.039	.107	.021	-.282	-.378	-.102	-.078
14	.383	.443	.086	.053	.343	-.240	.643	.635	-.380	.226
15	-.223	-.164	.070	-.104	.043	.001	-.149	-.013	-.197	.245
16	.589	.591	-.008	.210	.496	-.316	.698	.548	-.428	.170
17	.612	.601	.054	.137	.475	-.308	.766	.653	-.392	.205
18	.096	.060	.180	-.176	-.346	.470	.132	.265	.274	-.057
19	.388	.461	.143	.149	.330	-.191	.485	.493	-.348	.123
20	.127	.146	.047	-.048	-.006	.039	.149	.113	.029	-.102
21	.398	.481	.052	-.139	.141	-.117	.384	.455	-.297	.093
22	.362	.481	-.125	-.029	.454	-.278	.337	.349	-.532	.136
23	-.079	-.149	.040	-.110	-.326	.410	-.225	-.112	.390	-.164
24	-.127	-.159	.318	-.244	-.451	.234	-.152	-.102	.435	-.122
25	-.145	-.106	.134	-.240	-.169	.085	-.188	-.020	.125	-.038
26	-.019	.040	-.088	.051	.126	-.098	-.073	-.044	-.151	-.132
27	-.198	-.238	.104	-.185	-.244	.107	-.250	-.281	.295	.034
28	.935	.982	-.224	.209	.520	-.284	.656	.496	-.482	.064
29	.732	.796	-.295	.204	.674	-.371	.562	.426	-.614	.132
30	.625	.659	-.186	.151	.115	-.093	.296	.162	-.094	-.055
31	1.000	.960	-.111	.283	.367	-.156	.660	.483	-.322	.037
32		1.000	-.175	.286	.474	-.233	.682	.518	-.438	.071
33			1.000	-.335	-.426	.050	-.006	.205	.252	.041
34				1.000	.287	-.069	.203	-.002	-.175	.083
35					1.000	-.582	.345	.203	-.825	.163

36	1.000	-.173	-.087	.598	-.129
37		1.000	.714	-.282	.169
38			1.000	-.260	.334
39				1.000	-.177
40					1.000

TABLE D-1 (CONT.)

VARIABLE NUMBER	41	42	43	44	45	46	47	48	49
1	.127	.153	.268	.070	.065	-.127	.758	-.023	-.029
2	-.589	.450	.233	-.037	-.098	-.159	-.332	.076	.073
3	.740	-.658	-.093	-.123	.446	.000	.569	.198	.260
4	-.348	.203	-.055	.181	-.234	.113	-.477	.021	-.051
5	-.295	.136	-.068	.054	.027	-.127	-.251	.472	.490
6	-.241	.119	-.096	.045	-.032	-.061	-.193	.325	.344
7	.209	-.157	-.038	-.193	.283	-.220	.428	.291	.423
8	.134	-.132	-.023	-.173	.343	-.264	.336	.462	.586
9	.088	-.048	-.094	-.003	-.096	.157	.090	-.282	-.279
10	.284	.069	.236	.219	-.072	.032	.820	-.191	-.223
11	.341	-.227	.032	-.255	.453	-.365	.486	.355	.414
12	-.282	.231	-.026	.166	-.326	.381	-.431	-.428	-.471
13	.005	-.031	-.079	.155	-.273	.460	-.241	-.408	-.441
14	.528	-.471	-.087	-.118	.319	-.140	.512	.313	.351
15	.007	-.023	.637	-.081	-.177	-.162	-.058	-.096	-.047
16	.483	-.543	-.118	-.190	.634	.100	.250	.165	.187
17	.539	-.559	-.165	-.237	.658	.037	.399	.161	.216
18	.083	.158	.284	.100	-.053	-.082	.689	-.130	-.141
19	.486	-.391	-.169	.142	.111	.068	.352	-.127	-.027
20	.105	-.032	-.006	.173	.032	.062	.269	.006	.004
21	.560	-.262	.143	.136	-.023	.216	.563	-.425	-.361
22	.686	-.587	.172	.048	-.146	.196	.277	-.310	-.205
23	-.156	.182	.103	.057	-.141	-.052	.321	-.026	-.038
24	-.222	.454	.146	.265	-.021	-.044	.127	-.197	-.260
25	.108	.128	.140	.273	-.307	.018	.037	-.612	-.579
26	.111	-.109	-.047	.165	-.175	.163	-.115	-.352	-.403
27	-.128	.199	-.020	.021	-.144	-.052	-.289	-.307	-.236
28	.661	-.574	-.173	.001	.221	.694	.422	-.057	-.018
29	.700	-.699	-.194	-.009	.155	.517	.306	-.082	.001
30	.178	-.086	-.044	-.021	-.016	.645	.203	.085	.048
31	.545	-.457	-.180	-.026	.319	.638	.454	-.015	-.006
32	.645	-.549	-.155	.002	.237	.660	.466	-.037	-.004
33	-.140	.348	.132	.104	.159	-.361	.117	-.050	-.105
34	.026	-.207	-.272	-.103	.084	.165	-.063	.152	.195
35	.508	-.780	-.191	-.179	.084	.274	.030	.078	.204
36	-.210	.384	.132	.087	-.126	-.083	.128	-.166	-.226
37	.619	-.484	-.149	-.146	.567	.020	.500	.255	.289

38	.709	-.432	.059	-.103	.329	-.056	.596	-.134	-.092
39	-.520	.697	-.034	.161	.024	-.234	-.094	.042	-.078
40	.295	-.220	.165	-.221	.051	-.108	.056	-.034	.002
41	1.000	-.761	.083	-.051	.044	.184	.508	-.220	-.143
42		1.000	.097	.195	-.079	-.145	-.286	-.017	-.144
43			1.000	-.033	-.174	-.153	.027	-.253	-.272
44				1.000	-.204	.129	.051	-.168	-.251
45					1.000	-.144	.144	.385	.368
46						1.000	.018	-.288	-.295
47							1.000	-.034	-.002
48								1.000	.937
49									1.000

TABLE D-2

CORRELATION COEFFICIENTS: SOUTHEASTERN REGIONAL GROUPING

CORRELATION MATRIX

VARIABLE NUMBER	1	2	3	4	5	6	7	8	9	10
1	1.000	.202	.296	-.272	-.137	.097	.634	.269	.547	.817
2		1.000	-.500	.097	.135	.177	.103	.057	.070	-.157
3			1.000	-.407	-.266	-.210	.375	.324	.149	.274
4				1.000	.892	.828	-.300	-.256	-.136	-.147
5					1.000	.906	.015	.205	-.214	-.145
6						1.000	.282	.130	.216	.073
7							1.000	.664	.601	.386
8								1.000	-.197	-.019
9									1.000	.533
10										1.000

TABLE D-2 (CONT.)

VARIABLE NUMRER	11	12	13	14	15	16	17	18	19	20
1	.446	-.127	-.099	.152	-.078	-.030	.167	.739	-.055	.115
2	-.318	.515	.060	-.698	.325	-.422	-.403	.118	-.421	-.031
3	.539	-.743	-.451	.743	.048	.751	.786	.205	.503	.129
4	-.324	.405	.526	-.196	-.043	-.618	-.687	-.313	-.341	.144
5	-.244	.296	.447	-.097	-.044	-.588	-.630	-.187	-.250	.154
6	-.090	.260	.392	-.073	-.172	-.571	-.585	-.088	-.229	.134
7	.394	-.268	-.241	.236	-.239	.114	.207	.378	.242	.009
8	.174	-.251	-.197	.220	-.011	.096	.146	.261	.238	.022
9	.336	-.085	-.105	.078	-.296	.048	.126	.242	.056	-.021
10	.421	-.140	-.015	.239	-.190	-.021	.152	.653	.015	.139
11	1.000	-.713	-.490	.644	-.236	.291	.320	.304	.233	-.060
12		1.000	.726	-.843	-.009	-.599	-.601	-.077	-.457	.015
13			1.000	-.263	-.170	-.566	-.462	-.030	-.421	.102
14				1.000	-.167	.461	.536	.108	.373	.078
15					1.000	.111	.043	.021	-.269	.021
16						1.000	.901	-.052	.542	-.024
17							1.000	.208	.472	.010
18								1.000	-.125	.338
19									1.000	-.088
20										1.000

TABEE D-2 (CONT.)

VARIABLE NUMBER	21	22	23	24	25	26	27	28	29	30
1	.168	.063	.394	.219	.029	-.063	.006	.172	-.042	-.030
2	-.542	-.203	.245	-.039	-.094	-.286	.194	-.441	-.534	.091
3	.295	.492	.139	-.214	-.259	.065	-.370	.613	.663	-.182
4	-.350	-.340	-.293	.183	.096	-.216	.203	-.403	-.441	.185
5	-.317	-.286	-.154	.151	.039	-.129	.183	-.345	-.336	.093
6	-.276	-.257	-.076	.276	.140	-.170	.258	-.220	-.323	.177
7	.144	.152	.351	.165	.069	.064	.089	.332	.230	-.035
8	.083	.132	.274	-.077	-.120	.202	-.040	.132	.250	-.220
9	.109	.067	.181	.299	.223	-.120	.158	.302	.038	.198
10	.349	.040	.221	.377	.223	-.038	.018	.308	.013	.085
11	.183	.172	.159	-.187	-.015	.123	-.362	.330	.211	-.030
12	-.236	-.268	-.104	.414	.323	-.127	.595	-.463	-.481	.111
13	-.004	-.225	-.227	.433	.323	-.033	.357	-.300	-.249	.095
14	.373	.244	-.008	-.206	-.162	.158	-.544	.466	.537	-.132
15	-.324	.012	-.032	-.475	-.455	-.196	-.343	-.106	-.138	.079
16	.296	.545	.039	-.271	-.152	.056	-.322	.496	.689	-.313
17	.406	.559	.153	-.196	-.156	.065	-.337	.592	.733	-.249
18	.167	.098	.476	.076	-.061	-.054	-.157	.137	-.007	-.031
19	.459	.290	-.184	-.002	.151	.410	-.128	.483	.642	-.208
20	-.050	.163	.203	.029	-.142	-.373	-.292	.175	.142	.006
21	1.000	.488	-.168	.275	.393	.673	-.118	.604	.636	-.223
22		1.000	.196	.023	.056	.219	-.180	.553	.675	-.221
23			1.000	-.067	-.353	-.224	.053	.065	.007	-.051
24				1.000	.796	-.070	.585	.060	-.027	.103
25					1.000	.195	.424	.123	.064	.104
26						1.000	.062	.272	.341	-.134
27							1.000	-.225	-.300	.127
28								1.000	.800	.216
29									1.000	-.228
30										1.000

TABLE D-2 (CONT.)

VARIABLE NUMBER	31	32	33	34	35	36	37	38	39	40
1	.328	.218	.191	-.197	-.325	.331	.314	.307	.216	-.041
2	-.390	-.464	-.423	-.093	-.049	.225	-.548	-.447	.198	-.056
3	.619	.651	.402	.106	.225	-.097	.923	.661	-.243	.113
4	-.400	-.360	-.421	-.069	.012	-.111	-.363	-.642	.067	-.206
5	-.338	-.323	-.358	-.169	-.003	-.102	-.218	-.603	.049	-.275
6	-.171	-.177	-.267	-.115	-.134	.056	-.139	-.506	.233	-.291
7	.404	.330	.271	-.083	-.222	.269	.433	.251	.271	-.136
8	.134	.085	.146	-.217	-.013	.019	.343	.112	-.060	-.138
9	.391	.347	.198	.121	-.278	.332	.196	.217	.422	-.038
10	.442	.367	.270	-.078	-.313	.281	.332	.353	.202	-.079
11	.414	.397	.266	.021	-.098	.254	.548	.774	-.003	.098
12	-.424	-.468	-.301	-.059	-.236	.041	-.698	-.695	.321	-.119
13	-.326	-.308	-.187	-.268	-.129	-.114	-.419	-.530	.180	.030
14	.400	.470	.292	-.094	.207	-.129	.730	.610	-.280	.160
15	-.176	-.108	.000	.029	.339	-.282	-.067	-.057	-.460	.235
16	.449	.502	.338	.263	.250	-.113	.686	.599	-.273	.176
17	.527	.581	.341	.112	.250	-.112	.675	.623	-.249	.206
18	.193	.133	.098	-.289	-.141	.193	.141	.276	.075	-.061
19	.338	.429	.363	.216	.286	-.217	.571	.489	-.269	.052
20	.130	.178	-.022	-.009	.124	-.106	.160	-.054	-.057	-.148
21	.488	.544	.431	.008	.033	-.120	.325	.426	-.306	.027
22	.475	.552	.206	.279	.244	-.023	.374	.346	-.303	-.013
23	.226	.087	-.113	.046	-.209	.352	.047	.033	.309	-.206
24	.160	.106	.119	-.012	-.260	.155	-.139	-.232	.367	-.245
25	.111	.136	.141	.028	-.105	.081	-.158	-.032	.184	-.098
26	.137	.173	.301	-.105	-.097	-.037	.094	.276	-.195	.128
27	-.022	-.173	.036	.008	-.520	.262	-.313	-.417	.634	-.097
28	.820	.951	.497	.196	.179	-.090	.621	.528	-.155	.035
29	.575	.731	.393	.154	.318	-.191	.674	.508	-.340	.094
30	.049	.198	.005	-.098	.011	-.082	-.212	-.177	.249	-.109
31	1.000	.918	.614	.396	-.049	.052	.628	.539	.011	.043
32		1.000	.552	.340	.121	-.065	.665	.568	-.109	.061
33			1.000	.037	-.147	-.209	.454	.494	-.134	.247
34				1.000	.025	.049	.131	.147	-.026	-.061
35					1.000	-.560	.095	.073	-.732	.059
36						1.000	-.003	.118	.580	.013
37							1.000	.694	-.160	.137
38								1.000	-.205	.329
39									1.000	-.114
40										1.000

TABLE D-2 (CONT.)

VARIABLE NUMBER	41	42	43	44	45	46	47	48	49
1	.411	-.103	.259	.158	.181	-.125	.701	-.035	-.088
2	-.473	-.063	.349	-.098	-.369	.034	-.372	.063	.126
3	.761	-.586	-.079	.174	.481	-.383	.681	.191	.203
4	-.397	.176	.067	.041	.154	-.023	-.380	.335	.339
5	-.306	.103	.119	.092	.158	-.111	-.318	.444	.489
6	-.196	.158	.117	.153	.180	-.025	-.159	.368	.351
7	.354	-.043	.044	.205	.086	-.025	.405	.066	.029
8	.194	-.163	.098	.103	.023	-.203	.121	.220	.306
9	.265	.116	-.037	.153	.080	.189	.409	-.157	-.300
10	.426	.064	.050	.233	.267	.058	.774	-.173	-.256
11	.760	-.410	.051	.165	.111	-.208	.567	-.259	-.291
12	-.624	.466	.074	-.080	-.256	.276	-.529	-.111	-.108
13	-.301	.433	.053	.026	.030	.146	-.252	.020	-.027
14	.692	-.342	-.127	.186	.395	-.274	.609	.145	.107
15	-.192	-.265	.584	-.240	-.059	-.176	-.138	.266	.388
16	.485	-.496	-.263	.031	.139	-.247	.438	-.061	-.016
17	.576	-.497	-.223	.023	.246	-.172	.625	-.028	-.011
18	.290	-.188	.151	.093	.053	-.066	.643	-.025	-.042
19	.307	-.105	-.425	.320	.030	.011	.223	-.189	-.143
20	.051	-.179	-.205	.325	.167	.062	.241	.291	.301
21	.352	.209	-.234	.208	-.007	.381	.500	-.389	-.425
22	.353	-.343	-.158	.236	-.067	.105	.382	-.156	-.142
23	.161	-.278	.005	-.063	.014	-.077	.258	.145	.139
24	-.104	.444	-.066	.175	.130	.305	.102	-.247	-.317
25	-.053	.379	-.165	.248	-.190	.429	.007	-.548	-.573
26	.144	.271	-.127	.098	-.341	.246	.005	-.288	-.311
27	-.288	.459	-.065	-.104	-.038	.145	-.331	-.092	-.175
28	.594	-.152	-.225	.350	.161	.494	.523	-.123	-.156
29	.546	-.249	-.326	.348	.138	.206	.424	-.062	-.038
30	-.055	.224	.128	.067	-.092	.452	-.159	-.003	-.069
31	.612	-.200	-.137	.155	.411	.277	.582	-.113	-.177
32	.649	-.209	-.163	.304	.310	.395	.565	-.139	-.179
33	.338	.148	.092	.117	.218	.138	.301	-.160	-.211
34	.035	-.080	-.167	.035	.120	.112	-.055	-.166	-.165
35	-.026	-.440	-.060	.021	.084	-.038	.006	.039	.179
36	.131	.074	-.045	-.023	-.186	.001	.090	-.156	-.234

37	.759	-.412	-.134	.269	.491	-.290	.635	.133	.123
38	.766	-.362	-.086	.145	.097	-.110	.595	-.417	-.422
39	.019	.267	-.193	.069	-.082	.085	-.081	-.012	-.147
40	.246	-.110	.194	-.168	-.069	-.083	.033	-.084	-.151
41	1.000	-.481	-.052	.238	.276	-.143	.689	-.116	-.158
42		1.000	-.009	.035	-.222	.467	-.364	-.180	-.301
43			1.000	-.278	.094	-.176	-.101	.144	.160
44				1.000	-.133	.218	.214	-.071	-.089
45					1.000	-.341	.371	.387	.356
46						1.000	-.138	-.354	-.405
47							1.000	-.040	-.081
48								1.000	.945
49									1.000

TABLE D-3
CORRELATION COEFFICIENTS: NORTHEASTERN REGIONAL GROUPING

CORRELATION MATRIY

VARIABLE NUMBER	1	2	3	4	5	6	7	8	9	10
1	1.000	.256	.271	-.125	-.026	.068	.226	.108	.269	.755
2		1.000	-.587	.175	-.067	.111	-.106	-.295	.485	.057
3			1.000	-.411	-.129	-.219	.274	.385	-.226	.097
4				1.000	.696	.688	-.487	-.551	.047	.157
5					1.000	.942	.218	.199	-.072	.248
6						1.000	.295	.141	.261	.266
7							1.000	.908	.242	.113
8								1.000	-.150	.057
9									1.000	.089
10										1.000

TABLE D-3 (CONT.)

VARIABLE NUMBER	11	12	13	14	15	16	17	18	19	20
1	.357	.248	.262	-.141	-.297	-.160	-.029	.658	.353	.184
2	-.455	.240	.123	-.393	.396	-.229	-.342	-.134	-.271	-.033
3	.658	-.151	-.043	.371	-.494	.585	.767	.268	.432	.193
4	-.249	.444	.427	-.340	.283	-.308	-.475	-.036	-.192	-.193
5	.017	.181	.236	-.049	.025	-.329	-.353	.114	-.000	-.083
6	-.043	.266	.282	-.161	.049	-.416	-.443	.077	.039	-.071
7	.261	-.243	-.203	.237	-.294	-.118	.078	.140	.309	.133
8	.352	-.358	-.269	.387	-.321	.008	.223	.178	.272	.102
9	-.161	.253	.144	-.320	.048	-.286	-.279	-.071	.149	-.017
10	.247	.220	.241	-.135	-.199	-.328	-.260	.634	.297	.009
11	1.000	-.280	-.134	.498	-.526	.278	.428	.325	.221	.182
12		1.000	.918	-.735	.074	-.307	-.312	.178	.160	-.023
13			1.000	-.445	.065	-.241	-.222	.288	.205	-.063
14				1.000	-.093	.370	.431	.004	-.003	.007
15					1.000	-.070	-.247	-.260	-.370	-.135
16						1.000	.922	-.246	-.107	.191
17							1.000	-.086	.095	.167
18								1.000	.362	-.002
19									1.000	-.052
20										1.000

TABLE D-3 (CONT'D)

VARIABLE NUMBER	21	22	23	24	25	26	27	28	29	30
1	.226	.021	-.011	.316	.406	.058	.184	.326	.252	.135
2	.021	.224	.312	.242	.105	.591	.005	-.305	-.027	-.199
3	.332	-.109	-.471	.109	.130	-.401	.165	.700	.539	.133
4	-.145	.025	.284	.030	-.059	.003	-.138	-.378	-.334	-.076
5	-.130	.022	.162	-.049	.001	-.242	-.077	-.156	-.165	.076
6	.011	.163	.252	.087	.146	-.159	.063	-.181	-.152	.037
7	.226	.187	-.057	.063	.270	-.197	.282	.256	.255	.118
8	.062	.004	-.191	-.063	.101	-.284	.096	.307	.251	.169
9	.465	.460	.308	.436	.466	.231	.460	-.081	.058	-.125
10	.062	.077	.227	.202	.334	-.011	.081	.155	.152	.132
11	-.007	-.428	-.415	.179	-.041	-.425	-.214	.465	.243	.255
12	.198	.174	.037	-.058	.212	.183	.240	.011	.080	-.020
13	.200	.102	-.078	-.077	.140	.180	.181	.105	.093	.073
14	-.077	-.220	-.302	-.064	-.288	-.129	-.222	.234	.072	.175
15	.117	.265	.035	-.113	-.053	.157	.103	-.336	-.216	-.140
16	.018	-.216	-.441	-.078	-.372	-.123	-.242	.572	.409	.149
17	.156	-.233	-.540	.007	-.190	-.221	-.082	.644	.462	.114
18	.110	-.135	.034	.197	.258	-.034	.100	.289	.050	.298
19	.475	.208	-.047	.295	.598	-.222	.502	.313	.184	.042
20	-.267	-.179	-.161	-.185	-.102	-.109	-.186	.291	.164	.231
21	1.000	.687	-.033	.477	.703	.040	.892	.158	.372	-.305
22		1.000	.483	.257	.592	.278	.754	-.127	.329	-.360
23			1.000	.322	.259	.331	.105	-.431	-.205	-.203
24				1.000	.617	.080	.295	-.063	-.017	-.248
25					1.000	-.027	.784	-.094	.088	-.391
26						1.000	.015	-.189	.073	-.173
27							1.000	.016	.242	-.327
28								1.000	.630	.673
29									1.000	.086
30										1.000

TABLE D-3 (CONT.)

VARIABLE NUMBER	31	32	33	34	35	36	37	38	39	40
1	.371	.353	-.071	.038	-.364	-.008	.361	.423	.428	.205
2	-.318	-.329	-.485	-.110	.253	-.203	-.521	-.311	-.384	.310
3	.730	.677	.546	-.045	-.203	-.088	.908	.667	.561	-.119
4	-.430	-.328	-.449	.276	.055	.255	-.291	-.384	-.313	.208
5	-.266	-.127	-.399	.261	.128	.069	-.045	-.410	-.287	-.076
6	-.310	-.165	-.467	.228	.167	.014	-.138	-.442	-.316	.001
7	.171	.210	.017	-.065	.129	-.308	.213	-.030	.026	-.250
8	.253	.273	.124	-.043	.077	-.249	.332	.052	.086	-.306
9	-.146	-.110	-.215	-.051	.143	-.175	-.218	-.118	-.084	.226
10	.160	.207	-.240	.172	-.237	-.046	.173	.168	.163	.197
11	.516	.470	.345	-.021	-.374	.116	.743	.577	.633	-.103
12	.007	.050	-.384	.267	-.149	.314	-.073	.091	-.027	.369
13	.083	.145	-.339	.304	-.265	.399	.080	.250	.047	.413
14	.191	.205	.403	-.222	-.124	-.052	.382	.285	.177	-.084
15	-.435	-.346	-.330	-.037	.320	-.127	-.526	-.324	-.596	.455
16	.577	.515	.413	-.186	.048	-.129	.519	.478	.093	-.077
17	.683	.586	.527	-.248	-.058	-.114	.690	.598	.296	-.088
18	.346	.358	-.063	.214	-.425	.253	.404	.405	.418	.010
19	.237	.289	.241	.086	-.114	-.121	.306	.327	.347	.070
20	.313	.319	.128	.087	-.007	-.043	.165	.089	.036	-.253
21	.059	.072	.052	-.269	.084	-.180	.231	.248	.130	.337
22	-.282	-.202	-.321	-.162	.345	-.246	-.228	-.262	-.326	.210
23	-.446	-.405	-.382	.087	.101	-.044	-.480	-.507	-.223	-.132
24	-.045	-.090	.032	-.056	-.026	-.071	.132	.124	.253	.052
25	-.133	-.131	-.078	-.031	.029	-.144	.012	.024	.157	.177
26	-.194	-.202	-.325	-.189	-.028	.127	-.311	-.018	-.187	.183
27	-.078	-.056	.008	-.228	.114	-.197	.005	.024	.025	.268
28	.945	.981	.227	.105	-.105	-.102	.684	.653	.267	.061
29	.573	.561	-.119	-.095	.284	-.264	.474	.345	-.049	.146
30	.604	.728	.030	.390	-.092	.010	.224	.272	.074	.000
31	1.000	.953	.303	.121	-.241	-.017	.752	.711	.410	.009
32		1.000	.218	.211	-.171	-.038	.691	.651	.298	.050
33			1.000	-.317	-.336	-.105	.409	.412	.575	-.219
34				1.000	.135	.066	.057	-.034	-.132	.068
35					1.000	-.641	-.374	-.546	-.718	.042
36						1.000	.150	.307	.301	-.119
37							1.000	.754	.612	-.102
38								1.000	.616	.190
39									1.000	-.172
40										1.000

TABLE D-3 (CONT.)

VARIABLE NUMBER	41	42	43	44	45	46	47	48	49
1	.409	-.238	-.151	-.005	.059	.210	.689	-.191	-.247
2	.110	-.211	.628	.324	-.325	.106	-.461	-.252	-.274
3	.110	.240	-.487	-.243	.722	.073	.739	.158	.101
4	.142	-.149	.113	.225	-.260	-.156	-.286	.254	.206
5	.108	-.309	-.223	.007	-.210	-.100	.005	.454	.658
6	.165	-.368	-.160	.062	-.278	-.054	-.032	.306	.543
7	.032	-.257	-.332	-.219	-.003	.110	.325	.012	.375
8	-.037	-.164	-.384	-.261	.104	.081	.353	.146	.458
9	.184	-.199	.138	.191	-.212	.092	-.090	-.386	-.272
10	.410	-.454	-.134	.013	-.138	.128	.602	.060	.017
11	.060	.284	-.448	-.246	.513	.055	.686	.310	.176
12	.566	-.255	.023	.133	-.138	.152	-.082	-.345	-.318
13	.629	-.272	-.019	.142	-.110	.185	.028	-.317	-.311
14	-.190	.161	-.105	-.063	.198	-.009	.268	.252	.184
15	.140	-.264	.655	.007	-.280	-.023	-.513	-.308	-.174
16	-.028	.350	.077	-.203	.773	.270	.111	.157	-.045
17	.017	.377	-.114	-.212	.836	.206	.322	.098	-.052
18	.267	-.166	-.335	-.078	-.035	.161	.590	-.133	-.157
19	.066	-.065	-.587	-.093	.076	.047	.521	-.151	.017
20	-.043	.075	-.010	-.314	.123	.232	.181	.076	.112
21	.328	-.227	-.054	.086	.138	-.080	.248	-.501	-.302
22	.252	-.524	.252	.210	-.338	-.080	-.111	-.364	-.106
23	-.125	-.278	.218	.257	-.486	-.175	-.291	.056	.066
24	-.050	.076	.032	.271	.138	-.187	.170	-.064	-.114
25	.195	-.303	-.148	.201	-.124	-.249	.296	-.375	-.143
26	.131	-.179	.598	.402	-.347	.099	-.399	-.350	-.460
27	.245	-.335	-.117	.067	-.127	-.127	.178	-.565	-.260
28	.255	.002	-.291	-.264	.518	.763	.549	-.021	-.065
29	.402	-.243	-.012	-.133	.222	.393	.335	.005	.002
30	.002	.014	-.257	-.254	.052	.820	.240	.089	.060
31	.231	.152	-.304	-.242	.586	.660	.585	-.005	-.141
32	.255	.023	-.309	-.282	.483	.758	.566	.003	-.067
33	-.438	.608	-.350	-.037	.546	-.178	.333	.035	-.093
34	.102	-.111	-.223	-.131	-.188	.186	.048	.186	.215
35	-.186	-.234	.146	-.052	-.237	.038	-.374	.262	.452
36	.265	.106	.037	.100	-.067	-.063	-.025	-.230	-.356

37	.255	.228	-.455	-.144	.675	.133	.730	.159	.031
38	.404	.166	-.211	-.017	.520	.308	.577	-.291	-.498
39	-.084	.484	-.489	-.021	.477	-.136	.627	-.037	-.236
40	.542	-.373	.301	.077	-.135	.193	-.023	-.413	-.437
41	1.000	-.621	.187	.066	-.029	.257	.224	-.394	-.357
42		1.000	-.182	-.059	.470	-.215	-.018	.230	-.012
43			1.000	.197	-.179	.033	-.560	-.310	-.385
44				1.000	-.198	-.148	-.228	-.057	-.194
45					1.000	.070	.356	.192	.010
46						1.000	.099	-.171	-.182
47							1.000	.101	.069
48								1.000	.831
49									1.000

TABLE D-4
CORRELATION COEFFICIENTS: CENTRAL REGIONAL GROUPING

CORRELATION MATRIX

VARIABLE NUMBER	1	2	3	4	5	6	7	8	9	10
1	1.000	.374	.411	-.677	-.128	-.184	.705	.666	-.129	.551
2		1.000	-.420	-.264	.028	.006	.327	.326	-.114	-.412
3			1.000	-.416	.014	-.268	.283	.478	-.314	.624
4				1.000	.532	.638	-.687	-.652	.135	-.354
5					1.000	.655	-.088	.289	-.520	-.134
6						1.000	.109	-.117	.277	-.193
7							1.000	.727	.111	.274
8								1.000	-.583	.275
9									1.000	-.066
10										1.000

TABLE D-4 (CONT.)

VARIABLE NUMBER	11	12	13	14	15	16	17	18	19	20
1	.712	-.611	-.618	.398	.173	.095	.386	.736	.119	-.123
2	.093	.007	-.048	-.158	.214	-.313	-.115	.163	-.428	-.070
3	.649	-.745	-.719	.522	.172	.386	.562	.410	.600	.020
4	-.699	.673	.662	-.479	-.315	-.198	-.552	-.666	-.089	-.224
5	-.078	-.018	.004	.009	-.043	-.330	-.463	-.278	-.052	-.379
6	-.142	.205	.244	-.022	-.362	-.454	-.613	-.277	-.239	-.288
7	.762	-.667	-.609	.613	.085	-.141	.135	.598	-.111	.048
8	.726	-.780	-.746	.562	.324	-.064	.200	.508	.044	-.080
9	-.144	.310	.309	-.112	-.355	-.079	-.116	-.028	-.148	.136
10	.449	-.399	-.414	.257	.124	.220	.333	.564	.345	.023
11	1.000	-.917	-.899	.636	.157	.030	.395	.660	.192	-.086
12		1.000	.963	-.726	-.152	-.133	-.411	-.520	-.274	.040
13			1.000	-.520	-.154	-.102	-.434	-.586	-.264	.021
14				1.000	.043	.171	.212	.209	.180	-.045
15					1.000	.014	.228	.257	-.090	.175
16						1.000	.763	.106	.348	.139
17							1.000	.541	.405	.149
18								1.000	.108	.087
19									1.000	-.249
20										1.000

TABLE D-4 (CONT.)

VARIABLE NUMBER	21	22	23	24	25	26	27	28	29	30
1	-.074	.030	.024	.056	-.211	-.271	-.097	-.063	-.276	.270
2	-.691	-.449	.268	-.275	-.481	-.432	-.118	-.091	-.206	.238
3	.552	.580	-.087	.168	.218	-.149	.143	.224	.089	.062
4	.216	.109	.134	.144	.157	.287	.184	.011	.180	-.148
5	.115	.125	-.027	-.001	-.154	-.158	.052	.035	-.136	.244
6	.065	-.028	-.193	.122	-.016	.050	-.003	-.010	-.057	.154
7	-.204	-.151	-.375	-.046	-.189	-.314	-.222	-.045	-.306	.322
8	-.144	-.012	-.196	-.140	-.310	-.460	-.161	.001	-.348	.388
9	-.027	-.154	-.186	.200	.195	.323	-.048	-.041	.118	-.143
10	.526	.373	-.124	.308	.259	.292	-.086	.024	-.085	.071
11	.022	.120	-.296	.019	-.013	-.357	-.130	-.118	-.342	.145
12	-.077	-.144	.322	.094	.136	.405	.156	-.026	.253	-.235
13	-.014	-.089	.258	.085	.187	.368	.258	.004	.294	-.249
14	.171	.175	-.434	-.048	.030	-.287	.079	.127	-.049	.158
15	.050	.206	.293	.051	.203	-.261	.289	-.382	-.383	-.209
16	.189	.155	.109	-.043	.085	.037	.125	.114	.277	-.218
17	.087	.174	.209	.004	.026	-.186	.068	.071	.144	-.148
18	-.129	-.094	-.019	.006	-.171	-.226	-.264	-.118	-.319	.174
19	.594	.530	.003	.312	.302	.170	.220	.275	.283	-.036
20	-.057	-.013	.133	-.172	.119	-.068	-.109	.028	.128	-.159
21	1.000	.854	-.002	.510	.702	.325	.520	.097	.259	-.281
22		1.000	.272	.3[illegible]2	.672	.014	.693	.151	.323	-.275
23			1.000	-.118	-.005	-.141	.355	-.051	.191	-.234
24				1.000	.550	.263	.278	-.163	-.079	-.211
25					1.000	.344	.614	-.288	.120	-.711
26						1.000	-.157	-.073	.081	-.207
27							1.000	-.122	.258	-.539
28								1.000	.760	.600
29									1.000	-.023
30										1.000

TABLE D-4 (CONT.)

VARIABLE NUMBER	31	32	33	34	35	36	37	38	39	40
1	.078	-.018	.403	-.241	-.386	-.058	.372	.566	.381	.302
2	.090	-.064	-.263	.115	.141	.197	-.503	-.202	-.124	.023
3	.149	.197	.585	-.447	-.376	-.196	.854	.756	.228	.245
4	-.089	-.012	-.359	.167	.238	.150	-.427	-.757	-.331	-.371
5	.019	.033	-.065	-.028	-.178	-.012	-.214	-.429	-.117	-.225
6	-.052	.003	-.214	.008	-.131	-.079	-.324	-.489	.073	-.501
7	.048	-.003	.285	-.210	-.441	-.223	.244	.521	.525	.018
8	.105	.028	.367	-.223	-.445	-.153	.281	.474	.306	.206
9	-.071	-.015	-.154	.067	.095	-.023	-.104	-.056	.190	-.291
10	-.020	.061	.424	-.209	-.358	-.296	.703	.624	.348	.331
11	-.076	-.127	.492	-.415	-.544	-.315	.509	.802	.535	.311
12	-.052	-.007	-.472	.396	.480	.324	-.604	-.766	-.404	-.285
13	-.039	.013	-.441	.357	.441	.354	-.564	-.726	-.381	-.298
14	.099	.097	.371	-.328	-.393	-.114	.507	.617	.348	.137
15	-.322	-.325	.354	-.198	-.217	.220	.022	.295	.138	.480
16	.124	.121	.297	.100	.060	.203	.474	.351	.060	.093
17	.102	.082	.393	-.027	-.007	.134	.604	.632	.092	.294
18	-.018	-.046	.317	-.033	-.315	-.049	.419	.599	.391	.399
19	.109	.220	.304	-.110	-.146	-.066	.558	.352	-.048	-.038
20	-.022	.007	-.139	.018	.273	.125	.150	.118	.026	.202
21	-.152	.007	.321	-.389	-.269	-.108	.533	.279	.073	-.027
22	-.046	.053	.306	-.517	-.123	.057	.477	.315	-.055	.048
23	-.009	-.065	-.133	.032	.411	.407	-.119	-.196	-.275	.098
24	-.266	-.181	.492	-.253	-.458	-.031	.031	.164	.240	.114
25	-.521	-.379	.333	-.417	-.227	.019	.143	.264	.231	.111
26	-.226	-.085	-.102	.187	.078	-.134	.051	-.093	.115	-.303
27	-.226	-.209	.251	-.426	-.142	.353	-.023	.017	-.053	.056
28	.914	.966	-.365	.136	.499	.037	.388	-.042	-.628	-.307
29	.576	.658	-.356	.059	.598	.217	.238	-.112	-.576	-.306
30	.735	.687	-.265	.258	.103	-.155	.163	-.089	-.285	-.172
31	1.000	.960	-.325	.222	.470	.056	.292	-.095	-.622	-.233
32		1.000	-.334	.244	.478	.030	.370	-.070	-.609	-.278
33			1.000	-.539	-.742	-.143	.335	.601	.593	.333
34				1.000	.420	.187	-.206	-.439	-.246	-.067
35					1.000	.248	-.109	-.420	-.751	-.224
36						1.000	-.199	-.253	-.176	.045
37							1.000	.716	.087	.143
38								1.000	.492	.418
39									1.000	.209
40										1.000

TABLE D-4 (CONT.)

VARIABLE NUMBER	41	42	43	44	45	46	47	48	49
1	.130	.286	.303	-.297	.596	-.328	.691	.470	.436
2	-.406	.157	.179	-.305	.387	.194	-.266	.383	.423
3	.766	-.179	.215	.000	.276	-.454	.824	.205	.180
4	-.282	-.159	-.222	.282	-.558	.285	-.596	-.344	-.327
5	-.266	.183	.154	.028	-.156	.023	-.172	.195	.193
6	-.318	.135	-.067	-.048	-.285	.168	-.334	-.009	-.012
7	.062	.343	.244	-.402	.455	-.227	.457	.406	.378
8	.068	.366	.402	-.295	.500	-.314	.519	.560	.535
9	-.031	-.078	-.270	-.020	-.186	.169	-.199	-.294	-.304
10	.438	.107	.193	.141	-.001	-.390	.760	-.019	-.108
11	.368	.185	.439	-.417	.524	-.536	.735	.403	.393
12	-.421	-.171	-.287	.365	-.482	.467	-.762	-.513	-.472
13	-.371	-.150	-.306	.327	-.482	.478	-.727	-.553	-.505
14	.380	.191	.090	-.337	.287	-.228	.594	.215	.187
15	.090	.124	.552	-.096	.217	-.462	.157	-.112	-.009
16	.413	-.341	-.226	.175	.375	-.150	.410	-.002	-.003
17	.485	-.315	-.033	-.112	.572	-.305	.631	.186	.235
18	.135	.121	.202	-.255	.531	-.378	.670	.374	.378
19	.523	-.240	.084	.266	.036	-.144	.419	-.054	-.048
20	.189	-.204	-.142	.091	-.088	.012	.023	-.104	-.130
21	.623	-.185	.186	.252	-.375	-.275	.333	-.468	-.461
22	.707	-.380	.304	.151	-.182	-.244	.362	-.343	-.268
23	.070	-.370	-.031	.189	.117	.011	-.101	.026	.115
24	.078	.277	.417	.129	-.268	-.260	.018	-.514	-.555
25	.447	-.194	.379	.164	-.291	-.407	.065	-.784	-.672
26	-.036	.092	-.120	.447	-.543	.031	-.186	-.436	-.539
27	.394	-.300	.278	-.025	.072	-.206	-.009	-.489	-.282
28	.392	-.480	-.499	.121	-.195	.767	.132	.269	.181
29	.491	-.703	-.521	.209	-.216	.636	-.005	-.094	-.051
30	-.148	.153	-.210	-.116	-.032	.508	.104	.579	.401
31	.203	-.361	-.490	.069	.002	.738	.126	.461	.357
32	.282	-.409	-.512	.139	-.137	.754	.134	.338	.238
33	.239	.330	.483	.001	.408	-.719	.511	-.069	-.082
34	-.455	-.007	-.461	.039	-.057	.418	-.341	.166	.142
35	-.001	-.624	-.649	.149	-.227	.704	-.325	.082	.113
36	-.068	-.181	-.105	-.132	.206	.163	-.105	-.040	.079
37	.757	-.269	-.091	-.010	.139	-.208	.831	.209	.147

38	.647	.031	.342	-.173	.365	-.537	.808	.058	.039
39	-.022	.525	.420	-.132	.294	-.725	.314	-.087	-.121
40	.113	.126	.298	-.314	.263	-.442	.388	-.068	-.048
41	1.000	-.575	.052	.079	.044	-.146	.596	-.135	-.098
42		1.000	.380	-.110	.009	-.321	-.061	.075	-.048
43			1.000	-.028	.066	-.598	.101	-.210	-.187
44				1.000	-.386	.111	-.178	-.244	-.362
45					1.000	-.360	.443	.497	.636
46						1.000	-.422	.111	.047
47							1.000	.341	.323
48								1.000	.930
49									1.000

TABLE D-5
CORRELATION COEFFICIENTS: FAR WEST REGIONAL GROUPING

CORRELATION MATRIX

VARIABLE NUMBER	1	2	3	4	5	6	7	8	9	10
1	1.000	.479	.373	-.411	-.252	.143	.682	.341	.461	.908
2		1.000	-.106	-.675	-.691	-.482	.438	.194	.411	.301
3			1.000	-.252	-.008	.132	.497	.458	-.062	.220
4				1.000	.818	.704	-.702	-.574	-.263	-.086
5					1.000	.723	-.441	-.006	-.449	-.024
6						1.000	-.023	-.211	.163	.338
7							1.000	.596	.519	.395
8								1.000	-.195	.101
9									1.000	.381
10										1.000

TABLE D-5 (CONT.)

VARIABLE NUMBER	11	12	13	14	15	16	17	18	19	20
1	.569	-.402	-.198	.501	.484	.068	.114	.948	.540	.099
2	.353	-.207	-.328	-.030	.428	-.090	.083	.383	.247	-.002
3	.393	-.455	-.232	.530	-.170	.802	.787	.317	.432	.189
4	-.617	.613	.590	-.335	-.235	-.300	-.471	-.288	-.244	-.099
5	-.385	.481	.635	-.020	-.195	-.241	-.359	-.120	-.059	-.001
6	-.204	.335	.514	.119	-.040	-.182	-.267	.250	.110	-.027
7	.666	-.601	-.458	.527	.350	.263	.446	.643	.484	.121
8	.527	-.399	-.162	.530	.137	.198	.342	.321	.313	.145
9	.246	-.148	-.152	.126	.280	-.123	-.005	.447	.216	-.054
10	.318	-.166	.026	.365	.421	-.123	-.160	.865	.457	.056
11	1.000	-.637	-.368	.677	.157	.247	.464	.449	.204	.261
12		1.000	.850	-.655	-.140	-.428	-.512	-.367	-.445	-.014
13			1.000	-.164	-.162	-.369	-.451	-.164	-.308	.035
14				1.000	.078	.278	.320	.490	.422	.057
15					1.000	-.295	-.270	.627	.270	.068
16						1.000	.888	-.018	.278	.063
17							1.000	.015	.300	.168
18								1.000	.570	.056
19									1.000	.086
20										1.000

TABLE D-5 (CONT.)

VARIABLE NUMBER	21	22	23	24	25	26	27	28	29	30
1	.349	-.014	.330	-.076	-.106	-.204	-.255	.164	.121	.065
2	-.025	-.207	.175	-.004	-.075	-.223	-.102	-.202	-.246	-.149
3	.220	.079	.115	.001	-.348	-.159	-.139	.642	.543	.386
4	.043	.315	-.261	.004	.263	.495	.442	.131	.083	.156
5	-.026	.253	-.180	.055	.062	.343	.389	.254	.170	.247
6	.042	.194	-.104	-.144	-.018	.261	.154	.270	.224	.152
7	.044	-.202	.255	-.088	-.275	-.360	-.456	.088	.149	-.109
8	-.088	-.196	.167	.053	-.342	-.347	-.203	.166	.130	.112
9	.004	-.276	.172	-.069	-.196	-.291	-.275	-.013	.102	-.130
10	.390	.098	.188	-.109	.048	-.034	-.081	.160	.106	.108
11	.139	-.214	.342	-.009	-.426	-.367	-.403	.024	-.066	.062
12	-.238	.037	-.126	-.050	.058	.144	.339	.063	.031	.165
13	-.261	-.093	-.107	-.124	-.228	.032	.210	.146	.043	.271
14	.029	-.247	.064	-.104	-.458	-.236	-.353	.088	.003	.068
15	-.014	-.178	-.027	-.271	.166	.119	-.191	-.355	-.349	-.277
16	.176	.117	.074	.047	-.231	-.083	-.074	.491	.481	.241
17	.222	.030	.197	.132	-.336	-.159	-.075	.425	.460	.152
18	.266	-.077	.217	-.139	-.031	-.094	-.259	.104	.090	-.013
19	.221	.168	.064	.296	-.015	.061	.115	.233	.343	-.132
20	.143	.027	.108	.135	-.183	.099	.067	.072	-.010	.047
21	1.000	.636	.525	.436	.372	.232	.408	.225	.368	.014
22		1.000	.469	.605	.543	.171	.433	.220	.235	.098
23			1.000	.553	-.025	-.532	-.116	.300	.292	.237
24				1.000	.292	-.137	.380	.225	.335	.045
25					1.000	.460	.278	-.268	-.085	-.302
26						1.000	.635	-.303	-.133	-.438
27							1.000	-.039	.141	-.242
28								1.000	.835	.817
29									1.000	.416
30										1.000

TABLE D-5 (CONT.)

VARIABLE NUMBER	31	32	33	34	35	36	37	38	39	40
1	.264	.292	-.043	.232	-.232	.833	.552	.502	.684	.165
2	-.161	-.165	.239	-.125	.100	.149	.095	.421	.509	.184
3	.699	.704	-.217	.361	.094	.303	.917	.345	.286	.230
4	.092	.067	-.056	-.028	-.365	-.178	-.445	-.672	-.394	-.634
5	.235	.201	-.158	.061	-.379	-.049	-.192	-.558	-.390	-.536
6	.335	.292	-.263	.321	-.290	.246	.052	-.390	-.220	-.442
7	.210	.202	-.133	.275	.194	.505	.653	.595	.350	.437
8	.201	.196	-.144	.109	.088	.221	.515	.401	.164	.324
9	.034	.033	-.075	.042	.155	.335	.122	.241	.239	.192
10	.218	.272	-.097	.251	-.361	.777	.380	.307	.599	-.024
11	.070	.103	-.005	.008	-.048	.329	.601	.877	.371	.586
12	.013	-.020	-.217	.085	.045	-.409	-.533	-.700	-.324	-.639
13	.090	.078	-.301	.142	-.035	-.233	-.250	-.553	-.335	-.463
14	.113	.151	-.035	.046	-.110	.455	.659	.530	.135	.527
15	-.272	-.274	.234	-.221	-.075	.593	-.048	.159	.280	-.102
16	.540	.522	-.144	.340	.193	.084	.701	.285	.221	.322
17	.455	.447	-.005	.173	.228	-.001	.750	.468	.217	.488
18	.217	.223	.042	.132	-.244	.907	.451	.356	.590	.038
19	.268	.294	.219	.044	-.114	.533	.497	.285	.267	.205
20	.092	.128	.151	.020	-.079	.060	.288	.180	.146	-.041
21	.220	.274	.072	.051	-.572	.298	.193	.192	.543	.104
22	.249	.261	.095	.170	-.266	.073	-.021	-.177	.043	-.073
23	.329	.344	-.045	.143	.004	.193	.127	.188	.337	.286
24	.165	.203	.261	-.272	-.137	-.086	-.032	.015	.026	.147
25	-.257	-.242	.247	-.086	-.305	.106	-.414	-.248	.083	-.205
26	-.286	-.310	.262	-.121	-.603	-.034	-.240	-.240	-.090	-.425
27	-.082	-.106	.222	-.180	-.516	-.258	-.224	-.298	-.088	-.375
28	.966	.983	-.457	.381	.057	.084	.473	-.024	.320	-.052
29	.794	.809	-.466	.412	.043	.068	.383	-.018	.235	.036
30	.755	.791	-.404	.204	.080	-.009	.279	-.051	.275	-.055
31	1.000	.980	-.448	.477	.053	.212	.532	-.007	.365	-.117
32		1.000	-.457	.447	.042	.215	.563	.051	.390	-.026
33			1.000	-.700	-.120	.104	-.154	.007	-.054	.079
34				1.000	.146	.118	.335	-.033	.148	.005
35					1.000	-.268	.118	-.007	-.355	.306
36						1.000	.408	.254	.503	.033
37							1.000	.558	.347	.421
38								1.000	.433	.607
39									1.000	.044
40										1.000

TABLE D-5 (CONT.)

VARIABLE NUMBER	41	42	43	44	45	46	47	48	49
1	.437	.021	.574	-.196	.283	-.026	.897	-.297	-.202
2	.323	.128	.443	-.256	.185	-.192	.196	-.475	-.394
3	.422	-.367	-.052	-.072	.536	.188	.497	.287	.337
4	-.581	.198	-.308	.414	-.464	.328	-.198	.117	-.029
5	-.497	.133	-.265	.362	-.262	.331	-.025	.291	.186
6	-.125	-.090	-.103	.206	-.145	.262	.315	.047	.001
7	.703	-.331	.398	-.344	.534	-.203	.524	-.192	-.025
8	.298	-.129	.146	-.195	.450	-.078	.296	.220	.322
9	.386	-.231	.177	-.197	.245	.022	.375	-.263	-.121
10	.271	.120	.470	.033	.027	.066	.885	-.274	-.236
11	.568	-.054	.251	-.594	.727	-.219	.509	-.051	.096
12	-.508	.056	-.220	.262	-.324	.370	-.286	.106	.019
13	-.381	-.060	-.299	.185	-.151	.333	.007	.350	.279
14	.445	-.221	.006	-.236	.411	-.223	.556	.282	.347
15	.273	.061	.789	-.086	-.153	-.347	.206	-.468	-.444
16	.275	-.275	-.108	-.125	.494	.120	.120	.169	.199
17	.429	-.326	-.044	-.283	.702	.045	.164	.126	.236
18	.386	-.016	.614	-.113	.169	-.068	.827	-.301	-.236
19	.395	-.127	.383	.304	.224	.025	.449	-.296	-.236
20	.190	-.099	.051	-.047	.359	-.027	.197	-.122	-.025
21	-.142	.451	.353	.102	.152	.149	.441	-.321	-.220
22	-.185	.286	.252	.171	-.182	.232	.026	-.335	-.327
23	-.001	.123	.399	-.362	.362	.311	.341	-.200	-.029
24	-.104	.148	.043	.170	.237	.288	-.016	-.130	-.043
25	-.204	.372	.294	.304	-.473	-.123	-.213	-.512	-.596
26	-.306	.345	.046	.427	-.357	-.286	-.174	-.350	-.456
27	-.437	.389	-.093	.518	-.173	.038	-.120	-.171	-.189
28	-.104	-.081	-.202	.092	.416	.874	.360	.286	.326
29	-.075	-.134	-.129	.266	.434	.726	.323	.148	.235
30	-.187	.044	-.255	-.162	.234	.801	.218	.406	.396
31	-.053	-.095	-.112	.049	.420	.794	.410	.177	.219
32	-.004	-.102	-.096	.047	.430	.813	.459	.208	.258
33	.128	.009	.220	-.036	-.189	-.448	-.141	-.263	-.265
34	.068	-.132	-.016	-.016	.126	.259	.287	-.095	-.070
35	.482	-.756	-.160	-.182	.098	.013	-.287	.289	.330
36	.309	-.008	.606	-.112	.024	-.085	.722	-.278	-.239

37	.640	-.406	.047	-.204	.625	.025	.626	.189	.285
38	.609	.009	.241	-.326	.631	-.249	.407	-.187	-.059
39	.012	.449	.378	-.047	.331	.228	.581	-.370	-.296
40	.566	-.306	.066	-.474	.439	-.213	.158	.091	.258
41	1.000	-.667	.252	-.314	.392	-.401	.342	-.050	.054
42		1.000	.178	.166	-.170	.129	-.074	-.417	-.472
43			1.000	-.224	-.045	-.226	.306	-.651	-.583
44				1.000	-.317	.164	-.127	-.042	-.139
45					1.000	.193	.342	.065	.238
46						1.000	.145	.185	.204
47							1.000	-.038	.071
48								1.000	.956
49									1.000

Bibliography

BOOKS

Adelman, Irma and Cynthia Taft Morris. *Society Politics and Economic Development.* Baltimore: The John Hopkins Press, 1967.

American Economic Association and the Royal Economics Society. *Surveys of Economic Theory.* New York: St. Martin's Press, 1967.

Berry, Brian J.L., and Horton, Frank. *Perspectives on Urban Systems.* Englewood Cliffs, New Jersey: Prentice-Hall, 1970.

Bogue, Donald J. and Calvin L. Beale. *Economic Areas of the United States.* New York: The Free Press of Glencoe Inc., 1961.

Borts, George H. and Jerome L. Stein, *Economic Growth in a Free Market.* New York: Columbia University Press, 1964.

Boudeville, J.R. *Problems of Regional Economic Planning.* Edinburgh: Edinburgh University Press, 1966.

Campbell, Angus, Philip E. Converse, Warren E. Miller, and Donald E. Stokes. *The American Voter: An Abridgment.* New York: John Wiley and Sons, Inc., 1964.

Due, John F. *Government Finance: An Economic Analysis.* 3rd ed. Illinois: Richard D. Irwin, Inc., 1963.

Duesenberry, James S. *Business Cycles and Economic Growth.* New York: McGraw Hill Book Co., 1958.

Friedman, John, and William Alonso. *Regional Development and Planning: A Reader.* Cambridge: The M.I.T. Press, 1964.

Fuchs, Victor R. *The Service Economy.* New York: National Bureau of Economic Research, New York: Columbia University Press, 1968.

Goldberger, Arthur S. *Topics in Regression Analysis.* New York: John Wiley and Sons, Inc., 1968.

———— . *Econometric Theory.* New York: John Wiley and Sons, Inc., 1964.

Harris, Seymore E. (ed.). *American Economic History.* New York: McGraw Hill Book Co., 1961.

Higgins, Benjamin. *Economic Development: Principles, Problems and Policies.* Revised ed. New York: W.W. Norton and Co., 1968.

Hoover, Edgar M. *The Location of Economic Activity.* New York: McGraw Hill Book Co., 1948.

Hoover, Edgar M., and Raymond Vernon. *Anatomy of a Metropolis.* New Jersey: Doubleday and Co., 1962.

Iowa State University Center for Agricultural and Economic Development. *Research and Education for Regional and Area Development.* Iowa: State University Press, 1966.

Johnston, J. *Econometric Methods.* New York: McGraw Hill Book Co., 1963.

Kane, Edward J. *Economic Statistics and Econometrics: An Introduction to Quantitative Economics.* New York: Harper and Row, 1968.

Kendleberger, Charles P. *Economic Development.* 2nd ed. New York: McGraw Hill Book Co., 1965.

Life and Rand McNally. *Life World Library Atlas of the World.* New York: Time, Inc., 1966.

Meek, Ronald L. *Economics and Ideology and Other Essays, Studies in the Development of Economic Thought.* London: Chapman and Hall, Ltd., 1967.

Milbreth, Lester W. *Political Participation: How and Why Do People Get Involved in Politics?* Chicago: Rand McNally and Co., 1965.

Miernyk, William. *The Elements of Input-Output Analysis.* New York: Random House, 1965.

Moos, Malcom C. *Politics, Presidents and Coattails.* Baltimore: The John Hopkins Press, 1952.

McPhee, William N., and William A. Glaser. *Public Opinion and Congressional Elections.* The Free Press of Glencoe, 1963.

Needleman, L. *Regional Analysis: Selected Readings.* Baltimore: Penguin Books, 1968.

North, Douglas. *Growth and Welfare in the American Past: A New Economic History.* Englewood Cliffs, New Jersey: Prentice-Hall, Inc., 1966.

———. *The Economic Growth of the United States: 1790–1860.* New York: W.W. Norton and Co., 1966.

Nourse, Hugh O. *Regional Economics: A Study in the Economic Structure, Stability, and Growth of Regions.* New York: McGraw Hill Book Co., 1968.

Perloff, Harvey S., and Lowdon Wingo, Jr. (eds.). *Issues in Urban Economics.* Baltimore: The John Hopkins Press, 1968.

Perloff, Harvey S., Edgar S. Dunn, Jr., Eric E. Lampard, and Richard F. Muth. *Regions, Resources, and Economic Growth.* Baltimore: John Hopkins Press, 1960.

Perloff, Harvey S. and Vera W. Dodds. *How a Region Grows: Area Development in the U.S. Economy.* New York: Supplementary Paper No. 17, Committee for Economic Development, March 1963.

Perloff, Harvey S. "Problems of Assessing Regional Economic Progress," Regional Income, National Bureau of Economic Research, *Studies in Income and Wealth.* Vol. 21, Princeton: Princeton University Press, 1957.

Richardson, Harry W. *Regional Economics: Location Theory, Urban Structure, Regional Change.* New York: Praeger Publishers, 1969.

———. *Elements of Regional Economics.* Baltimore: Penguin Books, 1969.

Schaller, Howard G. (ed.). *Public Expenditure Decisions in the Urban Community.* Baltimore: The John Hopkins Press, 1963.

Thompson, Wilbur R. *A Preface to Urban Economics.* Baltimore: The John Hopkins Press, 1965.

Wilson, James Q. (ed.). *The Metropolitan Enigma.* New York: Anchor Books, 1970.

GOVERNMENT DOCUMENTS

Advisory Commission on Intergovernmental Relations. *Urban and Rural America: Policies for Future Growth.* Washington: Government Printing Office, 1968.

Netyer, Dick. *Impact of the Property Tax: Effect on Housing, Urban Land Use, Local Government Finance.* Washington: Government Printing Office, 1968.

U.S. Department of Commerce, Bureau of the Census. *Long Term Economic Growth, 1860–1965: A Statistical Compendium,* Washington: U.S. Government Printing Office, 1966.

U.S. Department of Commerce, Bureau of the Census. *County and City Data Book 1952: A Statistical Abstract Supplement.* Washington: Government Printing Office, 1953.

U.S. Department of Commerce, Bureau of the Census. *County and City Data Book 1962: A Statistical Abstract Supplement.* Washington: Government Printing Office, 1962.

U.S. Department of Commerce, Bureau of the Census. *County and City Data Book 1967: A Statistical Abstract Supplement.* Washington: Government Printing Office, 1967.

U.S. Department of Commerce, Bureau of the Census. *1967 Census of Governments,* Vol. 6, No. 5, Washington: Government Printing Office, 1970.

U.S. Department of Health, Education, and Welfare, Public Health Service, Division of Water Supply and Pollution Control, Basic Data Branch. *1962 Inventory (of) Municipal Waste Facilities.* 9 Vols. Public Health Service Publication No. 1065, Washington: Government Printing Office, 1963.

U.S. Department of Health, Education and Welfare, Public Health Service, Division of Water Supply and Pollution Control, Basic Data Branch. *1963 Inventory (of) Municipal Water Facilities.* 9 Vols. Public Health Service Publication No. 775. Washington: Government Printing Office, 1964.

PERIODICALS

Alonso, William. "Urban and Regional Imbalances in Economic Development," *Economic Development and Cultural Change,* Vol. 17, No. 1, October 1968, pp. 1–14.

Ashby, Lowell. "The Shift and Share Analysis: A Reply," *Southern Economics Journal,* 1968, pp. 423–425.

Berry, Brian J.L., "Introduction: The Logic Limitations of Comparative Factorial Ecology."*Economic Geography,* Vol. 47, No. 2, Supplement, (June 1971), pp. 210–219.

———— . "Cities as Systems Within Systems of Cities."*Papers of the Regional Science Association,* XIII (1964), 147–163.

Bourque, Philip J., and Millicent Cox, "An Inventory of Regional Input-Output Studies of the United States," *Occasional Paper No. 22,* Seattle, Washington: University of Washington, Graduate School of Business Administration, 1970.

Czamanski, Staneslaw and Emil E. Maliyia. "Applicability and Limitations in the Use of Natural Input-Output Tables for Regional Studies," *Papers of the Regional Science Association,* Volume XXIII, 1969.

Horton, John E. and Wayne E. Thompson. "Powerless and Political Negativism: A Study of Defeated Local Referendums," *The American Journal of Sociology,* LXVII, No. 5, March, 1962.

Houston, David. "The Shift and Share Analysis of Regional Growth: A Critique," *Southern Economics Journal,* February, 1967, pp. 577–581.

Kuehn, John A. and Lloyd D. Bender. "An Empirical Identification of Growth Centers," *Land Economics.* XL (March 1967).

Leggett, John G. "Working-Class Consciousness, Race, and Political Choice," *American Journal of Sociology,* LXIX, No. 3, Sept. 1963.

Mattila, John M. and Wilbur R. Thompson. "Measurement of the Economic Base," *Land Economics.* XXXI (January 1955), pp. 215–228.

Miernyk, William. "Comments on Czamanski and Maliyia," *Papers of the Regional Science Association,* Volume XXIII, 1969.

Perroux, Francois. "Economic Space: Theory and Applications," *Quarterly Journal of Economics,* February, 1950, pp. 90–97.

Schaffer, William A., and Kong Chu. "Nonsurvey Techniques for Constructing Regional Interindustry Models," *Papers of the Regional Science Association,* Volume XXIII, 1969.

Tilly, Charles, "Occupational Rank and Grade of Residence in a Metropolis," *American Journal of Sociology,* Vol. 67, No. 3, Nov. 1961, pp. 323–330.

Ullman, Edward L., and Michael F. Dacey. "The Minimum Requirements Approach to the Urban Economic Base," *Papers and Proceedings of the Regional Science Association,* Vol. VI, 1960.

UNPUBLISHED PAPERS

Berry, Brian J.L. "Spatial Organization and Levels of Welfare: Degree of Metropolitan Labor Market Participation as a Variable in Economic Development," Unpublished paper prepared for the Economic Development Administration, Draft, September 1967.

Consad Research Corporation. "A Study of the Effects of Public Investment," Unpublished report prepared under contract for the Office of Economic Research, Economic Development Administration, U.S. Department of Commerce, Pittsburgh, Pennsylvania, 1969.

Lankford, Philip M. "Regional Incomes in the United States, 1929–1967: Level, Distribution, Stability and Growth," Dissertation submitted to the faculty of the Department of Geography, University of California at Los Angeles, June 1971.

Rafuse, Robert. "Economic Development and the Economic Development Process in the Small Community," A Report Prepared for the Economic Development Administration, U.S. Department of Commerce by Mathematica, Princeton, New Jersey, August 1970.

Tanzi, Vito. "The Structure of the Individual Income Tax in Major Industrial Countries: An International Comparison," Ph. D. Dissertation, Harvard University, 1960.

Toborg, Mary A. "Growth Centers: Potential Focal Points for Development Policy?," unpublished paper written for the Economic Development Administration, October, 1967.

U.S. Congress, House Public Works Committee. "Estimating Unemployment in Small Labor Areas," undated, incomplete draft.

U.S. Department of Commerce, Office of Business Economics, Regional Economics Division. "OBE Economic Areas of the United States," Memo, September, 1967.

Notes

NOTES TO CHAPTER ONE

1. See John Meyer, "Regional Economics: A Survey," in *Surveys of Economic Theory,* Volume II, edited by the American Economic Association and the Royal Economic Society (New York: Saint Martins Press, 1967), p. 242 and John Friedman and William Alonso, ed. *Regional Development and Planning: A Reader,* (Cambridge: The M.I.T. Press, 1964), pp. 8–9.
2. Meyer, *op. cit.,* p. 242.
3. *Ibid.,* p. 245.

NOTES TO CHAPTER TWO

1. See Harvey S. Perloff, Edgar S. Dunn, Jr., Eric E. Lampard, and Richard F. Muth, *Regions, Resources and Economic Growth,* (Lincoln, University of Nebraska Press, 1960), pp. 4–8, Hugh O. Nourse, *Regional Economics,* (New York, McGraw Hill Book Co., 1968), pp. 129–136, Joseph Risher, "Concepts of Regional Economic Development," *P.P.R.S.A.,* Vol. I, (1955), pp. W2–W20, Harry W. Richardson, *Regional Economics: Location Theory, Urban Structure and Regional Change,* (New York, Praeger Publishers, 1969), pp. 223–231, Meyer, *op. cit.,* pp. 241–244 and Karl Fox, "Delineating Functional Economic Areas," *Research and Education for Research and Area Development,* ed. Iowa State University Center for Agricultural and Economic Development, (Aimes, Iowa: Iowa State University Press, 1966).
2. Richardson, *op. cit.,* p. 224 ff and Meyer, *op. cit.,* p. 243.
3. Richardson, *op. cit.,* pp. 224–225.
4. *Ibid.,* p. 227.
5. *Ibid.,* p. 230.

6. Harvey S. Perloff and Lowdon Wingo, Jr., "Introduction" in Perloff and Wingo, (eds.) *Issues in Urban Economics,* (Baltimore, The John Hopkins University Press, 1960), p. 5.
7. *Ibid.,* p. 5.
8. U.S. Department of Commerce, Office of Business Economics, "OBE Economic Areas of the United States," unpublished paper, September, 1967, p. 1.
9. *Ibid.,* p. 2.
10. Donald J. Bogue and Calvin L. Beale, *Economic Areas of the United States,* (New York, The Free Press of Glencoe, Inc. 1961), pp. xlii–xlviii and pp. 387–419.

NOTES TO CHAPTER THREE

1. See Perloff, *et al., op. cit.,* pp. 55–56, Advisory Commission on Intergovernmental Relations, *Urban and Rural America:* Policies for Future Growth, (Washington, D.C., G.P.O., April, 1968), pp. 30–53, and Harvey S. Perloff, "Problems of Assessing Regional Economic Progress," National Bureau of Economic Research, *Studies in Income and Wealth,* Vol. 21, (Princeton: Princeton University Press, 1957), pp. 35–62. (Hereafter referred to as Perloff, "Problems . . . "
2. The computation of the rate of increase used here assumes a constant annual rate of increase over the period 1950 to 1966. It is derived as follows:

$$Y = A(1+r)^n$$

where Y = value in final time period (1966).
A = value in the initial time period (1950).
r = rate of increase.
N = number of years (16).

conversion to logs yields

$$\log Y = \log A + N \log (1 + r)$$

$$\log (1 + r) = \left[\frac{\log Y - \log A}{N}\right]$$

$$1 + r = \text{antilog} \left[\frac{\log Y - \log A}{N}\right]$$

$$r = \text{antilog} \left[\frac{\log Y - \log A}{N} - 1\right]$$

3. Calculated as described by note 2 above.
4. Perloff, *et al., op. cit.,* p. 23.
5. Advisory Commission on Intergovernmental Relations, *op. cit.,* p. 32.

6. Perloff, *et al., op. cit.,* p. 25.
7. Benjamin Higgins, *Economic Development: Problems, Principles and Policies,* (New York: W.W. Norton and Co., Inc., 1968), p. 33.
8. The estimates used have not, to our knowledge, been published by OBE. They have been provided to us by the Regional Economic Division of the Office of Business Economics of the U.S. Department of Commerce for use in this study. We wish to express our appreciation to the Regional Economics Division of OBE (now called the Bureau of Economic Research) for their support.
9. C.L. Leven, "Regional and Interregional Accounts in Perspective," in Regional Analysis, L. Needleman, ed., (Baltimore: Penguin Books, 1968), pp. 68–9. Also see Nourse, *op. cit.,* pp. 149–154.
10. Harry Richardson, *Elements of Regional Economics,* (Baltimore: Penguin Books, 1969), p. 30. (Hereafter referred to as Richardson, *Elements*).
11. Charles M. Tiebout and Theodore Lane, "The Local Service Sector in Relation to Economic Growth," Iowa State Center for Agricultural and Economic Development, ed., *Research and Education for Regional and Area Development,* (Ames, Iowa: Iowa State University Press, 1966), pp. 96–97.
12. *Ibid.,* p. 96.
13. *Ibid.,* p. 96.
14. Calculated under the same assumptions as presented in note 2 of this chapter.
15. For a brief explanation of shift-share analysis see Perloff, *et al., op. cit.,* pp. 64–74, Richardson, *op. cit.,* pp. 342–347, David Houston, "The Shift-Share Analysis of Regional Growth: A Critique," *Southern Economic Journal,* 1967, pp. 577–581, and Lowell Ashby, "The Shift-Share Analysis: A Reply" *Southern Economic Journal,* 1968, pp. 423–425.
16. Calculated as discussed in note 2 of this chapter.
17. Thompson, *A Preface to Urban Economics,* (Baltimore, The John Hopkins University Press, 1965), pp. 15–16.
18. Richard L. Pfister, "External Trade and Regional Growth," in *Regional Development and Planning: A Reader,* John Friedman and William Alsono, ed., (Cambridge: The M.I.T. Press, 1964), pp. 298–301.
19. Douglas North, "A Reply," in Friedman and Alsono, ed., *op. cit.,* p. 261.
20. Michael Michaely, *Concentration in International Trade,* (Amsterdam: North Holland Publishing Co., 1962).
21. The lower limit (perfect diversification) using 32 employment sectors is defined as follows:

$$CC = 100\sqrt{\sum_{i=1}^{\tilde{}} \left[\frac{E_{ij}}{E_j}\right]^2}$$

where CC = coefficient concentration
E_{ij} = employment in industry i region j
E_j = total employment in region j.

where each E_{ij}, $(i = 1 - 32) = 1/32$

$$CC = 100 \sqrt{\sum_{i=1}^{32} \left(\frac{1}{32}\right)^2}$$

$$= 100 \sqrt{\frac{32}{1024}}$$

$$= 100\ (.1766)$$

$$= .17.66$$

This holds regardless of the absolute total level of employment. The only necessary assumption is that the employment is perfectly distributed.

22. Higgins, *op. cit.,* p. 468.
23. See Edgar M. Hoover, *The Location of Economic Activity,* (New York: McGraw Hill Book Co., 1948), pp. 186–312.
24. Higgins, *op. cit.,* p. 466.
25. Perloff, *et al., op. cit.,* p. 462.
26. Higgins, *op. cit.,* p. 466.
27. Richardson, *op. cit.,* p. 328.
28. *Ibid.,* p. 294.
29. Thompson, *op. cit.,* pp. 64–65.
30. *Ibid.,* p. 65.
31. Richardson, *op. cit.,* p. 354.
32. Thompson, *op. cit.,* p. 193.
33. Sidney Soneblum, "The Uses and Development of Regional Projections," *Issues in Urban Economics,* Harvey S. Perloff and Lowdon Wingo, Jr., eds. (Baltimore: John Hopkins University Press, 1968), p. 154 and John M. Mattila and Wilbur R. Thompson, "Toward an Econometric Model of Urban Economic Development," also in *Issues . . . ,* Perloff and Wingo, eds., p. 69.
34. Sonenblum, *op. cit.,* p. 154.
35. *Ibid.,* p. 155.
36. *Ibid.,* pp. 154–155 and Mattela and Thompson, *op. cit.,* p. 157.
37. Sonenblum, *op. cit.,* p. 157.
38. Duesenberry, Business Cycle and Economic Growth, (New York: McGraw Hill Book Co., 1958), Chapter 5.
39. Thompson, *op. cit.,* p. 52.
40. *Ibid.,* pp. 53–54.
41. Savings capital deposits are defined as financial deposits held by savings and loan institutions.
42. Thompson, *op. cit.,* p. 211.
43. *Ibid.,* p. 211.
44. Perloff, *et al., op. cit.,* p. 376.

45. *Ibid.*, p. 349.
46. *Ibid.*, p. 352. This could represent, as Perloff *et al.*, state, "a manifestation of the non-localized character of agricultural resources rather than an indication of the importance of non-resourse factors . . . " (p. 353). This possibility is then considered and rejected by Perloff, *et al.*, p. 353.
47. *Ibid.*, p. 354.
48. *Ibid.*, p. 355.
49. *Ibid.*, p. 355.
50. *Ibid.*, p. 355.
51. *Ibid.*, p. 355.
52. *Ibid.*, p. 560.
53. *Ibid.*, p. 560.
54. W.J. Baumol, "Urban Services: Interaction of Public and Private Decisions," *Public Expenditures Decisions in the Urban Community,* Howard Schaller, ed., (Baltimore: John Hopkins University Press, 1963), pp. 1–18.
55. *Ibid.*, p. 11.
56. Dick Netzer, *Impact of the Property Tax: Effect on Housing, Urban Land Use, Local Government Finance,* (Washington: U.S. Government Printing Office, 1968), p. 6.
57. *Ibid.*, p. 6.
58. John Meyer, "Urban Transportation," *The Metropolitan Enigma,* James Q. Wilson, ed., (Garden City, New York: Anchor Books, 1970), p. 56.
59. John F. Due, *Government Finance: An Introductory Analysis,* 3rd ed., (Homewood, Illinois: Richard D. Irwin, Inc., 1963), p. 360.
60. Netzer, *op. cit.*, p. 29.
61. U.S. Department of Commerce, Bureau of the Census, *1967 Census of Governments,* Vol. 6, No. 5, (Washington: U.S. Government Printing Office, 1967), p. 45.
62. The basis of this methodology is derived from Professor Vito Tonzi's Ph.D. dissertation entitled "The Structure of the Individual Income Tax in Major Industrial Countries: An International Comparison," (Harvard University, 1966), pp. 166–177.
63. Due, *op. cit.*, p. 490.
64. Annel Manuel, "Changing Patterns of Urban Expenditures," in Schaller, ed., *op. cit.*, pp. 23–24.
65. *Ibid.*, p. 24.
66. Due, *op. cit.*, p. 36.
67. *Ibid.*, pp. 36–37.
68. The statistical qualifications made for Table 3–1 must also be made for Table 3–2. Therefore, the conclusion that the expenditures have been allocated similarly since 1902 is open to some question.
69. Cited by Julius Margolis, "The Demand for Urban Public Services," in Perloff and Wingo, ed., *op. cit.*, p. 531.
70. *Ibid.*, p. 531.
71. *Ibid.*, p. 531.

72. For a discussion of the adjustments to local government expenditures that are needed to increase the accuracy of these statistics see Manual, *op. cit.*, pp. 20–23.
73. Seymore Sachs, "Spatial and Locational Aspects of Local Government Expenditures," in Shaller, ed., *op. cit.*, pp. 180–98.
74. Lester Milbrath, *Political Participation: How and Why Do People Get Involved in Politics?*,(Chicago: Rand McNally and Co., 1965), p. 17.
75. *Ibid.*, p. 17.
76. Angus Campbell, and others, *The American Voter: An Adbridgement*, (New York: John Witley and Sons, Inc. 1964).
77. William N. McPhee and William A. Glaser, eds., *Public Opinion and Congressional Elections*, (Glencoe, N.Y. , The Free Press of Glencoe, 1962).
78. Milbrath, *op. cit.*, p. 113.
79. *Ibid.*, pp. 110–141.
80. Campbell, *et al.*, *op. cit.*, p. 60.
81. *Ibid.*, pp. 55–64.
82. McPhee and Glaser, eds., *op. cit.*, p. 35.
83. John E. Horton and Wayne E. Thompson, "Powerlessness and Political Negativism: A Study of Defeated Local Referendums," *The American Journal of Sociology*, Vol. LXVII, No. 5, (March 1962), pp. 485–493.
84. *Ibid.*, p. 485.
85. There have been a large number of sociological studies that approach class attitudes in terms of the blue-collar–white-collar distinctions. For example, see Charles Tilly, "Occupational Rank and Grade of Residence in a Metropolis," *The American Journal of Sociology*, Vol. 67, No. 3, (Nov., 1961), pp. 323–330.
86. Robert Rafuse, *Economic Development and the Economic Development Process in the Small Community*, unpublished report by Mathematica Research Corp. for the Economic Development Administration, August, 1970, p. 28.
87. Alan Campbell and Jessee Burkhead, "Public Policy for Urban America," in Perloff and Wingo, eds., *op. cit.*, p. 609.
88. Mattila and Thompson, *op. cit.*, p. 68.
89. *Ibid.*, p. 68.
90. *Ibid.*, pp. 76–77.
91. Oscar Ornato, "Poverty in Cities," in Perloff and Wingo, eds., *op. cit.*, p. 355.
92. Thompson, *op. cit.*, p. 88.
93. Werner Z. Hirsch, "The Supply of Urban Public Services," in Perloff and Wingo, eds., p. 509.
94. *Ibid.*, p. 508. Also see The Advisory Commission on Intergovernmental Relations, *op. cit.*, p. 49.
95. The definition of an urban area as defined by the Bureau of the Census, *County and City Data Book 1967: A Statistical Supplement*, (Wash-

ington: U.S. Government Printing Office, 1967), p. XIX, is as follows:

The urban population comprises all persons living in (a) places of 2,500 inhabitants or more incorporated as cities, boroughs, villages, and towns (except towns) in New England, New York, and Wisconsin); (b) the densely settled urban fringe, whether incorporated or unincorporated, of urbanized areas; (c) towns in New England and townships in New Jersey, and Pennsylvania which contain no incorporated municipalities as sub-divisions and which have either 25,000 inhabitants or more, or a population of 2,500 to 25,000, and a density of 1,500 persons or more per square mile; (d) counties in States other than the New England States, New Jersey, and Pennsylvania that have no incorporated municipalities within their boundaries and have a density of 1,500 persons or more per square mile and (e) unincorporated places of 2,500 inhabitants or more.

NOTES TO CHAPTER FOUR

1. Ronald L. Meek, *Economics and Ideology and Other Essays, Studies in the Development of Economic Thought,* (London: Chapman and Hall, 1967), pp. 93–94.
2. This is one of the conclusions drawn by Philip Lankford in his Ph.D. dissertation, "Regional Incomes in the United States, 1929–1967: Level, Distribution, Stability and Growth," University of California at Los Angeles, June 1971.
3. George H. Borts and Jerome L. Stein, *Economic Growth in a Free Market,* (New York: Columbia University Press, 1964), pp. 53–55.
4. See Chapter 3, pp. 42–45.
5. Richard F. Muth and Richard C. Morey, "A Preliminary Analysis of the Impact of Out-migration on Income and Unemployment," Paper prepared for the Economic Development Administration, September, 1971.
6. Borts and Stein, *op. cit.,* pp. 50–55.
7. Council on Intergovernmental Relations, *op. cit.,* pp. 31–32.
8. Adelman and Morris, *op. cit.,* p. 148.
9. *Ibid.,* pp. 149–150.

NOTES TO CHAPTER FIVE

1. Advisory Commission on Intergovernmental Relations, *op. cit.,* p. 33.
2. Richard Easterlin, "Regional Income Trends, 1910–1950," *American Economic History,* Seymore Harris, ed., (New York: McGraw Hill Book Co., 1961), pp. 50–52.
3. *Ibid.,* p. 544.
4. *Ibid.,* p. 544.

5. Definitions of "the service sector" vary greatly. For the purposes of this study a relatively restrictive definition of the service sector was elected, which includes the sub-sectors of finance, insurance and real estate, lodging places, business and repair services, amusements and recreational, private households, and educational, professional, and medical services.
6. Victor Fuchs, *The Service Economy,* (New York: National Bureau of Economic Research, distributed by the Columbia University Press, 1968), pp. 2–3. Fuchs also argues that a growth of intermediate demand for services by goods producing industries as a result of an increased division of labor (i.e., business consulting firms) was cited as an important reason for this growth. He concludes, however, that this trend can account for less than 10 percent of the total change (p. 4). Fuchs includes public administration, wholesale and retail employment, as well as the sectors used in this study in the definition of services.
7. *Ibid.,* pp. 3–4.
8. *Ibid.,* p. 4.
9. *Ibid.,* p. 9.
10. Arthur Goldberger, *Topics in Regression Analysis,* (New York: John Wiley and Sons, Inc., 1964), p. 133.
11. This would require acceptance of the concensus that the problem of autocorrelation may only be applied to time series data.

NOTES TO CHAPTER SIX

1. The format for the discussion of the interpretation of the factor analysis results follows that of Adelman and Morris, *op. cit.,* pp. 150–153.

NOTES TO CHAPTER SEVEN

1. The percentage of tenant farmers is used as an indicator of the ownership characteristic of the agricultural production. As noted in previous chapters, this variable generally is clustered with other agricultural variables that measure desirable forces of agricultural production. The percent tenant farms may, therefore, be biased toward large scale commercial farming, rather than to "tenants" as they are usually known. Another possible explanation for the relationship with the other agricultural variables included in this factor is that tenant farmers in this regional grouping may specialize in the higher productivity growth sectors within agriculture. However, in this regional grouping the simple correlation between the percent tenant farms and the value of crops per total agricultural output was .295. Yet, when the second most rapid growth sub-sector in agriculture, livestock, is considered, a much closer association with the percent tenant farms is observed, the simple correlation jumps to .784. If

this is the case, the achieved productivity of the tenant farms may very well match that of owner occupied farms and thus not be an undesirable characteristic of the agricultural organization.

2. Two differences in variables exist between these two factors, but neither significantly affect the interpretation discussed above. The first factor of Table 7–5 includes the economic base rather than the index of the composition of growth industries that was included in the first factor of Table 7–4. The economic base (1950) has a negative factor loading, which suggests that the percent of total income earned in the non-basic or service sectors would be directly associated with the other variables. This is consistent with the urbanization element stressed with regard to this set of forces discussed above. Urban areas generally have a more service oriented economic structure. The negative factor loading on the economic base indicates this is present here. The second difference between these two factors is the inclusion of the percent change in agricultural output, also with a negative factor loading, in the first factor of Table 7–5. The OBE Economic Areas in this regional grouping that have had the greater growth in total agricultural output have been, as would be expected, the more rural areas. This represents the opposite type of economic structure than is represented by the other variables included in this factor.
3. The characteristics of the tenant farms in the Northeastern Regional Groupins are discussed in note 1 above.

NOTES TO CHAPTER EIGHT

1. The measure of the scale of agriculture production, the ratio of farms of 1,000 acres or more to farms of ten acres or less, is negatively related to these variables. A plausible explanation for this is that only 11 percent of the 971.9 thousand farms in 1964 fell into either one of these categories. This is also true with the measure of the percentage of tenant farms which, as discussed in previous chapters, most likely reflects the dominance of commercial farms in this category.
2. As noted above and in previous chapters, this category of ownership is most likely dominated by commercial farms.
3. The negative association of the percentage of change in bond investment and the other variables does not appear to represent any sound theoretical interrelationship.

NOTES TO CHAPTER NINE

1. The other two variables included in the first factor of Table 9–5, but not in the second factor of Table 9–4, are average manufacturing capital investment and the ratio of farms of 1,000 acres or more to farms of ten acres or less. Each has a relatively low negative factor loading and, most likely, is included in this factor because it is representative of areas with relatively low growth potential.

2. These areas were also characterized as being relatively more diversified in 1950. The more diversified areas at the initial point would also be the ones less likely to have even greater increases in diversity.
3. It is not surprising that the percentage of change in bond investment is inversely related to the average level of bonds outstanding and the other variables. It is suspected that the underlying statistical properties may influence this relationship more than the basic economic influences. In addition, the change variable is measured over a five-year period, which is most likely too short to indicate significant changes in attitude toward deficit financing.
4. It is argued in this study that the rate of increase in residentiary employment is a function of the growth in the economic base. In this case the percentage of change in the economic base is not included in the factor with the rate of growth of residentiary employment. However, it should be noted that the percentage of change in the economic base is positively correlated with the third factor with a factor loading of .496. In other words, although not included in the factor, the percentage of change in the economic base maintains the expected relationship with the rate of increase in residentiary employment. However, this relationship is not as strong as expected, especially based on the results of the export base model reported above.
5. Also included in this factor is the index of voting change. It is suspected that the large population increases as a result of the in-migration in the growth areas of this regional grouping resulted in significantly larger voter turnout in the 1964 election and therefore negated the use of this variable as a measure of erratic voting behavior.

NOTES TO CHAPTER TEN

1. This is true even when compared to the first equation for the Central Regional Grouping with the coefficient of concentration dropped from the equation. For this regional grouping the function becomes:

$$\frac{dTPY}{dt} = 5.597 + .065\,(\Delta EB)$$

Statistical Summary

Standard Error of Beta = .011
$F-$ Ratio = 39.5
R^2 = .497

where $\frac{dTPY}{dt}$ = average annual rate of increase in total personal income 1950–66.

ΔEB = percent change in the economic base, 1950–67.

2. The coefficient of variation of this variable in each regional grouping was as follows:

Northeastern:	.159
Southeastern:	.459
Central:	.837
Far West:	.514

NOTES TO CHAPTER ELEVEN

1. As noted in the first section of this chapter, the areas scoring higher on the scale of economic diversity are related to the urban orientation toward residentiary activities.

Index

Adelman, E. and Morris, H., 3
methodology, 62
Advisory Commission on Intergovernmental Relations, 61
aerospace industry, 20
agriculture, 117
central regional grouping, 127
commercial production, 144
commercial and total personal income in far west regional group, 168
and diversification, 23
employment growth, 72
farms in central regional group, 137
livestock component, 36
measures of, 34
northeast regional group, 104
output in southeastern regional group and total personal income, 96
participation rate, 26
shift to industrialization, 191
in southeastern regional group, 83, 88, 92
tenant farms, 89
worker output, 112
Alaska, 6
alienation, (*see* social negativism)
amusements, (*see* recreation)
area: geographical definitions, 5
armed forces: and civilian support services, 27
and diversification, 24
employment growth, 72
far west regional group, 152
northeastern regional group, 104

Baumol, W.J., 38
Berry, B., 6
blacks: and migration, 118
blue-collar workers: involvement and voting, 111
Bogue, D.J., and Beall, C.L., 8, 125
bonds: investment, 143
market, 30
borrowing, 30
Borts, G.H., 97
Borts, G.H. and Stein, J.L., 57–60
boundaries, 8

Campbell, A., 45, 46
Campbell, A. and Burkhead, J., 50
capital: accumulation, 133;
and agriculture, 35
availability in southeastern regional group, 89
formation, 33
investments and central regional group, 136
investment and northeastern regional group, 117
investment in southeastern regional group, 92
central regional group: boundary, 8
definition, 125
findings, 174
closure, 8
commodity market, 22
communications, 16
community: involvement, 91, 111
agriculture in far west regional grouping, 168
involvement and central regional group, 137
involvement and industrialization in far west regional group, 161

concentration, economic, 22
construction: and diversification, 23
  employment growth, 72
  far west regional group, 152
  northeastern regional group, 104
  residentiary sector, 18
consumption: pattern of, 15
convergence: concept of, 70
cost minimization, 31
credit: access to, 30

data: source of, 11
  Survey Research Center, 46
deficit financing, 118
  as component of economic change, 12
  by local governments, 41
Dennison, H., 33
development: conclusions of long-term economic, 176, 189
diversification, 22, 110, 178
  and central regional group, 132
  and export base theory, 57
  shift in industrial structure, 189
  in southeastern regional group, 90
  total personal income, 119
Due, John, 41

earnings: and productivity, 16
Easterlin, Richard, 70
economic base: comparative analysis, 176
  concept of, 8
  model, 73
  model and growth of total personal income, 83
economic change: measure in Perloff, 12
Economic Development Administration, 27
economies of scale, 52
education, 178
  and central regional group, 136
  diversity, 24
  expense between regions, 45
  and far west regional group, 149, 160
  and measure of achievement, 50
  and northeastern regional group, 104
  and per capita income, 110
  productivity, 89
  socioeconomic structure, 48
  total personal income, 116
  total personal income in central regional group, 143
  in southeastern regional group, 93
employment: in agriculture, 34
  blue-collar and white-collar, 48
  central regional group, 126
  change and distribution, 71
  characteristics and services, 44
  growth in far west regional group, 149
  growth rate by industry sector, 21
  growth in southeastern regional group, 82
  in northeastern regional group, 86
  participation rate, 24–28
  residentiary, 118, 174
  residentiary in far western regional group, 151
  residentiary and total personal income, 96
  residentiary and total personal income in central regional group, 139
  and total personal income in far western regional group, 167
  trends, 65
  white-collar, 110
  white-collar and central regional group, 136
  white-collar in far western regional group, 160
  white-collar in northeastern regional group, 108
  white-collar in southeastern regional group, 89–92
  white-collar and total personal income, 113
expenditures, pattern of, 15
export base model, 56, 129
  conclusions, 174–187
  far western regional group, 151
  for northeastern regional group, 102
  and southeastern regional group, 85
  theory, 2, 57
exports: closure, 8
  definition of sector, 16
  regional, 2
  in southeastern regional group, 83

far west regional grouping, 8, 149–170
  and agriculture, 34
  boundaries, 149
  findings, 175
  long-term economic development, 157
  total personal income, 65, 163
finance, 16; capital, 108, 119
  capital and per capita income, 121
  deposits, 97. 178
  deposits and far western regional group, 160
  deposits per capita in northeastern regional group, 108
  deposits and short-term economic growth, 182
  deposits and total personal income in central regional group, 139
  deposits and total personal income in far west regional group, 167
  diversification, 24

equity, 30
institutions, 30
institutions and employment growth, 72
in northeastern regional group, 104
fisheries: in southeastern regional group, 83
fluctuations, 22
food processing, 16
forestry: and diversification, 23
and far west regional group, 152
and southeastern regional group, 83
Fuchs, V., 71
furniture: southeastern regional group, 83

Glaser, W. A., 46
government: and definition of export sector, 17
federal and public welfare, 43
local and bond investment, 166
local bond investment and per capita income in central regional group, 145
local and deficit financing, 41
local and economies of scale, 53
local expenditures by function, 44
local and fiscal effort, 38
local and revenue per capita, 88
local and revenue per capita in northeastern regional group, 108
local services, 42
local services and central regional group, 143
growth industries, 118, 175–178
as component of economic change, 12
and export base theory, 58
and northeastern regional group, 108
and shift-share analysis, 20
short-term economic growth, 182
southeastern regional group, 89
total personal income, 96
total personal income in central regional group, 138
and total personal income in far west regional group, 163

Hawaii, 6
Higgins, B., 13, 25
Hirsch, W., 53
homogeneity: socioeconomic, 8
Horton, J. and Thompson, W., 48
hotels, 16
households: and diversification, 24
residentiary sector, 18
human capital, 116, 163
investment and per capita income in central regional group, 145
and far western regional group, 160
human resources, 190
in southeastern regional group, 89

income: distribution and education, 51
distribution and financial deposits, 142
elasticity, 70
export base theory, 57
interstate differentials, 26
per capita, 14, 59
per capita findings, 183, 194
growth in per capita, 68, 120
per capita in northeastern regional group, 109
per capita in southeastern regional group, 87, 91, 97
in Perloff, 13
and socioeconomic structure, 48
total personal, 113
total personal and central regional group, 125, 138
total personal and export base model, 188
total personal and far western regional group, 163
total personal and rate of growth, 63
total personal in southeastern regional group, 92
industrialization: and agriculture, 192
as component of economic change, 12
measures of, 25
in northeastern regional group, 101
residentiary in far west regional groups, 160
residentiary and total personal income, 113
and southeastern regional group, 90
and transportation, 25
insurance, 16
and diversification, 24
employment growth, 72
northeastern regional group, 104
interdependence: as economic concept, 62
Intermountain Region: definition by Bogue and Beale, 8
investment: manufacturing as component of economic change, 12
manufacturing, 33
social, 41

Kansas: agriculture, 34

labor force: and migration; participation rate, 26, 119
loan potential, 30
as component of economic change, 12
location quotient, 16
lumber: in southeastern regional group, 83

manufacturing: capital investment in
far western regional group, 163
diversification, 23
employment growth, 72
and far west regional group, 150–152
growth in northeastern regional group, 102
productivity in southeastern regional group, 88
southeastern regional group, 83
productivity and total personal income in far western regional group, 167
and total personal income in southeastern regional group, 93
Margolis, J., 43
Mattila, J. and Thompson, L., 50
medicine: diversification, 24
and far west regional group, 152
and northeastern regional group, 104
Meek, R., 55
methodology: and Adelman and Morris, 62
in Meek, 55
measurement of manufacturing productivity, 31
of OBE economic areas, 7
Meyer, J., 2; property tax, 38
Miami, 79
Michaely, M., 22
migration: as component of economic development, 12
and education, 111
findings, 190–197
and far western regional group, 149
growth of total personal income, 118
in-and per capita income, 121
net rate and total personal income, 96
net rate and total personal income in far west regional group, 167
net rate, 28
in northeastern regional group, 101
out–, 60
out–in central regional group, 125
out–in work of Richardson, 26
Milbroth, L., 45
mining: and diversification, 23
employment growth, 72
and southeastern regional group, 83
Morris, Cynthia Taft, 3
Morris, C.T. and Adelman, F., 173
Mountain Region, 66
Muth, R.F., 60, 97

Nebraska: agriculture, 34
Netzer, D., 39
North, Douglas, 22
northeastern regional group, 174
long-term economic development, 108–113
and total personal income, 101

OBE (Office of Business Economics), 6
economic areas, 6
economic area and definition of export sector, 16
estimate of economic base, 15
methodology of areas, 7
economic areas in southeastern regional groups, 84
Orlando, Florida, 79
Ornati, Oscar, 51
output: and employment data, 23

Pacific Region, 66
Perloff, H.S., and field crop sector, 34
Perloff, H.S., Dunn, E.S., Jr., Lampard, E.E. and Muth, R.F., 12
and manufacturing, 25
petroleum refining: in northeastern regional group, 102
Pfister, R.: and diversification, 22
politics: participation as component of economic change, 12
measures of participation, 45
voting and total personal income in southeastern regional group, 93
population: and central regional group, 125
density, 179
density and central regional group, 137
density as component of economic change, 12
density in northeastern regional group, 108
density and services, 44
density in southeastern regional group, 90
density and total personal income, 113
density and total personal income in central regional group, 139
far western regional group, 149
density and total personal income in central regional group, 139
measure of density, 52
and migration, 28
and total personal income, 66
printing and publishing, 16
productivity: agricultural, 35
analysis of regions, 16
export-oriented and central regional grouping, 129
and far western region group

agricultural sector, 162
inter-industry substitution, 119
manufacturing, 118
manufacturing and agriculture, 189
manufacturing as component of economic change, 12
measures of, 31
property tax, 38
and central regional group, 136
and far west regional group long-term development, 48
northeastern regional group, 108
and southeastern regional group, 88
and total personal income, 113
and total personal income in central regional group, 143
public administration: and diversification, 24
employment growth, 72
and far west regional group, 152
and northeastern regional group, 104
and residentiary sector, 18
public infrastructure, 58, 110, 175, 191
and central regional group, 131, 143
and far western regional group growth industries, 156
in southeastern regional group, 89
public investment, 110
long-term development in far western regional group, 157
public utilities, 16
and diversification, 23
employment growth, 72
and far west regional group, 152
and northeastern regional group, 104
and residentiary sector, 18

race, 111; and southeastern regional group, 91–93
and socioeconomic structure, 48
railroads, 16
real estate, 16
and diversification, 24
northeastern regional group, 104
recreation, 17;
and diversification, 24
employment growth, 72
far western regional group, 152
northeastern regional group, 104
and residentiary sector, 18
regions: and agricultural histories, 35
analysis and Adelman and Morris, 63
concept of, 5
definition by Bogue and Beale, 8
migration, 28
restaurants: and diversification, 24
employment growth, 72
far western regional growth, 152
northeastern regional group, 104
residentiary sector, 18
retail trade, 16
and far western regional group, 150
and residentiary sector, 18
revenue: and property tax, 39
sources, 178
Richardson, H.: location quotient, 16
labor force participation rate, 26
regional labor forces, 26
regions, 6
Rocky Mountain Region: definition by Bogue and Beale, 8

Sachs, S., 45
salary: and productivity, 16
savings: capital deposits definition, 282
sectors: and closure, 8
definition, 18
and per capita income, 121
residentiary, 190
in southeastern regional group, 90
in Tiebout and Lane, 19
services: definition, 71
in far western regional group, 150
in work of Fuchs, 73
governmental as component of economic change, 12
local government, 42
and socioeconomic structure, 49
variations, 44
shift-share analysis, 20
small business, 30
social capital: and infrastructure, 162
social negativism, 48
in Glaser, 46
in southeastern regional group, 91
social overhead, 178
capital, 157, 166, 189
social services, 191
Society Politics and Economic Development, 3
socioeconomics, 192
and agriculture, 35
measure of structure, 48
and political participation, 46
Sonenblum, S., 28
South: and agriculture, 35
South Atlantic Region, 66
southeastern regional grouping, 79
employment growth, 80
findings, 174
long-term economic development, 86
short-term economic growth, 97
Southeast: total personal income, 65
spatial units: concept of, 5
and OBE methodology, 7
sphere of influence: definition, 7

Standard Industrial Classification Manual, 32
Stein, M., 97
Stopler, S. and Tiebout, C.M., 22
suburbia, 38
Survey Research Center, 46

technology: agriculture as component of economic change, 18
textiles: mill products in northeastern regional group, 102
  mill products in southeastern regional group, 83
theory: development, 33
  export base, 2
  growth, 58
  international trade, 2
  investment, 30
  location, 2
  microeconomic and macroeconomic, 1, 31
Thompson, W.: credit access, 30
  diversification, 22
  labor force participation rate, 26
Tiebout, C.M. and Lane, T., 18
time series analysis, 98
transportation, 16
  and far west regional group, 152
  and northeastern regional group, 104
  trucking, 16

urbanization, 179
  and central regional group, 58
  definition, 284
  deterioration, 38
  diversity, 162
  and educational achievement, 50
  and far west regional group, 160
  and industrialization, 25
  and migration, 28
  and northeastern regional group, 110
  outmigration and deterioration, 60
  services variations, 44
  and southeastern regional group, 90

voting, 1960, 1964 elections, 47
  and central regional group, 136
  and community involvement in northeastern regional group, 111, 117
  and far western regional group, 161
  and political participation, 46
  southeastern regional group, 91
  total personal income in far western regional group, 167

wars, Civil War, 70
  World War II, 61
  and agriculture, 34
welfare, 169
  migration, 60
  patterns of growth and pattern of change, 62
  and per capita income, 144
  in Perloff, 13
  and socioeconomic strategy, 49
West South Central Region, 66
wholesale trade, 16

About the Author

Dr. James Sample is a senior economist with System Sciences, Inc. located in Bethesda, Maryland. He has previously held positions in the Economic Development Administration and the Special Action Office for Drug Abuse Prevention. Dr. Sample has also taught various courses in economics at the American University in Washington, D.C. He received his BA from Allegheny College and MA and Ph.D. degrees from the American University.